Second Edition

Strategic Enrollment Planning:
A Dynamic Collaboration

How higher education leaders can align mission, vision, and values with shifting market needs and expectations

Edited by Lewis W. Sanborne, PhD

RUFFALO℠
NOEL LEVITZ

i

Published by Ruffalo Noel Levitz, LLC.

ISBN: 978-0-9854281-1-2

Printed and bound in the United States of America.

Second Edition: June 2016
10 9 8 7 6 5 4 3 2 1

Copyeditors: Kevin Crockett, Jo Hillman, Pam Jennings, Fred Longenecker, Lewis Sanborne, Kylene Sommers, and Jennifer Wilson

Design: Curt Muntz

Ruffalo Noel Levitz
1025 Kirkwood Parkway SW
Cedar Rapids, Iowa 52404
800.756.7483

ContactUs@RuffaloNL.com
www.RuffaloNL.com

CONTENTS

Second Edition

Strategic Enrollment Planning: A Dynamic Collaboration

We all stand on the shoulders of those who came before us. Without the foresight and courage of Al Ruffalo, Lee Noel, Randi Levitz, and their partners over the last four decades, higher education would be a less vibrant place. For the majority of that time Ruffalo Noel Levitz has primarily focused its efforts on helping institutions develop annual plans for marketing, recruiting, retaining students, and engaging donors. As the first decade of the new millennium came to a close, however, the demographic and financial realities facing higher education forced institutions to move away from an annual focus and instead think of enrollment management holistically over multi-year periods. The Ruffalo Noel Levitz mission, "To provide strategic enrollment and fundraising solutions that support and guide our partner organizations to advance relationships, achieve their goals, and fulfill their missions," is at the heart of this book.

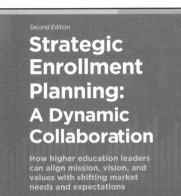

As with any project of this magnitude, many people contributed their talents to the book. The book would not exist without the planning concept, which found its origins in the collaborations of Dr. James Mager, formerly the associate vice president for enrollment management at The Ohio State University and vice president for consulting services at Noel-Levitz; and Kent Hopkins, vice provost for enrollment management at Arizona State University and formerly vice president and principal at Noel-Levitz. Without either of these gentlemen, the foundation for this book and the planning process it outlines would not have been created. It is the culmination of their substantive experience within enrollment management that validates the data-informed approach to enrollment management and distinguishes the strategic enrollment planning process from annual planning. This second edition of the book would also not exist without the dedication and energies of Dr. Jim Hundrieser whose hard work and leadership led to the creation of the first edition. Without data and leadership there is no plan.

In addition, there are several Ruffalo Noel Levitz team members to acknowledge: Kevin Crockett, Jo Hillman, Pam Jennings, Fred Longenecker, Curt Muntz, Kylene Sommers, and Jennifer Wilson all played instrumental roles to ensure this book happened.

And of course without the diligent, thoughtful work of each of the chapter authors, this book would not be possible. Their content expertise and patience throughout the process of developing this second edition has been invaluable. I offer them my heartfelt thanks.

–Lewis Sanborne

Second Edition

Strategic Enrollment Planning: A Dynamic Collaboration

By Lewis Sanborne

In the introduction to the first edition of this book, Jim Hundrieser observed that we were living in confusing times. If the pace of change was causing confusion in 2012, it only seems to be accelerating four years later. Years ago the development of the world wide web wrested control of the messages about colleges and universities away from the institutions and ceded it to prospective students and a host of other sources outside of colleges' and universities' control. That same trend is influencing the control of educational content, so that students are increasingly in the driver's seat, determining when and how learning opportunities occur. Students want education on demand, customized to their unique circumstances, on their own time frames, structured around their jobs and their family commitments. Learning opportunities abound, from MOOCs, to specialized training leading to badges, to countless YouTube channels, to synchronous and a-synchronous online courses, non-credit options, accelerated options, stackable credentials, credit-by-exam, and prior learning assessment, just for starters. It is little wonder that in the years since the first edition of this book was published, enrollment in higher education in the U.S. has declined each of the last seven terms (2015 National Student Clearinghouse. *Current Term Enrollment Estimates Spring 2015*). Colleges and universities are no longer the only educational game in town.

> **SEP refers to a complex and organized effort to connect mission, current state, and the changing environment to long-term enrollment and fiscal health, resulting in a concrete, written plan of action. It differs from traditional enrollment planning in that it brings academic and co-curricular planning into the center of the initiative.**

The timing of this decline in enrollment coincides with efforts by the Obama Administration and the Lumina Foundation to reach the goal of 60 percent of adults with a postsecondary credential by 2025. The good news is we are making progress, though it is slow. A 38.7 percent attainment rate in 2011 was followed by 39.4 percent in 2012 and 40.0 percent in 2013 (the last year for which we have data as of the publishing of this second edition) (http://strongernation.luminafoundation.org/report/). As we noted in 2012, the principles and concepts described in this book do not solve the challenges higher education faces as it strives to achieve the goal of producing a competent, credentialed workforce for 2025, but they do offer a context for planning that will help institutions evaluate their current state and establish measurable institutional goals for the future. For most institutions, this planning process should initiate a dialogue leading to the realization that current practices will not be sufficient to meet the demands of the majority of learners by 2025.

What is Strategic Enrollment Planning? SEP refers to a complex and organized effort to connect mission, current state, and the changing environment to long-term enrollment and fiscal health, resulting in a concrete, written plan of action. It differs from traditional enrollment planning in that it brings academic and co-curricular planning into the center of the initiative. SEP should not be considered an event or a time-bound project. The process is not linear. Rather, it should be viewed as a recursive process that proceeds through the phases described in the figure below, looping back as necessary, and then becoming part of the regular planning regimen of the institution. Chapter 8 describes the transition from SEP to strategic enrollment management, SEM.

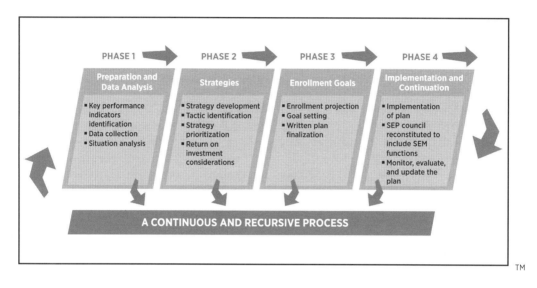

Architecture of the Book

This second edition is designed to walk college and university leaders through the strategic enrollment planning process while also providing a primer on the fundamentals of enrollment management.

Chapters 1 and 2 establish the imperative for strategic enrollment planning and explore how campuses can go about building a culture that facilitates the process. Chapters 3 through 8 describe the fundamentals of the SEP process Itself: building the organizational structures and constructing the process; developing a data-informed approach; integrating academic and co-curricular planning; developing strategies and action plans; establishing goals and determining return on investment; planning implementation, monitoring, and continuation of the cycle. While these chapters were all present in the first edition, they have been substantively upgraded to reflect current best practices and to capitalize on our experience since publication of the first edition.

Chapters 9 through 13 provide overviews of the fundamental elements of traditional enrollment planning: market positioning, financial aid and pricing, recruitment, student success, and planning for special populations. Two of these chapters—financial aid and pricing, and planning for special populations—are new to the second edition.

The final chapter concludes this edition through the lens of lessons learned from our work leading strategic enrollment planning initiatives on multiple campuses.

At the conclusion of most chapters, the authors have provided two- to three-paragraph summaries or lists of questions campus leaders may find helpful in prompting discussion within the campus community related to the topic or phase of the planning process described in that chapter. These concluding thoughts emphasize the importance of sharing the information and data learned through creation of the plan. These data may lead to immediate actions that can be implemented during the planning process. The dialogue may identify potential implications and/or challenges faced during the planning process and suggest ways to communicate these opportunities or challenges.

Final Thoughts Before We Begin

A colleague of mine recently recounted a position staked out to him by a faculty member during a campus visit. To paraphrase: "Faculty are responsible for the curriculum; the recruitment office is responsible for putting the students in the seats." If you are unequivocally attached to that perspective, then this book is likely not for you. Strategic enrollment planning is a dynamic collaboration because it puts the primary purpose of most colleges and universities—to educate students—at the center of the project. Enrollment planners must collaborate with academic planners, who must collaborate with space and facilities planners, with technology planners, with student success and residence life and co-curricular program planners, all of whom must collaborate with finance planners, while everyone pays attention to scanning the environment for the trends that are swirling around each institution. This book is predicated on the firm belief that we must all collaborate to plan for the long term health of our institutions. A siloed or divisionally insular approach will more likely lead to failure than to an adaptable, collaborative culture.

Ruffalo Noel Levitz consultants have been fortunate to deliver strategic enrollment planning on dozens of campuses over the last decade. More often than not the process is culturally transformative. We hear stories of faculty members asking for data on conversion and yield rates for their colleges and their programs; we see faculty partnering with service providers from across their institutions to support student learning and success and engaging in early alert programs. We see enrollment planners working with foundation staff to build strong funded scholarship programs and to plan for the next infrastructure project that will enable the next academic program or delivery model. We see chief financial officers welcomed into planning meetings because a shared understanding of the financial realities has taken root on a campus. In short, we see folks pulling the same direction on the rope. SEP can make that happen.

CHAPTER 1

The Future of Higher Education and the Strategic Enrollment Planning Imperative

By Kevin Crockett

It is always dangerous to look into a crystal ball with respect to the future of American higher education. Whenever the academy seems on the brink of fundamental change, or institutional closures/consolidations are predicted on a broad scale, we are reminded that our colleges and universities are remarkably resilient. Indeed, since World War II, the industry has either prospered from or suffered through events such as the introduction of Title IV aid programs, the substantial impact of Vietnam on both enrollment levels and campus culture, a massive expansion in the community/technical college sector, booms and busts in the number of high school graduates, large increases in the number of adult learners, explosive growth in the for-profit sector, the introduction and growth of online learning, and relatively severe recessions in the 1970s, 1980s, and 2000s.

CHAPTER HIGHLIGHTS

- **Changing enrollment patterns**

- **Enrollment forecasts to 2024**

- **Retention and completion take center stage**

Each of these events created winners and losers in our postsecondary system, but for the most part, the system itself grew and prospered. Indeed, most of these events resulted in increased access to higher education, and that has led to more people than ever before attending college and holding postsecondary credentials. In 1949, there were 2.4 million individuals enrolled in postsecondary institutions, 70 percent of whom were men. By fall 2014, those figures had increased to 20.2 million students, 57 percent of whom were *women* (NCES, 2015). During roughly the same period, the number of degrees conferred on an annual basis increased from 497,000 to more than 3.8 million (NCES, 2015). Importantly, the percentage of young adults (age 25 to 29) with a bachelor's degree or higher increased from 8 percent of the population in 1950 to 36 percent by 2015 (NCES, 2015). To say that the last 65 years have been a gilded age for American higher education is an understatement.

But the current environment is probably more challenging than any previous period. Between fall 2010 and fall 2014, total enrollment declined by over 800,000 students, an unprecedented four-year decline in the post-World War II era (NCES, 2016). As the United States and other developed nations continue to struggle with relatively weak economic growth in the wake of the Great Recession, perhaps our colleges and universities will emerge stronger than ever; or maybe economic and demographic pressures will lead to a fundamental transformation of our postsecondary system. In either case, institutions that develop strong strategic enrollment planning (SEP) systems will have the best chance of capitalizing on an increasingly turbulent environment. Those that fail to adapt may find themselves closed, consolidated, or considerably weaker.

The purpose of this chapter is to briefly review some of the issues and trends confronting enrollment planners and discuss why these trends make strategic enrollment planning an imperative for colleges and universities that wish to thrive in the years ahead.

Slowing enrollment growth

Table 1-1 shows the enrollment growth of American higher education by type of institution. It also displays the market share for each sector. Between 1964 and 2014, total fall enrollment increased 283 percent from 5.3 million students to 20.2 million students. This growth was largely driven by the emergence of the public two-year sector, which grew by 631 percent and increased its market share from 17 percent of total enrollment in 1964 to 32 percent in fall 2014. While the growth in the public two-year sector is impressive, it is worth noting that, as a share of total enrollment, this group of institutions achieved its maximum market share in 1992 (38 percent), and that figure has since declined to 32 percent. In an era of escalating college costs, it is interesting that our lowest-cost providers are experiencing a decline in their share of total enrollment.

Meanwhile, the four-year public sector experienced growth of 218 percent during this period, while its share of total enrollment declined from 49 percent to 41 percent. The growth rate for the four-year private sector mirrored the four-year public trends, with 208 percent overall growth and a decline in its share of total enrollment from 32 percent to 26 percent. The erosion in market share for private colleges continues a long trend. If you look at the data as far back as 1950, enrollments in public and private institutions were within a few thousand students of each other (NCES, 2015). Today, public institutions control 73 percent of the market, and that share would be greater were it not for the emergence of the private for-profit sector during recent decades.

Table 1-1: Total Fall Enrollment in Degree-Granting Institutions by Type of Institution: Selected Years, 1964 Through 2014 (in Thousands)

Year	Total enrollment	4-year public	Percent of total enrollment	2-year public	Percent of total enrollment	4-year private	Percent of total enrollment	2-year private	Percent of total enrollment
1964	5,280	2,593	49%	875	17%	1,698	32%	114	2%
1974	10,224	4,703	46%	3,285	32%	2,117	21%	119	1%
1984	12,242	5,198	43%	4,279	35%	2,513	21%	252	2%
1994	14,279	5,825	41%	5,308	37%	2,924	21%	221	2%
2004	17,272	6,737	39%	6,244	36%	3,990	23%	302	2%
2014	20,207	8,257	41%	6,398	32%	5,236	26%	317	2%
Growth percent	283%	218%		631%		208%		177%	
Compounded annual growth rate	2.7%	2.3%		4.1%		2.3%		2.0%	

TM

Source: 2015/2010 Digest of Education Statistics

The data in Table 1-1 mask an important trend, namely the explosive growth of the for-profit sector within the private college arena. As Table 1-2 shows, since 1980, the for-profit sector grew from 112,000 students to 1,656,000 students in 2013, for a compounded annual growth rate of 8.5 percent, and its share of total college enrollment has increased from just under 1 percent to 8 percent. This increase in market share appears to have largely come at the expense of the public sector, which lost 5 percentage points of market share between 2000 and 2013. That said, the for-profit sector has contracted 18 percent since 2010 as regulatory and financial pressures have led to steep enrollment declines that show no signs of abating. It will be interesting to see whether this group of schools can reverse these trends or if their best days are behind them.

The slowest growth sector over the last three decades is the independent not-for-profit group, which grew by 37 percent, while the other portion of the not-for-profit sector, religiously affiliated schools, experienced a relatively healthy 87 percent increase (Table 1-2). The growth in the latter group is divided between institutions affiliated with the Roman Catholic Church, which accounted for 36 percent of the growth, and institutions affiliated with various Evangelical Protestant denominations, which accounted for 64 percent of the growth (NCES, 2014). These shifts within the private college sector should be interpreted with some caution, as it totally depends on how institutions chose to self-report their status for more than 30 years.

Table 1-2: Fall Enrollment by Control and Affiliation of Institution: Selected Years, 1980 Through 2013 (in Thousands)

Year	Total enrollment	Public institutions	Percent of total enrollment	Independent not-for-profit	Percent of total enrollment	Religiously affiliated not-for-profit	Percent of total enrollment	For-profit	Percent of total enrollment
1980	12,097	9,457	78%	1,522	13%	1,006	8%	112	1%
1990	13,819	10,845	78%	1,475	11%	1,285	9%	214	2%
2000	15,312	11,753	77%	1,577	10%	1,532	10%	450	4%
2010	21,016	15,142	72%	1,995	11%	1,860	9%	2,018	10%
2012	20,643	14,880	72%	2,064	10%	1,890	9%	1,809	9%
2013	20,376	14,746	72%	2,089	10%	1,885	9%	1,656	8%
Growth percent	68%	56%		37%		87%		1,383%	
Compounded annual growth rate	1.6%	1.3%		1.1%		1.9%		8.5%	

TM

Source: 2015 Digest of Education Statistics

In summary, over the last 50 years (1964-2014), enrollments have increased 326 percent for an annual compounded growth rate of 2.7 percent. That growth was initially fueled by the rapid expansion in the two-year public sector during the 1960s and 1970s, followed by growth in the for-profit sector. Since 1980, the public sector and independent not-for-profits have been losing market share to both the for-profit sector and religiously affiliated not-for-profits.

Enrollment forecasts: 2014 to 2024

According to the National Center for Education Statistics (NCES), total enrollment is expected to increase from 20.2 million in 2014 to 23.1 million in fall 2024. This represents growth of 14 percent overall and a compounded annual growth rate of just 1.4 percent, compared to 4.3 percent between 1964 and 1984 and 3.2 percent between 2000 and 2010, after which we began a four-year enrollment decline. While these decreases may appear modest at first glance, they represent declines of 67 percent and 46 percent in the respective compounded annual growth rates. Here's another way to look at the data: Between 2000 and 2010, total enrollment grew 37 percent, compared to projected growth of 14 percent through 2024. That's 62 percent less growth than colleges actually experienced in the preceding decade (NCES, 2015). The projections do not forecast any significant shifts in market share among sectors, but that may have more to do with NCES methodology than anything else. Importantly, in the private college category, NCES does not distinguish between the for-profit and not-for-profit sectors in its forecasts. It is difficult to imagine existing market share ratios remaining relatively stable over the next decade given past changes.

If the preceding forecasts materialize, then higher education will have to adapt to slower growth rates. This will represent a paradigm shift for many institutions that have relied on enrollment growth to fund campus improvements and academic and co-curricular program expansion. It also underscores the importance of localizing the preceding trends in your enrollment planning efforts.

In the event you do not believe the federal projections cited above, we need to look no further than recent reports from the National Student Clearinghouse, which has become an important source of enrollment data because they are able to report enrollment trends in advance of the federal data. The Clearinghouse fall 2015 enrollment report indicates another year of enrollment decline, which means we likely added a fifth consecutive year of enrollment contraction dating back to fall 2010. They report the most severe declines in the two-year public and four-year for-profit sectors (National Student Clearinghouse, 2015). Five years of enrollment contraction is an alarming and unprecedented development. In fact, since 1947 there was only been one other multiyear decline, from 1993-95, although that was more a leveling, as the total enrollment declined by less than 45,000 students (NCES, 2015).

I am routinely amazed at how little schools know about the market share trends in their student markets or how their growth patterns compare to those of major competitors. I recently visited a college that was experiencing enrollment declines in its adult undergraduate programs. Although campus leaders were convinced they were losing market share to several for-profit competitors that had entered their primary recruitment markets, they had no data on the size or scope of this erosion in market share.

Moreover, it is rare for institutions to have developed enrollment forecasts based on current and projected market share data in their region. These data are foundational to the SEP process. Strategic enrollment plans cannot be based on what you would like to see happen or what you might need to strengthen your institution's financial position. Rather, they should be based on an empirical analysis of past trends and future forecasts in your markets.

Demographic shifts

Coming demographic shifts will lead to regional variations in enrollment levels and ongoing challenges in student preparation and ability to pay for college. The preceding data on projected college enrollments do not include regional projections, but it is safe to assume the underlying projections of high school graduates by geographic region will have a significant impact on college enrollments. The vast majority of college freshmen enroll at colleges/universities within 250 miles of their home, and transfer students tend to be even more local in their enrollment behavior. Enrollment of young adults (age 24 to 30) in both undergraduate and graduate programs is also impacted by these projections, although they lag the high school projections by six to 12 years.

Tables 1-3 and 1-4 show the projected change in high school graduates from 2008-09 through 2027-28 by geographic region and race/ethnicity (note: the race/ethnicity data are for public high school graduates only).

Table 1-3: Actual and Projected Numbers of High School Graduates (Public and Non-public) by Region: 2008-09 to 2027-28 (in Thousands)

Region	2008-09 actual	2018-19 projected	Percent change (from 2008-09)	2027-28 projected	Percent change (from 2018-19)
Northeast	642	605	-6.1%	576	-4.7%
Midwest	768	722	-6.0%	676	-6.4%
South	1,166	1,221	+4.7%	1,230	+0.8%
West	772	762	-1.3%	760	-0.3%
Total	**3,348**	3,310	-1.1%	3,242	-2.1%

TM

Source: Western Interstate Commission for Higher Education (WICHE), 2016

The number of high school graduates increased nationally by 21 percent between 1998-99 and 2008-09, from 2,760,000 to 3,348,000 (WICHE, 2016). This increase fueled substantial enrollment growth during the first decade of the millennium, as noted above. A decrease of 1.1 percent is expected between 2008-09 and 2018-19, after which graduates will decline 2.1 percent between 2018-19 and 2027-28. However, the regional variations are substantial, with the Northeast and Midwest experiencing substantial decreases. Meanwhile, the West will experience a very modest decline and the South will actually increase 5.5 percent between 2008-09 and 2027-28. It is important for institutions to look inside these regional trends by focusing on their own student catchment areas. For example, in the Northeast, New York State's projected decline by 2027-28 is less than 2 percent, whereas New Jersey is expected to decline by 15 percent. In the South, Texas is expected to grow by 25 percent, whereas Louisiana is projected to grow by only 5 percent. In the West, California is expected to decline by 9 percent, while Colorado is projected to increase by 14 percent between 2008-09 and 2027-28 (WICHE, 2016).

If your institution serves large numbers of transfer and adult students, population projections are typically available from state planning offices. These can be used to infer future enrollments based on your current and projected market share of students within specific age groupings. For example, if your state had 1,000,000 persons age 25 to 29 with 50,000 enrolled in college, and your institution enrolled 500 of those students, your market share would be 1 percent of the 25- to 29-year-old college population. These data can be compared to future population projections to infer potential changes in enrollment based on changes in the age cohorts of the general population.

Table 1-4: Actual and Projected Numbers of Public High School Graduates by Race/Ethnicity: 2008-09 to 2027-28 (in Thousands)

Race/ethnicity	2008-09 actual	2018-19 projected	Percent change (from 2008-09)	2027-28 projected	Percent change (from 2018-19)
Caucasian	1,889	1,690	-10.5%	1,530	-9.5%
Black/African American	452	419	-7.4%	418	-0.3%
Hispanic	482	667	+38.5%	718	+7.6%
Asian/Pacific Islander	162	208	+28.3%	254	+22.1%
American Indian/Alaska Native	34	33	-3.1%	36	+8.4%

TM

Source: Western Interstate Commission for Higher Education (WICHE), 2016

The race/ethnicity data also contain significant underlying trends, namely a projected 19 percent decline in the Caucasian population (by 2027-28) accompanied by substantial increases in the number of Hispanic and Asian/Pacific Islanders (Table 1-4).

The increase in Hispanic high school graduates, coupled with the decline in Caucasian students, is significant, as it relates to preparation for college. According to 2015 ACT data, Hispanic test takers had an average ACT composite score of 18.9 vs. 22.4 for Caucasian students. Moreover, while 50 percent of Caucasian students met three or more ACT college-readiness benchmarks in 2015, only 16 percent of Hispanics met at least three benchmarks. These benchmarks are based on achieving specific scores on ACT sub-tests, which correlate to the statistical probability of achieving a C or higher in college coursework (ACT, 2015).

Meanwhile, the increase in Asian/Pacific Islanders is encouraging, at least as it relates to the Asian portion of this population. Fifty-nine percent of Asian students met three or more college readiness benchmarks, the highest of any group. Meanwhile, 26 percent of Pacific Islanders met at least three college readiness benchmarks (ACT, 2015).

© 2016 Ruffalo Noel Levitz

When it comes to remediation, 29 percent of first-year Caucasian students took a remedial course in 2011-12. The corresponding figure for Hispanic students was 36 percent and 38 percent for African American students (NCES, 2014). Thirty-three percent of Asian students required a remedial course in 2011-12 despite their relatively strong ACT composite and college readiness statistics. It is fair to conclude that institutions that will serve growing numbers of non-Caucasian students will need to **allocate additional resources** for developmental education programs and related academic support services in the years ahead.

> It is fair to conclude that institutions that will serve growing numbers of non-Caucasian students will need to **allocate additional resources** for developmental education programs and related academic support services in the years ahead.

Finally, demographic shifts are likely to place additional pressure on students' ability to pay for college. In 2014, median family incomes were highest among Asian families ($82,732), followed by Caucasians ($76,658), Hispanics ($45,114), and African Americans ($43,151). Indeed, Hispanic and African American families earn approximately 43 percent less than the typical Caucasian family (College Board, 2015). This promises to place additional strain on federal, state, and institutional financial aid resources as we experience a contraction in Caucasian students and substantial growth in Hispanic students. This will make the college financing environment particularly challenging in those regions of the country where these demographic shifts are most pronounced.

Rapidly changing economic models

The traditional economic model for both public and private institutions is changing rapidly. While enrollment growth rates are projected to slow over the next decade, it is highly likely that resources to fund the enterprise will also remain constrained. Indeed, in virtually every sector, reliance on net tuition revenue has increased while state and federal support has either contracted or increased only modestly. As Table 1-5 shows, at all types of institutions, the average share of revenues coming from net tuition and fees increased between 2002-03 and 2012-13 (College Board, 2015).

Table 1-5: Percentage of Institutional Revenue per FTE Student in Constant 2012 Dollars at Public and Private (Nonprofit) Institutions by Revenue Source: 2002-03 vs. 2012-13

Note: Revenues from private gifts, investment returns, and endowment income are not included in these percentages.

Institution type	Federal appropriations and federal, state, and local grants and contracts		State and local appropriations		Net tuition and fee revenue	
	2002-03	2012-13	2002-03	2012-13	2002-03	2012-13
Public doctoral	34%	34%	40%	26%	26%	40%
Public master's	13%	12%	52%	35%	35%	53%
Public bachelor's	16%	14%	49%	37%	35%	49%
Public two-year	16%	14%	60%	51%	24%	35%
Private doctoral	39%	36%	3%	1%	57%	63%
Private master's	7%	4%	3%	0%	90%	96%
Private bachelor's	9%	4%	3%	0%	88%	95%

™

Source: College Board, 2015 Trends in College Pricing

These shifts were most pronounced in the public sector, where reliance on net tuition and fee revenue increased by 11 percentage points in the two-year sector and 18 percent for the master's degree-granting institutions. These trends over the past decade reflect a longer-term shift in the financing of public postsecondary education, changing what was once a largely public entity to one that is increasingly financed by students and their families. Looking across all public institutions in 1990, net tuition revenue as a percentage of public higher education total revenue was 25 percent. By fall 2014, that figure had increased to 47 percent. Moreover, in constant dollars, the amount students contributed to finance public postsecondary education through net tuition and fees increased 203 percent during the period, from $20.9 billion to $63.3 billion (SHEEO, 2015).

Meanwhile, net tuition revenue constitutes a much larger percentage of total revenue for private nonprofit colleges and universities than for public institutions. Bachelor's and master's degree-granting institutions derive over 94 percent of their revenue (excluding gift and investment income) from net tuition and fees, while doctoral institutions are somewhat less dependent on net tuition revenue.

So if we assume colleges and universities will continue to be increasingly dependent on net tuition and fee revenue to finance operations, what are the prospects that students and families will be willing and able to pay an ever-increasing share of college costs?

It is well-documented that college costs have risen faster than both family incomes and the consumer price index for at least the last 30 years. As Table 1-6 shows, the average annual percentage increase in *inflation-adjusted* published tuition and fee prices increased in each of the past three decades. While price increases have slowed during the last decade, they continue to increase faster than family incomes.

Table 1-6: Average Annual Percentage Increases in Inflation-Adjusted Published Prices by Decade, 1985-86 to 2015-16

Institution type	1985-86 to 1995-96	1995-96 to 2005-06	2005-06 to 2015-16
Private nonprofit four-year	3.5%	3.0%	2.4%
Public four-year	4.2%	4.3%	3.4%
Public two-year	3.9%	2.5%	2.6%

TM

Source: College Board, 2015 Trends in College Pricing

However, published prices are less meaningful than net tuition and fees, the amount that students actually pay after subtracting grant aid from all sources and federal education tax credits and deductions. As Table 1-7 shows, over the past decade, net prices have actually declined in the two-year public sector while increasing 38 percent in the public four-year sector and a mere 1.3 percent in the four-year private sector. Remember, all figures are adjusted for inflation. It is also important to recognize that large increases in federal Pell Grants and veterans' benefits in 2009-10, combined with the 2009 implementation of the American Opportunity Tax Credit, had a significant impact on the net prices paid by students who benefit from these programs (College Board, 2015). In the case of tuition tax credits, it is debatable whether these funds truly impact student enrollment decisions because families experience these "savings" within the context of their individual tax return, not when they are initially evaluating college costs and financial aid offers.

Table 1-7: Net Tuition and Fees in Constant 2015 Dollars for Full-Time Undergraduate Students: 1995-96, 2005-06, and 2015-16 (Estimated)

Institution type	1995-96	2005-06	2015-16
Private nonprofit four-year	$11,270	$14,700	$14,890
Public four-year	$2,300	$2,880	$3,980
Public two-year	$770	-$300	-$840

Source: College Board, 2015 Trends in College Pricing

Nevertheless, these relatively modest increases in net tuition and fees have come at a price, especially in the four-year private sector where tuition discount rates have been on the rise. In fact, between fall 2004 and fall 2014, the average tuition discount rate increased from 38.1 percent to 47.0 percent for first-time, full-time freshmen while increasing from 34.3 percent to 41.3 percent for all undergraduate students (NACUBO, 2016). When nearly 50 cents of every tuition dollar collected is returned in the form of institutional financial aid, we are clearly seeing price resistance manifested in the form of increased discounting.

Finally, family borrowing, which increased from $54.3 billion in 2000-02 to $124.0 billion in 2010-11, has declined four consecutive years and currently stands at $106.1 billion in constant dollars (College Board, 2015). While some of this is attributable to the aforementioned enrollment declines, per-student borrowing declined by $840 between 2009-10 and 2014-15 (College Board, 2015). Although some observers applaud this modest reduction in student debt, these trends suggest we may have reached an upper limit with respect to families' willingness to finance college through debt.

In my judgment, the next decade promises to be very challenging for colleges and universities as they attempt to help students manage net cost of attendance. The industry received some necessary relief in 2009 with increased Pell Grant funding and the American Opportunity Tax Credit, expanding the number of families eligible for tuition tax credits. Given the federal budget deficit and very tight fiscal conditions in the states, the best-case scenario is probably static funding on an inflation-adjusted basis at the state and federal levels. What does this mean for strategic enrollment planners and students?

Four-year public institutions are likely to continue increasing tuition rates at well above inflationary levels, assuming policy makers do not constrain their ability to do so, as is happening in some states. This will require them to adopt financial models more akin to the private four-year sector, charging some families more so that they can provide adequate financial aid to families with lower incomes. Private institutions, which have already experienced erosion in net tuition and fee revenue, are likely to face a prolonged period of very modest growth in net tuition revenue, forcing them to make difficult choices regarding program offerings and the types of students they serve.

Community colleges continue to offer the most favorable financial proposition for students. This is unlikely to change in the years ahead, but they will also contend with tight fiscal conditions in most states.

It will be important to aggressively monitor student borrowing levels across sectors in the years ahead. Increased borrowing enabled colleges and universities to increase tuition without significant increases in institutional aid, at least until 2009-10 when tuition discounting started to increase in the private sector. If students and their parents are unwilling to gradually increase the amount of debt they take on, as evidenced by the recent decline in overall and per-student borrowing, then the system will lose an important funding mechanism that has fueled revenue growth for decades.

This environment makes it imperative that enrollment planners understand how various segments of their student population pay for college and develop targeted financing strategies for these populations in the years ahead. Indeed, it is far too common for colleges to raise tuition and fees in the context of their own internal cost pressures with little regard for how various student groups will finance those cost increases. Therefore, a central focus of SEP in the years ahead will be devising multiyear strategies to make certain that the target student markets have a viable means of managing their portion of college costs.

Growing pressure for improved retention and completion rates

Not only are we facing a difficult demographic and financial environment, the demand for public accountability is on the rise, especially in the form of improving college completion rates. The Obama Administration has had a stated goal of increasing the percentage of young Americans with a college degree from 41 percent in 2009 to 60 percent by 2025. If successful, that would produce about 8 million more college graduates than the 2 million that are currently projected through modest growth in college enrollments (U.S. Department of Education, 2011). Large foundations, such as Lumina and the Bill and Melinda Gates Foundation, have aligned themselves with the President's completion agenda and are investing tens of millions of dollars in programs aimed at helping to increase college access and attainment rates. State legislatures and higher education coordinating boards are also demanding increased completion rates from the institutions they fund and oversee. Dozens of states have announced plans to increase college attainment rates, and with that comes increased pressure on enrollment planners to develop viable strategies for reaching these goals.

The focus on increased college attainment has strong rationale. Consider the following data compiled by the Lumina Foundation and reported on their website.

- Four out of five jobs lost during the 2007-09 recession were those requiring high school education or less.
- By 2020, two-thirds of all jobs will require postsecondary education.
- Young adults are continuing to enter the labor force ill prepared. At a mere 42 percent, the United States currently ranks 13th among developed countries in college attainment rates for young adults.
- The postsecondary attainment rate for adults is 40 percent. Adults who identify as Asian are leading in attainment with 59 percent, while whites come in at 44 percent. African American attainment rates are as low as 27 percent. Native American and Latino Americans complete postsecondary programs at even lower rates, 23 percent and 20 percent, respectively.

On a macroeconomic level, if the United States wishes to remain competitive with the rest of the world, it will need a workforce with increasing levels of postsecondary education—hence the sharp focus on increasing attainment rates at the federal level. At the state level, we are likely to see increased accountability in the form of funding mechanisms that reward institutions on the basis of course and degree completions instead of enrollment levels, which have driven these formulas in the past. According to the National Conference of State Legislatures, "Thirty-two states have a funding formula or policy in place to allocate a portion of funding based on performance indicators such as course completion, time to degree, transfer rates, the number of degrees awarded, or the number of low-income and minority graduates. Five states are currently transitioning to some type of performance funding, meaning the Legislature or governing board has approved a performance funding program and the details are currently being worked out" (NCSL, 2016).

At an institutional level, strategic enrollment planners will be motivated by more than just state and federal calls to improve completion rates, especially if they are in markets with flat or declining demographics. Indeed, if you are faced with a relatively flat or even shrinking student market, one way to maintain existing enrollment levels is to increase student retention through to graduation as a means of mitigating potential losses in new students. Unfortunately, this is no small task, but one that can be accomplished when data are used to create programmatic and student-level strategies.

Despite decades of increased focus on student retention and completion, little progress has occurred in improving either retention or graduation rates. Table 1-8 displays data from ACT on the retention rates of first-year students at four-year colleges from 1994 to 2014. Among all institutions, the first- to second-year retention rate has dropped from 74.1 percent to 73.7 percent with a slight improvement at public institutions and a decline at private institutions.

Table 1-8: Percentage of First-Year Students at Four-Year Colleges Who Return for a Second Year: 1994-2014 (in Five-Year Increments)

	1994	1999	2004	2009	2014
Public institutions	71.7%	71.9%	73.5%	72.9%	72.3%
Private institutions	75.2%	75.1%	75.1%	73.0%	74.4%
All four-year institutions	74.1%	74.1%	74.5%	73.0%	73.7%

TM

Source: 2015 ACT Retention Completion Summary Tables

Table 1-9 contains data on the five-year graduation rates among first-year students at four-year colleges by year. Among all institutions, just slightly over half (52.6 percent) of first-time, full-time students who begin at a four-year school graduate within five years.

Table 1-9: Percentage of Four-Year College Students Who Earn a Degree Within Five Years of Entry: 1994-2014 (in Five-Year Increments)

	1994	1999	2004	2009	2014
Public institutions	45.6%	42.2%	42.3%	44.0%	44.2%
Private institutions	57.2%	55.8%	57.9%	57.6%	57.6%
All four-year institutions	53.7%	51.6%	52.0%	52.7%	52.6%

Source: 2015 ACT Retention Completion Summary Tables

While ACT does not provide year-to-year data on the two-year sector, they do report that for the 2013 cohort of first-time students, 55 percent returned for their second year (ACT, 2013). And the National Center for Education Statistics reports that since 2000, the number of students completing a certificate or associate degree within 150 percent of normal time has declined from 31 percent to 28 percent (NCES, 2015).

Table 1-10: Percentage of Two-Year College Students Who Earn a Certificate or Associate Degree Within 150 Percent of Normal Time: Selected Years 2000-2011 Cohorts

	2000	2005	2010	2011
All two-year institutions	30.5%	27.5%	29.4%	27.9%

Source: 2015 Digest of Education Statistics

Of course, these figures do not consider students who move on to a four-year college prior to completion of an associate degree, and more states are counting this outcome as a successful two-year student. Nevertheless, it represents a significant attainment gap when fewer than one in three full-time, degree-seeking students at two-year schools successfully completes a degree within 150 percent of normal time.

Faced with pressure from state and federal governments to improve student success rates and relatively flat numbers of high school graduates in many regions of the country, strategic enrollment planners cannot afford to ignore the critical issues surrounding persistence, progression, retention, and completion in their work. In fact, it is likely that these issues will consume an increasing portion of the SEP agenda on most campuses, whereas in the past, they have all too often taken a backseat to marketing and recruitment strategies.

Changing learning modalities

The National Center for Educational Statistics only recently began tracking the proportion of enrollments in online courses. They actually track the data as students enrolled in "distance education," which includes students enrolled in more conventional distance delivery systems; but most observers logically assume the vast majority of these courses are either fully or partially online. As Table 1-11 shows, approximately 28 percent of all college students took at least one distance course in fall 2014. And while total enrollment continued its multiyear contraction, enrollment in distance courses increased 4.1 percent, including a 6.2 percent increase in those enrolled in exclusively distance courses and a 2.2 percent increase in students taking at least one distance course. These data support a long-term trend we have observed—a growing student preference for online courses that essentially replaces traditional, classroom-based instruction.

Ruffalo Noel Levitz worked with a state system a few years ago that had placed a lot of emphasis on building their online delivery capacity as part of their effort to reverse a multiyear enrollment decline. However, as their online enrollments grew, they experienced commensurate declines in their other learning modalities. Therefore, as strategic enrollment planners consider the role and scope of online learning in crafting their academic strategy, they should bear in mind that, unless an online program represents an entirely new academic program or is targeted at an entirely new student market, the potential to cannibalize existing enrollments is high.

Table 1-11: Number of Students Enrolled in Degree-Granting Postsecondary Institutions, by Distance Education Participation: Fall 2013 and Fall 2014

	2013	2014	Percent change
Total enrollment	20,375,789	20,207,369	-0.8%
No distance education	14,853,595	14,456,952	-2.7%
Total, any distance education course(s)	5,522,194	5,750,417	+4.1%
At least one, but not all, of student's courses	2,862,991	2,926,083	+2.2%
Exclusively distance education courses	2,659,203	2,824,334	+6.2%

TM

Source: 2015 Digest of Education Statistics

There are also significant gaps between attitudes and implementation of online learning. For example, in its annual survey of campus leaders, the 2016 *Online Report Card* found that, while 63 percent of leaders reported that "Online education is critical to the long-term strategy of my institution," the percentage that had distance education in their strategic plans was only 41 percent, a 22-point gap (Allen and Seaman, 2016). This suggests a fairly significant gap between perceived importance of online learning and what is actually making it into institutional strategic plans. It is also clear that faculty skepticism regarding online learning remains a problem. In fact, less than 30 percent of the survey respondents in the *Online Report Card* said that, "Faculty at my school accepts the value and legitimacy of online education" (Allen and Seaman, 2016).

Unfortunately, we still lack normative national data on the retention and graduation rates of students in online courses. Since retention and completion rates are tracked by student cohort, and many students take a mixture of face-to-face, fully online, or hybrid courses, there is simply no reliable source of data on student success rates in these courses. The lack of national normative data makes it even more important that strategic enrollment planners evaluate student success metrics in their own online courses compared to students enrolled in more traditional course delivery formats.

Finally, any discussion of online learning would be incomplete without commentary on student satisfaction. The Ruffalo Noel Levitz Priorities Survey for Online Learners™ (PSOL) provides some insight into the satisfaction of online learners and suggests areas that represent challenges to institutions offering online course work (Ruffalo Noel Levitz, 2016). In our *2015-16 National Online Learners Satisfaction and Priorities Report*, we identified the strengths and challenges for online learners specifically at four-year and two-year institutions. The national data set for the combination of institution types provides the following perspective on perceived strengths and challenges for online learners. Strengths were defined as those items ranked above the mid-point in student importance and in the top quartile of satisfaction. The following strengths were identified by online learners as a whole (in order of importance):

- Registration for online courses is convenient.
- Billing and payment procedures are convenient for me.
- Adequate online library resources are provided.

Challenges were areas ranked above the mid-point in importance and in the bottom quartile of satisfaction—or in other words, the top quartile of performance gaps. Listed in order of importance, the following were the top challenges identified by online learners as a whole:

- Student assignments are clearly defined in the syllabus.
- The quality of instruction is excellent.
- Faculty are responsive to student needs.
- Tuition paid is a worthwhile investment.
- Program requirements are clear and reasonable.
- Faculty provide timely feedback about student's progress.

These high-level findings suggest that schools have done a good job of perfecting the transactional aspects of online learning such as registration, billing, and making library resources available to online learners. On the other hand, students are expressing dissatisfaction with some important parts of the actual learning experience, including instructional quality, faculty responsiveness, and the overall value received for tuition paid. These are significant issues that should be addressed in any SEP process, especially for schools that are exploring significant expansion of their online offerings.

Conclusion

In this chapter, I have outlined some of the major trends impacting higher education. They can be summarized as follows.

- Postsecondary enrollment in the United States is contracting, and any future growth is expected to be very slow by historical standards. This means institutions that have previously relied on enrollment growth to fund campus improvements and academic and co-curricular program expansion may have to adapt their thinking based on likely student demand in their primary student catchment areas.

- Demographic shifts will lead to regional variations in enrollment levels and ongoing challenges in student preparation and ability to pay for college. The traditional student cohort is becoming more ethnically diverse, less able to pay for college, and less prepared for the rigors of postsecondary education. These trends need to be localized, and strategies should be developed to respond to the needs of future students. Schools should also develop programs to serve students in their 20s and 30s. These students fueled enrollment growth from 2000-10, and they will have needs for graduate education as well as continuing education in the years ahead.

- The traditional economic model for both public and private institutions is changing rapidly. Public institutions will become increasingly reliant on net tuition and fee revenue, and the privates will have to contend with slower growth in net tuition revenue than they are accustomed. This environment makes it imperative that enrollment planners understand how various segments of their student population pay for college and develop financing strategies for these student populations in the years ahead.

- Pressure to improve retention and completion rates will intensify. For some institutions, this will represent an economic imperative based on the demographics of their primary student markets. For others, the pressure will come from legislatures and higher education coordinating boards discontented with the lack of meaningful progress in improving student success rates over the past several decades.

- Online learning will offer both opportunity and challenge. Schools that harness online technology to develop new academic programs and open new markets will prosper. Those that simply shift students from one learning modality to another may see their cost structures increase as they attempt to maintain multiple delivery systems without any significant increase in enrollment and net tuition revenue.

As the United States and other developed nations struggle with anemic economic growth and unfavorable demographics, perhaps our colleges and universities will deal with the challenges outlined in this chapter and emerge stronger than ever; or maybe these structural, economic, and demographic changes will lead to a fundamental transformation of our postsecondary system. In either case, institutions that engage in meaningful strategic enrollment planning and shift institutional thinking from annual planning to strategic enrollment management with a longer-range (three-to-five-year minimum) focus will have the best chance of thriving in this environment. Those that rely on traditional planning models, with their inherently inward focus, are likely to fall victim to the market forces.

I hope this chapter both motivates your campus to engage in an SEP process and provides some initial guidance about the environmental data you should be collecting in the first phase of that process. In closing, it is well to heed the admonition of the 19th century English essayist and reformer John Ruskin: "What we think, or what we know, or what we believe is, in the end, of little consequence. The only consequence is what we do."

CHAPTER 2

Building a Culture of Strategic Enrollment Planning

By Jim Hundrieser

Why is effective strategic planning so rare on campuses?

In *The Chronicle of Higher Education in 2011*, Benjamin Ginsberg, professor at Johns Hopkins University and author of *The Fall of the Faculty: The Rise of the All-Administrative University and Why It Matters*, stated that faculty members often view the strategic plan as "neither strategic nor a plan, but a waste of time" (Ginsberg, 2011). Over an eight-year period, surveys of enrollment managers conducted by Ruffalo Noel Levitz show about 70 percent of four- year public and private colleges have a multi-year strategic enrollment plan (SEP), yet fewer than half consider it to be of good or excellent quality (Ruffalo Noel Levitz, 2016). A quick web search using the words "plan to grow enrollment" provides links to pages and pages of college and university strategic plans where a major priority is to grow enrollment. This observation is in a time where, as stated in Chapter 1, enrollment in many regions is not expected to grow for potentially the next decade or longer.

> **CHAPTER HIGHLIGHTS**
>
> ■ **People create the process**
>
> ■ **Process is as important (or more important) than the plan**
>
> ■ **The plan sets the direction for a future state**

Many institutions make student enrollment and its relevant metrics a top priority. The metrics include such things as total enrollment numbers, academic profiles, diversity profile numbers, student success measures such as retention and graduation rates, and many others. These metrics are discussed at board meetings, presidential cabinet meetings, deans' meetings, faculty meetings, and with the media. In fact, these enrollment metrics define each institution—its reputation, its learning environment, its culture, and its fiscal health.

The reality is that most institutions, as reported by their own enrollment leaders (Ruffalo Noel Levitz, 2016) do not have effective enrollment plans. Why? The fault typically lies with a poor planning process, no planning process, or a history of plans that were made but not implemented. Many times, an enrollment plan may be called "strategic" but was produced by a process that was not really strategic or linked to budget reallocation. The reason excellent enrollment plans are the exception is because true strategic enrollment planning is rare. Indeed, if the planning process is not done right, the plan will be a waste of time.

So how does an enrollment plan become a strategic enrollment plan? How do campus leaders get administrators, faculty, and staff to see it as an active, intelligent, realistic vision of what the campus could (and should) become? In this chapter, we will explore how to create an environment where strategic enrollment plans can thrive—from the elements of a successful plan to the acceptance of the plan by campus stakeholders.

Seeking alignment with a future state

In the early 1990s, President James Young of Elon University told his faculty and staff, "A fine-quality institution is never static" (Keller, 2004). The same can be said for first-rate strategic enrollment planning processes. With fast-paced changes in technology, the need to attract and graduate a more diverse student body, and the challenges identified in Chapter 1, planning must be more than a periodic exercise conducted by an organization to maintain legitimacy (Bolman and Deal, 1997). Good planning needs to shift paradigms and provide a roadmap to the future. This is not a task to be delegated. Plans should be shepherded by top leaders, well-lived through active review, and carefully monitored by institutional leaders along with key faculty, staff, and other administrators.

Given the profound external challenges universities face, transformational SEP leaders must not only master the strategic and organizational framework of the organization, but also establish patterns that bring out the deep talents and gifts of the people within that organization. A useful management construct that may apply here is the "flywheel," explained by management researcher and author Jim Collins in his executive leadership book, *Good to Great: Why Some Companies Make the Leap and Others Don't* (2001). Collins noted that effective organizations foster a culture of deliberate, consistent action toward a common goal. To illustrate this point, Collins uses the metaphor of a flywheel, "a massive metal disk mounted horizontally on an axle, about 30 feet in diameter, two feet thick, and weighing about 5,000 pounds" (Collins, 2001). Members of the organization attempt to rotate the disk, yet the weight of the wheel makes the initial pushing almost backbreaking. Finally, the wheel moves an inch, then two, then a quarter turn, and then, with considerable and sustained force, the wheel finally makes a full rotation. At this point, the momentum of the massive disk begins to compound the efforts, making the pushing no less sustained, but less intense with each and every push. Eventually, the wheel is humming.

This is the kind of disciplined culture that SEP represents and facilitates as long as trust and interdependence are fostered with the ongoing intentionality Collins describes. While many variables may differ by institutional type and governance structure, the initial movement in a truly collaborative SEP process is usually imperceptible and agonizing for all those leaning into that wheel of change. Depending on an institution's history and experience with enrollment planning, the path toward trustful collaboration may take many years.

As various stakeholders and university divisions battle to avoid vulnerability and maintain control—both perceived and real—the effort needed to move the enormous disk may be prolonged. However, if we are going to move an institution forward, we must seek to build a symbiotic solution to the challenges faced by the academy and, indeed, by higher education collectively.

The case for connectivity and alignment

SEP is the alignment of an institution's strategic planning core with the collective mission, vision, and values of the college/university thereby generating meaningful collaboration to achieve common goals and integrated strategies. It is tempting for the casual observer to compartmentalize the influence of a well-functioning SEP enterprise within an institution in spheres surrounding the student application and enrollment processes. In fact, the fully realized SEP engages the entire mission, vision, and values of an institution, aligning academic and co-curricular programming with the student lifecycle from initial interest through completion. Figure 2-1 illustrates the central role of the institutional mission, as well as the interconnectedness of the SEP on every level of college/university management.

Figure 2-1: The Interconnectivity of Effective SEP

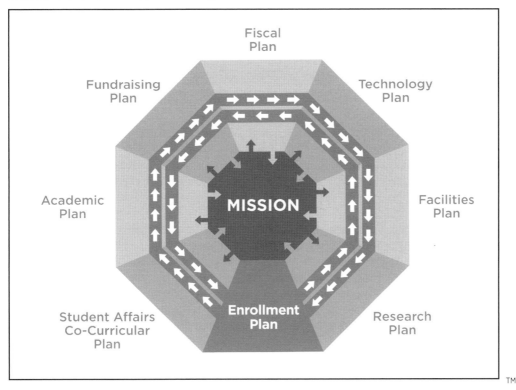

TM

This level of interconnectedness ensures each functional unit is integrated so the academic, co-curricular, and enrollment plans, in effect, become a unified whole. For example, a community college might establish a mission of outreach to a local neighborhood with a large Kurdish immigrant population. If only embraced by the admissions staff, a few local open houses and community events may take place, but the resulting outreach has minimal effectiveness. However, if also embraced by the foreign language department as part of its educational mission, native speakers from the department may begin educational programming in the community while the alumni office engages young alumni from that neighborhood to host campus tours.

In an authentic sense, a well-crafted SEP process answers who we educate, while the academic plan establishes how we will educate them, and the co-curricular plan seeks to link together an expanded community experience. The bottom line is that these three concepts (SEP, academic plan, and co-curricular plan) are interrelated and must be viewed in this manner to realize the educational goals of the institution. While answers to these questions form the essence of an organization's purpose and are at the center of mission-driven SEP effectiveness, they are only part of a complex process of interdependent SEP leadership. In order to foster innovative collaboration, the bond felt by a campus community to the academic mission of the institution must extend beyond the surface to provide engagement at a deeper, human level.

The establishment of trust-based SEP collaboration is an important goal; however, it is not the end goal. SEP advocates for the accomplishment of sustainable success through a highly collaborative, long-term process allowing a college/university to thrive in a multitude of market conditions. A pattern thus emerges from the combined campus interactions—a type of upward spiral of increasing mutual faith, in which the level of positive empathy and cooperation grows. As the collaborative process grows, the loops decrease in circumference as the trusting process becomes easier and easier with each rotation. Research and experience consistently confirm that educational organizations featuring higher levels of trust are able to instill an ongoing confidence that the institution will act "reliably and competently" (Bryk and Schneider, 2003, as quoted in Schmidt, 2010). Trust reduces inner complexity, as individuals engage in repeated interactions where what was expected to happen has come to pass (Lane, 1998).

Considerations for starting a strategic enrollment plan

As institutions contemplate creating strategic enrollment plans for their campuses, practitioners must consider how this planning process can strengthen enrollment management and align academic and co-curricular trends, demands, and capacities with graduate academic programs, employment, and workforce needs. Leaders must also consider how this process can educate diverse audiences about enrollment planning, the important linkage that quality programs bring to building enrollments, and the value of planning and implementation. This process should be transparent and be a process that builds trust and collaboration between cross-functional units.

SEP is a data-informed and ongoing process that identifies, evaluates, and modifies strategies and enrollment goals in light of internal and external forces that may influence the direction of the institution. The planning process addresses:

- The institution's mission and goals, as well as its competitive position in the higher education environment;
- The institution's ability to serve students, both currently and in the future;
- The changing marketplace and environment and their relative impact on the institution's vision; and
- The potential to adapt within the context of an institution's current mission and the expected future state.

Ultimately, SEP should align enrollment goals with a stable future fiscal state that allows the institution to achieve optimal long-term enrollment levels and fiscal health.

The initial process involves innovative thinking by a cross-section of strategic individuals who can determine institutional direction and allocation of resources as well as use data to inform their strategic direction and action. It also entails communicating with all constituencies and earning their confidence and support. After a strategic enrollment plan has been developed, a campus must shift efforts from planning to implementation. Strategic enrollment management becomes an ongoing and routine planning process to ensure the plan's strategic vision and goals are effectively and efficiently pursued. The results of strategies and tactics must be continuously monitored, evaluated, and modified when necessary. As the internal and external environments change, additional information and data need to be collected, analyzed, and integrated into the ongoing management process.

Higher education serves a variety of markets (undergraduate, traditional, transfer, adult, graduate, and those seeking certification for specific skill sets), and its practitioners need to better understand the evolving marketplace in order to create a sustainable future. The current state of higher education suggests that few of the thousands of colleges and universities in existence have done enough to adapt to changing market conditions since those institutions were founded 50 to 200 years ago. Despite extensive research and high-level theorizing, higher education has made progress toward its ultimate mission—moving more students toward degree attainment—but only at a rate of approximately 34 percent completion nationally, with the majority of improvement among female students (National Center for Education Statistics, 2014). As institutional leaders prepare to launch an SEP process, they must consider the involvement of stakeholders, the realities of higher education's future, and the use of data to determine their position relative to peer and aspirational institutions.

> "The role of SEP is to identify...disruptions and determine how the individual institution can optimize its market niche within the higher education marketplace."

Harvard business professor Clayton Christensen has written numerous books about innovative solutions and practices. In *The Innovative University*, he discusses the innovator's dilemma: when industry leaders focus on better serving their most prized customers and matching their toughest competitors, they may overlook what is happening among their broader base of potential consumers (students). In an educational context, this suggests that two things are likely occurring: 1) growth in the number of potential students who cannot afford an enhanced but increasingly expensive product (a college education) and thus become non-consumers of that product, either by transferring to another institution or withdrawing completely; and 2) the emergence of technologies that allow new competitors to serve this disenfranchised group of non-consumers (Christensen, 2011).

As Chapter 1 explained, focusing on the best and brightest students who have the time and ability to pay for a traditional college education has two negative outcomes for institutions. First, the non-consumer group of students is likely to grow as they are overlooked and priced out of a college education. Second, institutions pursuing an inordinate number of top-quality students may endanger their fiscal health as they have to offer steep discounts to enroll those students. The romanticized idea of four years at a residential college will still have a place in higher education, but it will be a smaller piece of the overall picture (Van Der Werf, Sabatier, 2009). It is likely this shifting paradigm will continue to cause disruptions to the higher education marketplace.

The role of SEP is to identify those disruptions and determine how the individual institution can optimize its market niche within the higher education marketplace. Institutions must hone their program offerings and key marketing messages while also aligning those offerings and messages with market demand and student preferences. They must also understand how they can distinguish their programs, services, activities, or community experiences from their competition, and convey the value and benefits of their offerings to students.

Finally, the campus must rethink its product and how it is delivered. In a complex market, institutions must consider multiple types of program delivery (online learning, face-to-face instruction, hybrid class offerings) and understand the implications of changing or limiting their product delivery methods. That said, the institution must also link budgetary realities to offering multiple delivery options. Furthermore, in seeking to find the point where market, competition, and product align, each institution must compare its own offerings and delivery modes to those of its peer institutions, competitors, and aspirant institutions.

Peer vs. aspirational institutions

As campuses begin the planning process, it is critical to conduct an honest and data-informed review of institutional competitors within the marketplace. Campuses should determine which institutions are considered their peers, which are their competitors, and which institutions they aspire to be more like.

- Peer institutions are those that have comparable programs, often they have similar student characteristics, and are of comparable size and resources. Peer institutions become the group against which a campus benchmarks its data in order to gauge its performance.

- Competing institutions may not be in an institution's peer grouping. An analysis of National Student Clearinghouse, FASFA filing, and cross application data show students are enrolling at or expressing interest in other institutions that seem very different on the surface.

- Aspirant institutions are those that an institution strives to be more like in terms of enrollments, student profiles, research goals/initiatives, athletic affiliations, academic or co-curricular product offerings, size, endowments, and/or resources.

Campuses need an accurate assessment of their peers, competitors, and aspirant institutions. It is essential to base these comparisons on solid data rather than assumptions or perceptions. Numerous national surveys allow an institution to compare their data with that of peer, competitor, and aspirant institutional types. Figure 2-2 provides a snapshot of the type of data points to be collected. As part of the planning process, an institution must assess whether it is below, above, or at the stated averages of its comparator institutions. If below or at stated averages, an institution must set goals to move above peer averages before it can set data goals that focus on reaching aspirant institution benchmarks.

Part of the reason for this comparison is to answer four questions:

1. Who are your competitors (including peers, aspirants, community colleges, regional comprehensives, local privates, institutions establishing a new site or advertising online programs in your primary or secondary markets)?
2. What is causing a student to enroll at institutions other than your own?
3. Are there changes you can realistically and budgetarily make to be competitive with lost admitted students?
4. How far are your metrics from those of your aspirant institutions?

The data comparisons should help you understand the realities of your current state and the points of difference between your campus and other institutions. Campuses must accept this reality and provide the educational experience and support services that will produce student success and strong outcomes. Therefore, the SEP process aligns both the current state of a campus and its desired future state. It also provides a data-informed process for making the transition between those two states. If a campus aspires to seek a different type of student, SEP establishes comparison benchmarks that are carefully monitored while also illuminating the necessary realignment of academic and co-curricular offerings, enrollment and marketing practices, and fiscal strategies to grow revenues as the institution progresses toward that desired future state.

Figure 2-2: Peer Institution Data Benchmarks

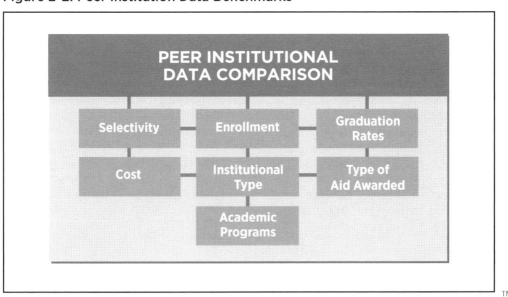

Peer institution data benchmarks are the foundation of SEP. They inform decisions in key areas of enrollment management, ensuring that these areas are aligned and working in harmony toward common institutional goals.

Engaging stakeholders

Much of the literature on how to generate campuswide collaboration focuses on identifying and constructing the optimal institutional structure and the strategic planning practices necessary to ensure the sustainability and success of that structure (Henderson, 2005). From the original conception of enrollment management, the fulcrum of success hinged on a structure that would generate synergy among college/university enrollment functions such as admissions, financial aid, and retention programming (Henderson, 2005). Today's chief enrollment officer leads an immensely sophisticated network: steering committees of high-level administrators and deans; planning groups with enrollment management directors; marketing task forces; retention roundtables; and a range of formal and informal partnerships with external constituents, alumni, parents, and students. The current state of shared governance seeks to draw in key campus voices to the enrollment management process, thus requiring their "skin in the game," which moves them toward mutual accountability.

Within the context of a highly complex institution where an employee's experience is itself largely compartmentalized, individuals readily accept that they simply cannot know every piece of relevant information about the organization. Staff and faculty, even at the middle and senior levels, perpetually operate with incomplete knowledge of the scope and depth of the broader organization. Therefore, it is not surprising that these staff members do not readily or frequently consider their daily actions as interdependently linked to the greater mission of their college/university, a basic condition of SEP. The SEP process seeks to force key institutional leaders to think beyond silos. At its best, the SEP process moves institutional leaders to seek ways to actively engage and connect efforts focused on the student in order to promote a learning-based experience with measurable outcomes.

The goal of this process is to align enrollment efforts with other key institutional priorities and to interlink academic and co-curricular offerings with future enrollment trends and demands.

Every institution has internal and external stakeholders with differing levels of investment in the institution and in the SEP process. Some external stakeholders might welcome growth and understand its economic benefits—boards of trustees or governors, local officials, alumni, or donors within a smaller community who see the institution as a positive contributor to the community's quality of life. Other external stakeholders may resist growth and, despite data demonstrating the positive results of growth, may view it as a net negative. For example, smaller communities may consider an institution setting a goal that is enrollment-growth oriented as a negative because this growth may be perceived to affect the charm or character of the community. In either case, building or sustaining effective working relationships with these external constituencies is an important condition for success (Anderson and Anderson, 2001).

Within a campus, all institutional community members should be considered internal stakeholders, even though not everyone will be involved in implementing all parts of the enrollment plan.

Internal and external stakeholders should be included in the strategic planning process, especially if the planning team expects to link academic and/or co-curricular program demands and trends with institutional or employer needs, or if campus planning includes a significant growth in residential facilities. External stakeholders may play a significant role in shaping the quality of the local community, engaging students through internships, and providing a welcoming environment for campus visitors. Internal stakeholders are essential for coordinating and implementing the elements of the plan—they are the ones who will be turning the plan's vision into action.

However, this inclusion does not mean all stakeholders are equal. At the start of the planning process, institutional leaders should determine which stakeholders must be active participants and which merely require updates as the plan progresses. See Chapter 3 for a list of typical stakeholders to include.

Alignment with basic funnel management

The growth of the Internet and the changing nature of the ways prospective students research possible colleges and universities, and then interact with them, have led higher education theorists and practitioners to expand their conception of the traditional enrollment funnel (Figure 2-3) into a more robust student engagement stream. For a full treatment of this conceptual shift, see *Navigating the Student Engagement Stream: The Evolution of the Funnel for Enrollment and Beyond* (Ruffalo Noel Levitz, 2015).

Figure 2-3: The Traditional Enrollment Funnel

No matter how an institution frames the student decision-making journey, a key step in effective enrollment management is consistently measuring the number and percentage of students from pre-enrollment through graduation. This stream or funnel analysis measures stages in the progression from initial interest through completion, identifies where gaps occur, and provides insights about where to focus efforts to increase new student enrollment and/or completion strategies.

Approaches to the student engagement stream must include separate or sophisticated funnel metrics that measure yield, persistence, and completion rates at different points in the funnel, because prospective students no longer enter the funnel in the traditional, linear prospect/inquiry/applicant fashion. For example, we know an increasing number of prospective students first contact an institution through an application, even if they were first in the prospect pool, but never inquired. Institutions must not lose the opportunity to continually communicate with high-affinity prospects who do not inquire, and must redesign their admissions communication process to build relationships with students whose first contact is the application, using specific communications that connect prospective students with the institution and their major or other areas of interest they identified on the application. The communication and recruitment process can no longer be generic and only triggered by a prospective student's interaction with the institution. Prospective student data must be carefully analyzed, and self-provided information and preferences integrated into the data stream so that campuses can use that information to create customized communications to improve yield among students who enter and re-appear at any stage along the traditional enrollment funnel or within the student engagement stream. Consider Figure 2-4.

Figure 2-4: Enrollment Funnel With Multiple Entry Channels

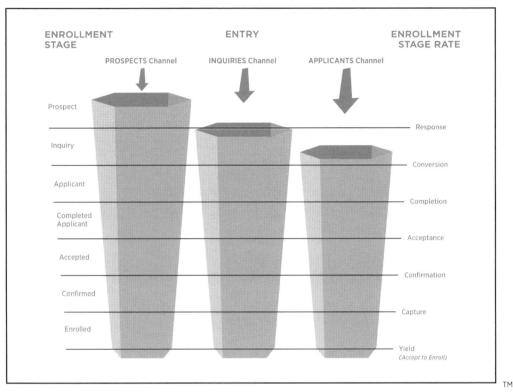

TM

Notice that this new set of funnels has multiple entry points and may be dominated by students who remain anonymous before applying. Yet the goal for campuses—generating the same number of high-quality applicants—remains. This requires a strategic shift in marketing, perhaps one that emphasizes good outcomes (i.e., graduates prepared for graduate school or employment) rather than first-year experience programs or the value of attending an institution that provides small class sizes. Other than acceptance and financial aid, the sophisticated applicant of the future may be looking to the end of the student engagement stream (graduation) and not worried much about what happens when they first dip their toes into the student engagement stream.

As we consider the rest of the SEP process, it is essential to consider how each variable discussed affects some segment of the engagement stream. Remember that the goal is to enroll the optimal mix of students, provide them with the necessary programs, support, and connections to achieve their goals, and graduate them with degrees that prepare them for their future endeavors.

What makes excellent enrollment plans and outcomes?

Bernard Ginsberg (2011) emphasized the importance of the process. "Occasionally a college or university does, in fact, present a grand design for the next decade…. Such a plan typically presents concrete objectives, a timetable for their realization, an outline of the tactics that will be employed, a precise assignment of staff responsibilities, and a budget." He states, "The 2007 strategic plan of the University of Illinois, for example, put forward explicit objectives, benchmarks, timetables, and budgets." Obviously, it was the process that resulted in these explicit objectives, benchmarks, timetables, and budgets.

Since 2008, Ruffalo Noel Levitz consultants have studied a large number of institutional strategic plans and strategic enrollment plans. In addition, they have engaged in an extensive review of strategic planning literature and conducted numerous dialogues with college/university campuses regarding SEP. Based on these contacts, literature reviews, observations, and experiences on many campuses, one maxim has become perfectly clear: Excellent, long-range, strategic enrollment plans are the result of a collaborative, data-informed process.

What goes into that process? We have identified the most common characteristics of successful strategic enrollment plans, which generally include most, if not all, of the following:

- Clearly defined strategic planning phases, where strategies, tactics, and return-on-investment prioritization lead to goal setting, rather than the traditional approach of setting goals first and then planning strategies and steps;

- A comprehensive and integrated scope that considers multiple types of student enrollments and programs, as well as the interaction of these components with a focus on the entire institution, not just enrollment per se;

- Futuristic focus, using external data and environmental scanning to direct the institutional community to use emerging best practices and develop relevant programs to construct a realistic future state;

- An academic- and co-curricular-oriented process, rather than a primary focus on marketing, recruitment, and retention tactics. Academic programs form the heart of the institution, and so enrollment functions support academic and co-curricular programs;

- Data-informed strategies, tactics, and enrollment goals;

- Fiscally minded strategies, tactics, and goals;

- Interconnection with facilities planning to ensure appropriate academic and co-curricular spaces;

- Current technologies, in terms of delivery of learning systems as well as systems that support effective institutional processes;

- High participation and buy-in across the institution;

- High-quality implementation of the plan with clear timelines, responsibilities, and accountability;

- A continuous process that develops, implements, evaluates, and refreshes the plans; and

- An experienced and strong leader of the strategic process, one with a track record of successful outcomes.

These essentials not only agree with the principles and trends that have been identified for a number of years as components of successful planning processes, but also address the most common reasons plans fail. In addition, the essentials are aligned with the significant factors cited in respected strategic planning literature (Bryson, 1995 and 2004; Steiner, Miner, and Gray, 1992; Haines, 2000; and Lake, 2006) and higher education strategic planning literature (Bean, 1990; Rowley, Lujan, and Dolence, 1997; Cope, 1981; Sevier, 2000; and Norris and Poulton, 2008).

As an institution seeks to create a Strategic Enrollment Plan, the planning process is a great opportunity to change campus culture, encourage a greater understanding of the fundamentals of planning, and demonstrate that planning is more than an exercise. The goal of the planning process is to create a vibrant, living plan that describes an ongoing and continuous process aligning strategy implementation with resource allocation to create a stronger future state. By actively managing and implementing the plan, institutional leadership has an enormous opportunity to demonstrate the value and meaningfulness of SEP to the campus community.

Aligning organizational strategic plans with strategic enrollment plans

Strategic planning is the disciplined effort to produce fundamental decisions and actions that shape and guide an organization's identity as well as its mission, its purpose, and its menu of programs and services (Bryson, 1995). Most campuses have a strategic plan—some are used well and some sit on the proverbial shelf. The most effective strategic enrollment plans draw from the overall institutional strategic plan to set direction for the SEP process.

If, when created, the strategic planning process was data informed, the enrollment planning process should roll seamlessly into the institutional strategic plan. However, the strategic planning process is often not data informed. In that case, the SEP process, if done correctly, will confirm or deny the assumptions, perceptions, and other non-qualitative measures that were used to establish enrollment and fiscal goals in the strategic plan. For example, many strategic plans call for an enrollment goal of XX by YY year, but often no data have been used to inform these enrollment goals. The SEP process can determine specific strategies, tactics, and anticipated costs to reach the stated enrollment goals or will provide evidence that the campus should realign expectations.

In its purest form, the institutional strategic plan should establish mission, vision, and ways to ensure institutional effectiveness. The strategic enrollment plan should determine key performance indicators (KPIs) (Chapter 4), key strategies (Chapter 6), and enrollment goals (Chapter 7) to be reached through implementation of the plan. Annual plans take the operational items identified through the planning process and move these tactics to action. The effective organizational model ensures that the institutional strategic plan blends with the strategic enrollment plan and that key operational staff use both of these plans to pursue priorities through annual planning and implementation efforts, see Figure 2-5.

Figure 2-5: The Strategic Enrollment Plan as a Part of the Overall Strategic Plan

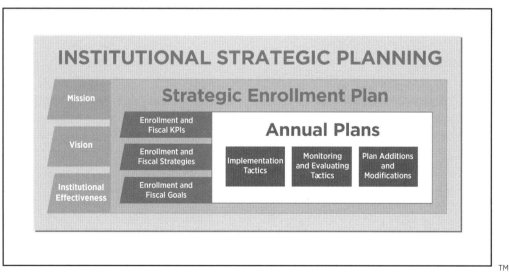

Strategic enrollment planning and strategic enrollment management

Today, institutional leaders face two competing demands. They must execute immediate actions in order to meet today's enrollment challenges, and they must adapt the ways they execute and achieve enrollment efficiencies in order to thrive in tomorrow's world. They must develop tomorrow's innovative practices while excelling at today's best practices (Heifetz, Grashow, and Linsky, 2009).

Higher education is averse to change (Selingo, 2013). It is not uncommon for mature enterprises to become increasingly risk-averse, complacent, and perhaps unduly expensive, and not make the advancements necessary to compete in a future marketplace (Christensen and Eyring, 2011). SEP can rectify this organizational inertia by challenging a passive approach with data. Institutions may use the SEP process to devise a plan coupling best practices with emerging practices, relying on external data, imagination, and dynamic conversation to envision a future state unimaginable by some. This requires a careful review of competitors and recommended best practices to understand how to become an innovative college/university, rather than simply a survivor, in the next five to seven years.

The great majority of efforts to strategically shape enrollment at colleges and universities fall under the umbrella of strategic enrollment management (SEM). Institutions attempt to achieve desired enrollment outcomes and goals through some combination of marketing, recruitment, retention, and financial aid/discounts. What distinguishes the Ruffalo Noel Levitz approach to SEP from SEM is our significantly more comprehensive scope, which includes such elements as academic and co-curricular programs and their locations, delivery modalities, and times to deliver; facilities; technology; and all the institutional fiscal and planning consequences of all of these elements. SEP has a longer planning horizon— three to five years—than most SEM initiatives. The great majority of SEM officers and SEM committees are not addressing these comprehensive SEP issues, and therefore not optimizing enrollment outcomes at their institutions.

In order for the SEP process to be successful, it requires the embedding of SEM. Often, after the initial strategic enrollment plan is completed, efforts are recast as SEM. SEM is the ongoing effort focused on ensuring that strategies and tactics are implemented; the monitoring of key performance indicators; and the reviewing of data to ensure responsiveness to changes in competition, market share, or demand (if the market demand aligns with the institution's vision, mission, goals, values, and available institutional resources).

SEM is monitored through an oversight body such as an enrollment management council and not delegated exclusively to a vice president for enrollment management or dean/ director of admissions. The goal of the council and the institutional leadership is keeping the institution focused on the future state described in the plan that aligns with the institutional strategic plan and other identified institutional priorities. In Chapter 8, we will define the role and purpose of the council in greater detail.

There are four fundamental components of the SEP process:

1. Creation of the plan, which serves to prioritize activities, programs, and initiatives to ensure future success. The plan is based on an understanding of how the institution is characterized, differentiated, and competitively positioned.

2. Implementation of the plan, which employs the best methods/procedures to accomplish enrollment goals and institutional outcomes. This is based on an understanding of how the institution functions as a coordinated system with maximum campus involvement, shared leadership, and commitment to educational excellence and institutional effectiveness.

3. Institutionalization and systemic integration of the SEP and the conversion to the SEM process, which focuses on integrating SEP into the university's routine planning structures and is based on a commitment to the continuous improvement process.

4. Linkage of the ongoing planning process to the institution strategic plan and budget planning, which moves the institution from a planning document to a guiding action document where priorities are linked to budget allocation (or reallocation).

SEP and SEM systems include institutional databases, external data sources, data reports, and analytical tools that allow institutions to continuously develop, manage, evaluate, and modify well-conceived enrollment strategies and activities.

Taking a more realistic approach to setting goals

In creating a strategic enrollment planning process for campuses, Ruffalo Noel Levitz has identified two underlying principles. The first is that leadership matters. While this seems like common knowledge throughout higher education, analysis of highly effective organizations shows that, due to a lack of leadership, few campuses live by their strategic enrollment plans—if they exist at all. Campus leaders play a crucial role in creating the plan and monitoring progress toward it.

Second, the strategic enrollment plan must be led by a change agent. This person may be an academic dean, vice president, or someone who has a campus reputation to make sustainable change and the ability to lead the process, with a commitment to doing what is good for the overall organization and using the plan as a tool to transform the institution to its desired future state (Anderson and Anderson, 2001).

The planning model described in subsequent chapters advises campuses to review their data first; align their data with a situation analysis that informs the development of strategies, tactics, cost, and return-on-investment projections; and then develop enrollment goals linking academic and co-curricular priorities that have been determined through assessment of demand and capacity. Based on our analysis of realistic goal setting, the Ruffalo Noel Levitz approach diverges from traditional planning models by asserting that institutions must identify key strategies, tactics, costs (human, technological, and actual dollars), and expected return-on-investments before setting goals. This is a truly strategic approach informed by the SEP literature (see Chapter 3). Without a clear understanding of the action plans and resources needed to implement the strategies, goals are meaningless. Goals must be realistic and achievable based on campus readiness and resource allocation (or re-allocation) to support the activities needed to drive the institution to its desired future state.

Fundamental approaches

As the planning process progresses, an institution must evaluate whether current demand and market penetration strategies are working effectively to lead the campus to its desired future state. Dickeson (2010) identifies five fundamental challenges that institutions confront as they incorporate this type of analysis into their planning activities:

1. The power of legacy;
2. The realities of the marketplace, which will force differentiation;
3. Wrestling with the true quest for excellence;
4. Local reconciliation of higher education's function (teaching, research, and service); and
5. The specific ways to fulfill their most essential purpose.

A comprehensive planning process will address these fundamental issues.

As campuses consider academic and co-curricular demand and market penetration, they must set internal and external benchmarks to track programs and activities in their current and evolving future state. For example, there are several national benchmarks related to limiting classroom size; yet numerous studies have shown the effectiveness of instruction for class sizes in the hundreds when technology, lab experiences, and teaching assistants supplement the course lectures. While best practices provide a solid strategic foundation, a campus must set its own internal benchmarks and align them with expected outcomes in order to be truly strategic.

Institutions must also look at the financial viability of each program, future program demand, employment trends, and other factors (described in Chapter 4) when examining program demand and areas of future focus. Figure 2-6 shows an approach focused on aligning programs with a variety of internal and external factors. This process may lead to the elimination or restructuring of certain programs to align with future student demand and employment/graduate school needs.

Figure 2-6: Connecting Academic and Co-Curricular Programs

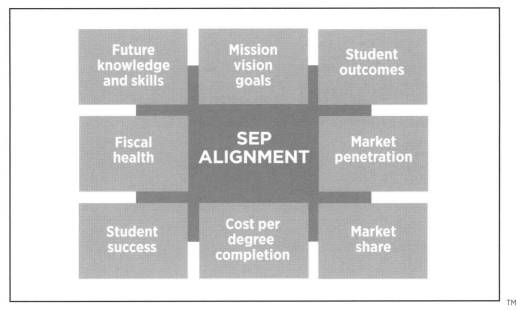

Conclusion

If completed with diligence and strong leadership, the planning process can build a culture of SEP within which the resulting plan is used as a tool to guide the institution toward a desired future state. As noted earlier, few campuses report having a strategic enrollment plan or effectively using their current plan to guide their institution's efforts in this manner. The goal of this planning process, and indeed of this book, is to help institutions think through the importance of planning, the process of planning, and the value of moving from a planning mode to a management mode. Ultimately, successful institutions will adopt a data-informed management model using a process that is continuously refreshed in order to ensure the campus reaches its desired future state.

Dialogue

As campus leaders consider embarking on an SEP process, they should first discuss at the cabinet or senior-staff level whether this is the right time to pursue such an initiative. Key to the SEP is a living institutional strategic plan. Without that plan, it is difficult to frame the enrollment plan with strategies that align and guide actions. If the campus is ready for SEP, the team should:

- Discuss the expected outcomes of the plan;
- Review data sources that might be available;
- Discuss the availability of institutional research to support the planning process;
- Agree that the institution is ready to prioritize and potentially make tough choices; and
- Identify key stakeholders to engage in the planning process.

Of particular note, the leadership should determine whether this planning exercise should include a review and prioritization of existing academic and co-curricular programs and their trends, demands, and capacities. If the process does not include prioritization, it shifts from true SEP to a long-range enrollment planning process. While all the elements of the planning process (as described in Chapter 3) remain valid, the planning team will not address changes in current program offerings or consider program reduction activities.

As leaders discuss the potential of the planning process, they should consider whom else to engage in a discussion of the value and benefits of the planning process.

Lastly, institutional leaders should discuss the value of the planning process, the reason for planning, and the need to establish a long-term plan with deans, directors, and department chairs, ensuring them of the institution's commitment to moving from planning to an active institutional management process after the plan is completed.

CHAPTER 3

The Planning Process

By James Mager

What makes for excellence in a strategic enrollment plan (SEP) and the strategic enrollment planning process? While this question may be answered in many ways by individuals at different institutions, most would agree that the plan and the process should lead to enrollment outcomes and student success metrics that meet or exceed the goals developed during the planning process. In addition, an excellent plan is one that pushes the institution to increase performance or advance levels of practice and also has enough detail to ensure the plan will be implemented.

CHAPTER HIGHLIGHTS

- **Planning phases define the process**
- **SEP scope is determined early**
- **Six P's outline the planning topics**
- **Dialogue links the process with the plan**

However, it is unwise to tie planning excellence and success exclusively with the achievement of enrollment goals. If an institution exceeds its enrollment goals, but the goals were conservative and set in an external environment that provided ample enrollment growth opportunities, achievement of those goals may simply be the result of demographic factors rather than a comprehensive enrollment plan that encouraged innovative actions and sophisticated practices.

Many higher education institutions (and other organizations) call their planning process strategic when they are, in fact, conducting traditional planning under the trendy guise of "strategic planning." Traditional planning typically involves setting goals, either short- or long-term, and then developing steps to achieve those goals (Bean, 1990, and Rowley, Lujan, and Dolence, 1997). This type of planning can succeed in some circumstances, but is fraught with risks, including the example of conservative goal achievement cited above. Others risk setting enrollment goals that are unrealistic or arbitrary; creating a plan that is not aligned with demographic realities, the competition, or the institution's strengths and weaknesses; or having a plan with a narrow scope, to name but a few.

Strategic planning primarily aligns an institution with its external and internal environment (Rowley et al., 1997; and Steiner, Miner, and Gray, 1992). Unlike traditional planning, goals are set toward the end of the process, after analyzing the environment, strategy development, and business investment decisions, rather than at the beginning.

Recommended process phases and steps

Strategic planning phases, as opposed to traditional planning phases, are critical to a successful SEP process. These phases align with fundamental planning elements that ensure successful SEP processes are integrated into planning. They also align with best practices identified in strategic planning literature (Bryson, 1995 and 2004; Lake, 2006; Haines, 2000; and Steiner et al., 1992) and higher education strategic planning literature (Bean, 1990; Rowley et al., 1997; Massey, 2001; Dickeson, 1999; Dolence and Norris, 1994; and Sevier, 2000).

The scope or details of the plan may be aligned with strategies defined within six categories—the Six P's—that link other plans (academic, technology, fundraising) and are framed within a concept of: 1) the product (academic and/or co-curricular programs); 2) place and delivery (sites and delivery modes); 3) price (tuition, fees, and discounts); 4) promotion (marketing and recruitment); 5) purpose and identity (mission and brand); and 6) process (how things are accomplished and linked to other institutional planning and management processes). These will be addressed in more detail later in the chapter.

The following phases and steps provide a recommended starting point for SEP process design. The four interactive phases have inherent feedback loops. See Figure 3-1.

Figure 3-1: Strategic Enrollment Planning Phases

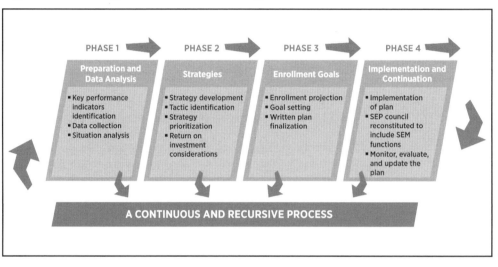

Phase one: Preparation and data analysis

In phase one, the institution determines Key Performance Indicators (KPIs), completes a thorough data analysis (which includes an intensive review of internal and external data), and creates a new or updated situation analysis framed from an enrollment perspective. This situation analysis sets the stage and reason for the institution to commit to a strategic enrollment planning process.

This phase may include:

- Reviewing the Institutional Strategic Plan (if one exists);
- Defining the scope of the planning process;
- Organizing the leaders and participants for a successful process, as demanded by its scope;
- Defining the KPIs for the planning process;
- Collecting and reviewing data related to the current and future state of each KPI; and
- Conducting a data-informed situation or strengths, weaknesses, opportunities, and threats (SWOT) analysis related to the identified KPIs.

Phase two: Strategy development

Phase two is an output of the situation analysis. Strategy development should maximize institutional effectiveness across the defined strategic areas as well as provide impetus to the overall realization of institutional mission and vision.

During phase two, the planning process includes:

- Brainstorming strategies to optimize the KPIs;
- Identifying the major tactics for each possible strategy (Note: strategies are larger initiatives, while tactics are specific action items or activities needed to complete or accomplish a strategy);
- Determining estimated costs, impacts, and return on investment (ROI) for each of the possible major tactics;
- Identifying additional data for collection in order to refine the possible strategies, major tactics, costs, and ROI; and
- Prioritizing the strategies and major tactics based on attractive ROI and other considerations.

Phase three: Enrollment goal setting and plan finalization

Goals are established during phase three. Goal setting includes two key items: 1) a thorough review of the anticipated ROI based on each strategy implemented, and 2) enrollment projections to determine specific enrollment goals.

Additional action items during this phase include:

- Conducting enrollment and fiscal projection scenarios;
- Determining multiyear KPI goals based on the most attractive scenario;
- Finalizing a written plan; and
- Conducting the appropriate approval process for the plan.

Phase four: Plan implementation and modification

During phase four, the planning team implements and monitors the plan. In addition, the campus recasts the SEP council to include SEM functions: monitoring KPIs and requesting quarterly progress reports on strategy implementation, insuring adherence to annual SEP and SEM cycles, refreshing the environmental scan, and continually updating the plan.

Action items for this phase include:

- Forming a strategic enrollment management council and affiliated committees;
- Thoroughly implementing the plan at every level;
- Monitoring and evaluating the plan's outcomes;
- Continuing the planning process to align with new data or environmental changes that were unanticipated when the initial plan was created; and
- Updating the plan based on monitoring and the continuous planning process.

The importance of communication

It is essential that campuses communicate with stakeholders throughout these four phases. Primary stakeholders will need to be actively involved; secondary stakeholders should be informed as planning and implementation progress. While the steps may be modified to meet the needs of particular institutions, planners should keep these fundamental phases and components in mind as they design their own processes.

Points of emphasis for planning process success: leaders and timetable

The process phases and activities described within this chapter are based on sound fundamentals, but merely following the recommended process will not ensure success. There are a number of other important factors that affect the outcome of the process.

Process leaders and the planning participants are critical to the ultimate success of the planning process. The process leader is an institutional expert in the specific area of strategy or tactic development and implementation. The planner-participants (those involved in implementing the strategy or tactic) bring not only their particular expertise to the planning process, but also contribute analytic, innovative, and big-picture skills. The process should not be seen as a means of garnering buy-in from naysayers; rather, it should bring together the best campus minds, those who understand the larger view and the value and importance of the planning process. Therefore, these personnel decisions should be made with extreme care at the beginning of phase one.

Decisions regarding the respective roles and organization of these leaders and planning participants are also important to the ultimate success of the process. Having dynamic leaders and planning participants without clear roles and responsibilities can lead to unsatisfactory results or even a collapse of the process. Dynamic leaders and planners working as a coordinated team can result in tremendous success with the planning process, implementation, and ultimately enrollment. (A section dedicated to the important topic of organizing for a successful planning process is covered later in this chapter.)

These personnel and organizational decisions must be preceded by a preliminary decision regarding the scope of the process, because this scope determines the kind of expertise and representation that will be required throughout the planning process. The scope also determines *what long-range enrollment issues will be addressed in a strategic, integrated manner* for the next three to five years and which issues will not be addressed. Therefore, in making decisions regarding scope, the benefits of addressing certain issues and types of student enrollment must be weighed against the risks of choosing not to address certain issues in an integrated, strategic manner. The topic of determining process scope is addressed more fully later in this chapter.

Planning timetable and outcomes

The strategic enrollment planning process that leads to the initial plan document should take nine to 15 months, though it may take as long as 18 months. Completing this process in a thorough, high-quality manner requires time. Taking less time will almost certainly result in a plan that is not fully data-informed, is deficient in participation and buy-in, and has not fully analyzed cost/ROI. As a result, the plan will not lead to the desired enrollment outcomes with minimal or even reasonable risks. Schools with already well-established key performance indicators (see Chapter 4), robust data collection and analysis systems, and effective dashboards (see Chapter 8), are more likely to move through the process faster. Those without a data-centric culture are likely to take longer, as are smaller schools where SEP leaders are likely to be managing multiple job responsibilities. Ensuring that the process is data-informed, collaborative, and productive is more important than the number of months it takes to complete the process.

However, the intensity and involvement of this process also requires it to be finished in a reasonable amount of time. If the planning process produces nothing tangible to affect an institution's enrollment future within 12 months, the negatives will quickly begin to outweigh the benefits of prolonging the process to produce a more perfect plan. In this case, the planning process is vulnerable to being bogged down and moving from an action-oriented group focused on creating a plan to one that becomes paralyzed. The plan is unable to move forward with strategies or tactics because it is waiting for more data than is necessary. In addition, those not central to the process (trustees, academic leaders, faculty, and staff) may become impatient and/or lose confidence in the process when nothing tangible is produced.

Keep in mind that the goal of the situation analysis is to understand trends, patterns, and behaviors, and should spur creative thinking and action. While more data can always be collected, it is essential that the planning leaders remain focused on established priorities and understand that the plan is a living document.

The best initial strategic enrollment plans are dynamic efforts, produced and approved within nine to 15 months, and consist of the following:

- Strategies and tactics prioritized by target years for implementation. Each of these strategies and tactics includes timetables, resource needs (fiscal and human), and individuals responsible for high-quality implementation.

- Expected ROI and multiyear KPI goals related to the implementation of these strategies and tactics.

- Planning topics that are still in the process of analysis, strategy development, or evaluation, including timetables, resources, and individual responsibilities.

- Enrollment projections based on institutional readiness and the realities of the current state vs. the desired state.

- Regular updates to the campus community regarding the planning process, with relevant data sent to appropriate units to help jumpstart activities or gain further unit buy-in by explaining the implications of data.

- Steps for monitoring, evaluating, and updating the plan—it should be a living document supported by an ongoing strategic enrollment management process.

After the first edition of the plan has been produced and approved for implementation, the SEM council—or reconstituted SEP council—should be created and the nature and composition of the working groups reconsidered, and if appropriate, refreshed. There will be committee members and leaders who want to stay involved in the process (or at least are willing to stay engaged) and others who wish to be relieved. However, senior leaders must remain actively involved in managing implementation. Strategic enrollment planning is not a one-and-done process. The SEM council should be charged not just with evaluating the first edition of the plan, but with regular refreshing of the environmental scan and situation analysis, continual identification of new strategies to respond to external opportunities and the changing internal context, and so revisions and updates to the plan on at least an annual basis.

The enrollment successes that come from the planning process are more dependent on high-quality implementation than on the plan itself. These enrollment successes start with decisions about who will lead the implementation of each strategy and each tactic. They continue with detailed quality-control systems that are implemented not only by the leader of each tactic, but also by those with other levels of involvement.

Leaders and doers who are successful at meeting high-quality implementation standards need to be recognized, rewarded, and retained. Those who are not meeting these standards need to be counseled, mentored, and possibly relieved of their planning responsibilities. Sometimes the actions that must be taken are not pleasant; however, too much valuable time and money has been invested in the planning to allow the enrollment and fiscal success to break down at the implementation phase. For these reasons, decisions regarding the leadership and monitoring of the implementation processes are extremely important to the plan's ultimate success.

In summary, long-term enrollment and fiscal success require strong institutional leaders to provide detailed attention to the planning process, essentials, and points of emphasis listed above. Failure to do so can result in an SEP process that does not produce results or is never completed.

SEP scope defines the boundaries of the process

Before the strategic planning process begins, institutional leaders must have thoughtful discussions about its scope, because these discussions will determine who should be involved in the planning process. Decisions about scope will also determine which long-range enrollment issues will be addressed in a strategic, integrated manner for the next three to five years, and which issues will not. Although there may be valid reasons to modify the scope later in the process, this creates significant inefficiencies that are best avoided, if possible.

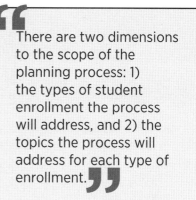

There are two dimensions to the scope of the planning process: 1) the types of student enrollment the process will address, and 2) the topics the process will address for each type of enrollment.

There are two dimensions to the scope of the planning process: 1) the types of student enrollment the process will address, and 2) the topics the process will address for each type of enrollment.

Enrollment types included in planning scope

What types of enrollment will the planning process address? Will it target only traditional undergraduate enrollment or include other populations such as nontraditional undergraduates, non-degree enrollments, graduate students, or professional school students? Will the process only address traditional, on-campus enrollment, or will it also address enrollments in online and hybrid courses and programs? Will the process include enrollments at remote sites and branch campuses? Finally, will it address how these enrollments interact with each other?

Taking a comprehensive approach by answering "yes" to all or most of these questions is recommended unless this would make the planning process too large and unwieldy. Be aware that data collection for all subpopulations can bog down the process, so institutional priorities must be set to ensure that data for each population can be collected in a timely manner.

Why take such a comprehensive approach? Colleges and universities are comprised mostly of departments and programs: academic, student life, student support, and administrative. Each of these departments and programs has its own physical facilities, utilities, and technology applications. It is important for each department to have clear strategic enrollment plans and expectations for every type of student it serves, not just for certain types of students. Not having clear plans and expectations for other students who use these same departmental resources will likely lead to costly inefficiencies in the future at the departmental level and, in turn, for the institution as a whole.

For example, assume there is a strategic plan and an expectation that business undergraduate students will grow significantly in the next five years. What kind of physical facility will the College of Business need to serve not only these students, but MBA students (not addressed by the strategic plan) who will be using the same facility? Moreover, what implications might this have for an adjacent academic department that is competing for the same expansion space?

The hazards of not planning comprehensively are many and multiply quickly when considering the interactions among departments and programs. An overarching plan that encompasses each department and program, as well as a comprehensive plan that addresses the interactions of these departments and programs, will help avoid these types of inefficiencies.

On the other hand, a comprehensive approach to strategic enrollment planning can be very challenging to manage because of all the distinct parts and how they interact. This is especially true at larger institutions with hundreds of moving parts that need to be addressed both separately and interactively. All of these interactions will need to be addressed by planning subcommittees that represent clusters of these parts, and in turn, these subcommittees must be efficiently and effectively coordinated by the planning process leaders.

As a result of these planning challenges, some institutions might be better off initially focusing on certain types of enrollments and programs, such as traditional undergraduates, then addressing the enrollments of other student populations later. This sequential approach worked for The Ohio State University in the 1990s, when the focus of the enrollment planning process was first on traditional undergraduate enrollments at the main campus. Later, processes were developed to address graduate student and branch campus enrollments.

The bottom line for making decisions about the scope of the process for different types of students is that there is no right or wrong decision for a comprehensive approach vs. a more concentrated approach. The advantages and risks must be carefully weighed before determining the scope. It is best to change the scope of this continuous planning process as few times as possible and only after carefully weighing the advantages, challenges, and risks of scope change as the project progresses. During the initial planning process, data collection and review may help senior leaders determine the plan's scope.

Enrollment topics included in planning scope

The second dimension of scope entails determining the topics that the process will address for each type of enrollment that is selected. These are known as the Six P's:

1. **Product and program strategies** related to academic programs and courses; student life; co-curricular and extracurricular programs; and student success, retention, and graduation programs.

2. **Place and delivery strategies** related to program and course delivery innovations/ options (e.g., off-site, online, and executive format strategies) and the integration of enrollment planning with physical facility and technology planning.

3. **Price strategies** related to tuition, fees, and discounts such as scholarships, assistantships, and need-based financial aid.

4. **Promotion strategies** related to institutional and program marketing, student recruitment, and prospective student influencers such as parents, guidance counselors, advisors, and teachers.

5. **Purpose and identity strategies** related to effective realization and illumination of mission, distinctiveness, and brand of the institution.

6. **Process strategies** related to fiscal planning and management, data and information systems, institutional effectiveness assessment systems, institutionwide engagement, organizational strength of the campus community, and systemic coordination of planning, including determination of priorities and strategic direction.

One of the most common mistakes that institutions make is conducting an enrollment planning process that primarily or exclusively addresses marketing, recruiting, student persistence and success, and scholarships/financial aid. The foundation of each higher education institution—and, therefore, the foundation of institutional strategic enrollment planning—is the viability and effectiveness of its product, including its academic programs and courses, co-curricular and extracurricular programs, student life opportunities, and support for student success. The content and quality of this product either meet or do not meet the wants and needs of its students. The reputation and content of the programs are the main influencers for prospective students choosing to enroll.

The strategic enrollment planning process should address the following questions for each academic, student life, and student support program:

- Has the program been effective in attracting, satisfying, retaining, and graduating students in the past and present? Why or why not?

- In the future, can the program be effective in attracting, satisfying, retaining, and graduating students given recent and projected external demographic trends, competition, opportunities, and threats in light of the institution's internal strengths and weaknesses?

Even though institutional programs are the foundation of enrollment success and therefore the basis for a successful enrollment planning process, it is often the most elusive area for an enrollment manager to control (Lesick, 2009). Therefore, developing program-related strategies needs to be at the forefront of the SEP process and must involve the academic program leaders. Institutions must have effective program plans and strategies before they can effectively and efficiently complete the development of pricing and promotion strategies.

Where and how these courses are delivered is also an important topic in the strategic enrollment planning process. Will each program and course be delivered in convenient and attractive ways to its students? What are the costs and advantages to making them more convenient and attractive in the future? Does the institution offer an attractive mix of program and course delivery options such as on-campus, remote sites, online, hybrid, and executive format delivery modes? If so, what is the cost and return on investment?

> " Institutions must have effective program plans and strategies before they can effectively and efficiently complete the development of pricing and promotion strategies. "

During the planning process, the greater the emphasis on the development of high-quality and attractive programs, places, and modes of delivery, the more likely it is to produce enrollment success. This is the whole point: providing first-rate, highly sought-after programs at convenient places for a chosen subset of the market. That is why the institution exists and why successful strategic enrollment planning is largely about aligning an institution with its external and internal environment.

Strategic pricing of the institution's programs, places, and modes of delivery is another important part of strategic enrollment planning. The pricing (and net tuition) approach includes the development of data-informed strategies for discounting prices for certain student populations (at some types of institutions), or even assigning pricing premiums for certain programs (see Chapter 10). However, it is crucial for an institution to have the best possible understanding not only of its current and future programs, places, and modes of delivery, but also how attractive these are in comparison to competing institutions' programs, places, and modes of delivery before developing its pricing strategies.

With strategies for programs, places, and price in place, promotion strategies can be addressed. These typically take the form of both institutional and individual program marketing strategies as well as more targeted prospective student recruitment strategies. The process of developing promotion strategies also takes into account the role of prospective student influencers such as parents, guidance counselors, spouses, employers, advisors, and teachers.

As the strategic enrollment planning process continues, the planning team should be constantly confirming or modifying the institution's purpose or identity, aiming for more effective realization and illumination of the mission, distinctiveness, and brand of the institution. Keep in mind that there may be external opportunities and threats or emerging internal strengths and weaknesses that make a case for using the planning process to modify the institution's purpose, identity, or even its mission. The institutional mission, distinctiveness, and brand should coincide with the institution's strengths, keeping the process aligned with those characteristics.

Finally, the scope of the planning process should address the institution's ongoing, internal process strategies in the areas of fiscal planning and management, data and information systems, systems for assessing institutional effectiveness, institutionwide engagement, campuswide organizational strengths, planning priorities, and strategic direction. These ongoing processes must provide for the continuous integration of strategic planning, enrollment planning, physical facility planning, technology planning, fundraising planning, budget planning, and assessment. A strategic enrollment planning process can be a major force in ensuring this integration. Without this integration across all of these processes, the institution is vulnerable to enormous enrollment planning inefficiencies that can cost millions of dollars in facility and technology expenditures alone.

Organizing for a successful planning process

Once the scope of the process has been established, institutional leaders will be ready to determine the best leaders, planner-participants, and the organization of the SEP process. The SEP process can be organized in many different ways; however, there are a number of principles to keep in mind. The following observations and recommendations have emerged through Ruffalo Noel Levitz formal consultations and informal conversations with higher education professionals regarding the most effective ways to organize the planning process.

The president plays a critical role in setting the tone regarding the importance of this process for the institution's future. True strategic enrollment planning requires a significant investment of time on the part of participants, institutional leaders, and departmental leaders. The president must leave no doubt that this process is so critical to the institution's future that the planner-participants and the process leaders must be fully engaged. (See the dialogue section of this chapter for more on how the president can set this tone.)

At least one of the leaders of the process should have experience in successful strategic planning, not just traditional planning. If the institution does not have one or more leaders who have strategic planning success in their background, an outside facilitator who has this experience should be identified to partner with the appropriate institutional leaders in managing the SEP process.

It is human nature for people to support what they build. Therefore, institutional leaders must design a planning organization that will reach as many people as possible. Communication efforts must reach those who are not on one of the process-planning committees, with special attention to communicating with and involving deans, faculty, administrators, and staff. One way to accomplish this is for the planning council and the committees (described in the next section) to include planning participants who not only bring their own expertise to the planning process, but also can communicate outside of the formal planning meetings with their colleagues and/or constituents and then contribute their feedback. Another way is to continuously provide updates and ask for feedback at different venues, such as departmental staff meetings, deans' meetings, faculty councils, student affairs councils, and trustee meetings. Other means for spreading the word include developing and maintaining a high-quality, up-to-date SEP website and a high-quality, consistent SEP newsletter.

The planning process includes topic-specific working groups. An effective process not only explores large concepts and directions, but also analyzes numerous external and internal factors, trends, and issues in order to develop effective, reality-based strategies. Topic-specific subcommittees might be formed to address areas such as academic program planning and delivery modes, graduate student enrollment, international student enrollment, nontraditional enrollment, pricing strategies, and marketing strategies. Detailed expertise is needed to inform each topic and guide the work of these subcommittees.

With an array of planning committees and broad, institutionwide representation, a small steering committee is needed to lead and manage the process. This committee is the hub that connects all the working subcommittees/groups, the SEP council, the president, and the president's cabinet.

The process and its participants must have an academic and co-curricular orientation, be fiscal-minded, and be data-informed. It is important to have high-level, fully engaged participants from academic affairs, academic colleges and departments, student affairs, fiscal affairs, and the appropriate data analysts, typically from institutional affairs and enrollment services. If these leaders indicate they are too busy to be fully engaged, then their availability should be addressed with the president, because either the message that this process is extremely important to the institution's health has not been received, or the president must authorize alternative topic-specific leaders who can fully engage in the process. The planning process requires leaders with high-level authority to speak for a particular administrative or academic division, college, or department.

Responsibility and accountability are the centerpieces of this process. Typically, each planner-participant serves one or more of the following roles:

- Provides expertise on a given topic;
- Communicates with constituents and brings feedback to the process;
- Is seen as a campus leader and someone who seeks to improve the entire institution, not just his or her own department;
- Serves as chair of a working group determined through the planning process; and
- Has the authority to speak and/or make decisions for a department, college, division, or institutional governing body.

Figure 3-2: Example of SEP Organization

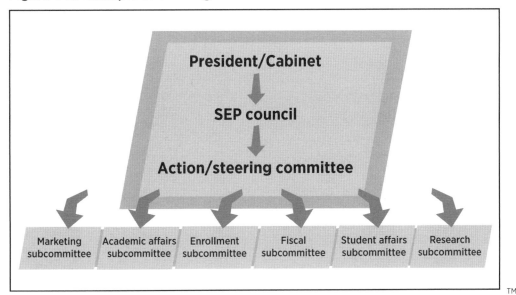

TM

The following outline provides an overview of a recommended structure for a successful SEP process that has worked for numerous campuses.

Focus on oversight: The SEP council

The SEP council composed mainly of campus leaders, in conjunction with its action/steering subcommittee, directs the process and ensures institutionwide processes for communication, participation, endorsements, and approvals. It should have representatives from the following:

- Academic affairs and selected deans (one of these chairs or co-chairs the council);
- Enrollment (facilitates and possibly co-chairs the council);
- Fiscal services;
- Institutional research/planning;
- Student affairs;
- Selected faculty (typically from faculty-governing bodies such as the faculty council and the curriculum committee);
- Specialists (e.g., graduate, adult learner, campus technology); and
- Others based on the institution's culture (e.g., president, chief of staff, student, etc.).

Focus on planning details: The steering committee

An action/steering group coordinates the planning process and ensures that the details of the planning process are followed. This team keeps the process moving forward in a timely manner, reports to the SEP council, and ensures that each action subcommittee is supported during the planning process.

The steering group will address a variety of topics. Topics might include academic program planning, student life, student retention, distance learning, pricing, and promotion. Institutions may need to consider subpopulations when determining work process (e.g., traditional undergraduate, nontraditional, graduate, and international).

The steering group directs the process, coordinates the subcommittees, determines the agenda items for the council, and keeps the president, chancellor, or other senior-level leaders highly involved in the SEP process. It is important that the steering committee has high-level representation from academics, enrollment, business or financial affairs, student affairs, and institutional research. In addition, the committee should continue to link activities back to ROI considerations and have the systems in place to measure and monitor results.

The president or chancellor typically provides direction for the SEP council and the steering committee or is an active member of one or both of these groups.

An alternative conceptualization

The four-level team structure described in Figure 3-2 is effective at large, comprehensive universities or systems with multiple campuses and large administrative structures. Many Ruffalo Noel Levitz SEP partners have adopted a more streamlined model that requires a high level of engagement by the president's cabinet and an expanded role of the steering committee. In this alternate structure, captured in Figure 3-3, chairs of each working group serve on the steering team to support coordination, and the entire project is supported by a data team and communication specialists.

Figure 3-3: SEP Steering Team Model

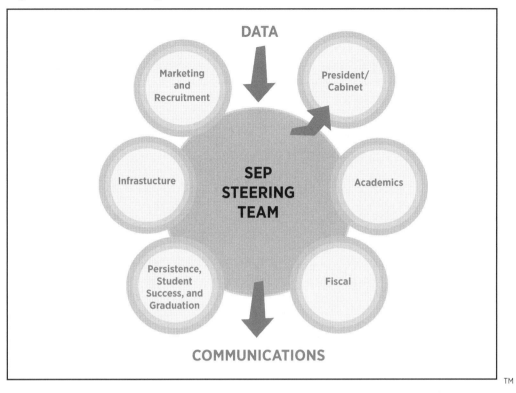

TM

Governing bodies that endorse or approve the plan

The faculty senate, council of deans, and others, depending on institutional culture, coordinate their agenda with this planning process and provide appropriate direction, feedback, endorsements, and/or approvals.

The board of trustees should provide vision, feedback, and appropriate approvals throughout the planning process.

Summary

Successful strategic enrollment planning is a complex, intensive process that is not intuitive for institutions. This is why the great majority of enrollment professionals report that their respective institutions do not have an excellent strategic enrollment plan in this very challenging higher education environment (Ruffalo Noel Levitz, 2016).

Successful strategic enrollment planning and long-range enrollment and fiscal success rely on a chain of events that guide the process and lead to success. To ensure enrollment and fiscal success, institutions should rigorously implement an excellent, multiyear, strategic enrollment plan. Finally, to develop and implement a successful process, institutions must execute the process essentials that are outlined in this chapter, with emphasis on choosing the right process leaders and organizing them effectively, while also conducting continuous high-quality dialogue, both formally and informally, among process participants and throughout the institution.

Dialogue

This chapter has made the case that it is the process that determines whether an institution produces a successful strategic enrollment plan with excellent outcomes or an ineffective plan that may be nothing more than a tremendous waste of time. Along with this, it is important to emphasize that dialogue (Figure 3-4) makes the process and its essentials work.

Figure 3-4: Dialogue Links the SEP Process With the Plan

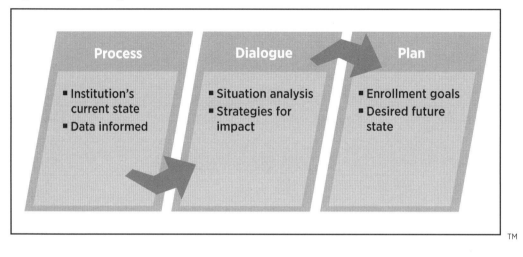

Specifically, dialogue occurs among many different parties: 1) the president and the president's cabinet, the deans, the institutional community, and the board; 2) the chief academic officer, the chief enrollment officer, and the chief fiscal officer; and 3) academic affairs including academic department chairs and faculty. Moreover, it includes dialogue that the SEP process leaders have with other key department heads and staff who support students. Throughout this experience, the informal conversations among all these parties may have as much impact as the formal dialogue process.

Both formal meetings and informal dialogue between colleagues are so important to the success of the process that they need to be continuously nurtured and even orchestrated by the process leaders as part of the SEP process design and implementation. In fact, each week, process leaders should be asking themselves, "What have we done this past week to encourage critical informal and formal dialogue? What are we coordinating for the next week and the next month to nurture dialogue about the SEP process?" It should be a topic of discussion at many deans' council meetings, faculty council meetings, staff meetings at all levels, president and provost speeches, and numerous day-to-day informal conversations.

The following approaches will ensure a high level of dialogue regarding the SEP process. Implementation of these approaches must be planned and monitored—they are too important to the success of the process to be left to chance.

President/Chancellor communication: Just as the SEP council and its action committee are at the center of the SEP process, the president/chancellor plays the key role in setting the tone for institutionwide dialogue about the process and the expected outcomes from the process. The president creates the buzz that this SEP process will make significant impact on the enrollment and fiscal health of the institution, as well as its culture and image. The president talks about these topics continuously in individual conversations with board members, vice presidents, deans, faculty members, and staff. The president also speaks about these topics in speeches and written communications. However, care must be taken that the expected outcomes are discussed in general terms, not in terms of precise numbers, until the SEP process produces quantifiable goals that are supported by strategies, tactics, and fiscal and human resources.

Academic dialogue: Because the SEP process should be academic-oriented, the dialogue among process leaders and deans, academic department chairs, and faculty is paramount. At most institutions, deans and faculty members are more likely to buy into an SEP process that is being led by an academic leader (i.e., the provost, an associate provost, or a respected dean) than one that is led by another administrator. It is important for the SEP council to be chaired, or at least co-chaired, by an academic leader. For example, at The Ohio State University, the SEP council (under a different name) was chaired by a respected dean who spoke frequently about the SEP process at council of deans' meetings, faculty senate meetings, and academic department chair meetings, as well as in informal conversations with deans, department chairs, and faculty. This continuous dialogue with the academic community not only reset the priorities and the culture for undergraduate students and their enrollment trends, but also created buy-in for investments in key enrollment strategies and tactics—investments that may have been redirected away from other important academic initiatives. This academic leader must be highly knowledgeable about external and internal trends that affect enrollment in order to be a credible communicator with the academic community. Therefore, dialogue between the academic leader and the chief enrollment officer is also a key component.

Co-curricular dialogue: Because the planning process covers co-curricular issues, student life, and student success, the SEP process leaders should be in constant dialogue with department heads in student affairs, student advising, and student success centers. To ensure this happens, have key individuals from these departments on the SEP council and action committee. These individuals not only serve as the dialogue links between the SEP process leaders and the student support departments, they also bring valuable insights and expertise to the development of the strategies, tactics, estimated costs, and estimated return on investment. These leaders can interact in two ways: 1) through formal contact with the institution's student support departments, and 2) informal, day-to-day contact through individual conversations and staff meeting discussions.

Fiscal dialogue: The fiscal aspect of the SEP process requires frequent dialogue with the chief fiscal officer, as well as communication with other fiscal officers (e.g., associate vice presidents, budget directors, and fiscal officers in departments such as academic affairs, student affairs, and academic colleges). The SEP plan will not be successful without innovative resource planning that is supported by institutional and departmental fiscal officers.

Data/research dialogue: To ensure the process is data-informed, there must be continuous dialogue with the individuals who provide the data that drive the SEP process. At many institutions, the primary individual responsible for providing this data is the director of institutional research. At some institutions, there are data analysts within the office of enrollment services who also contribute valuable data and analysis to the process. No matter how the institution is organized to retrieve and analyze enrollment and environmental data, formal and informal dialogue on a daily basis is a must for the success of the process. See Chapter 4 for more on ensuring a data-informed SEP.

KPIs, Data Collection, and the Situation Analysis

By Gary Fretwell and Robert Van Cleef

***"The future is embedded in the present."*—John Naisbitt**

A rigorous assessment of the institution and its environment is at the heart of strategic enrollment planning (SEP). Many institutions have a wealth of internal and external data at their disposal, but do not use this data in a meaningful way to drive actions or interconnect numerous data points to make strategic decisions. Campus leaders are unable or unwilling to make appropriate use of the considerable resources that could help them effectively navigate their challenges to ensure long-term growth and stability. They are *data-rich and information-poor*. Other institutions turn data into usable information, but too often succumb to the old habits of decision making and strategic direction setting; they rely on intuition and anecdote, and often defer to the strongest personality or loudest voice in the room. Truly strategic and effective institutions have processes and systems in place to collect, analyze, and effectively interpret data, and then use that data to support decision making and to set strategic direction.

CHAPTER HIGHLIGHTS

- ■ **Data is a resource that can be neglected, exploited, or understood**

- ■ **Data collection should be purpose-driven**

- ■ **A strategic enrollment plan should contain *metrics* stated as Key Performance Indicators**

The imperative of a data-informed campus culture

Most institutions collect data. Few institutions use that data to understand trends or patterns that warrant strategic responses and instead only use data to support annual enrollment plans. Leaders may look at a particular data element and set a goal to change it, deciding, for instance, to set a goal to increase the number of inquiries or applicants. Other campus leaders may fail to align both internal and external data with trend data to determine the real issues the institution faces. For example, few institutions are prepared for the student demographic changes happening in many regions (see Chapter 1).

A data-informed institution, on the other hand, takes the all-important next step of analyzing its data and developing a more informed awareness of its situation and environment. The institution uses that awareness to make decisions that align with its mission while allowing it to adapt intentionally to the future instead of simply reacting to it. A data-informed institution asks, "Does our data allow us to understand our context and draw implications about how we will need to change in order to fulfill our mission and vision in the future? Does our current state align with the emerging needs, demands, and trends? If not, can our institution sustain itself?" Such institutions, in effect, develop a kind of data wisdom that provides an impetus to move forward and drives the SEP process.

As challenging as this might seem, there is nothing magical about data. It is simply a resource that can be neglected, exploited, or understood. Frequently, a campus will have reams and reams of data with no one purposefully assessing it, considering its implications, or suggesting ways to change institutional behavior based on what it indicates. A campus must charge appropriate personnel with taking the data and drawing conclusions from it, as illustrated in Figure 4-1.

Figure 4-1: Using Data to Inform Decisions

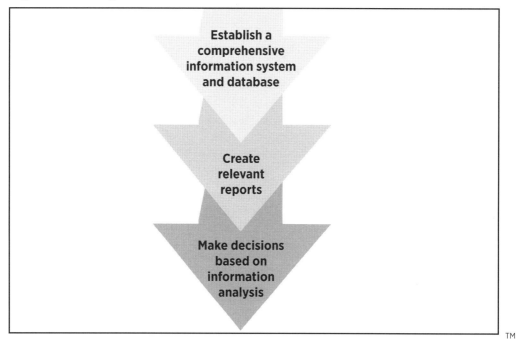

The process begins with the establishment of a comprehensive database of internal and external information that an institution can use to better understand its current situation and the context within which it operates. From these sources, the institution must extract relevant reports that enable campus leaders to understand institutional contexts, trends, strengths, and challenges. Finally, the institution takes that information and uses it to make decisions that will guide its operation on both strategic and tactical levels.

Within this framework, it becomes plain that it is not enough to simply collect data. It is essential to understand what data reveal about an institution's state and environment, and then use that data sagely and with integrity.

Building a data-informed campus culture

Let's take a closer look at what is involved in the development of a data-informed campus culture. Institutions that have the skill, discipline, and teamwork to make decisions informed by data will actually increase the focus and velocity of institutional progress. Leaders will learn to quantify and define problems and use data to make decisions based on appropriate assessments of risk.

First, campus leadership needs to understand the distinction between being data-informed and being data-driven. Those who are, by nature, driven by narrative may fear that becoming a data-informed culture requires an utter submission of human intuition and wisdom to reams of reports with nothing but numbers. They fear a data-informed culture means giving up the human element for computers. This ought not to be the case. Rather, a data-informed culture means that organizational leaders posit a theory or problem; arguments and possible solutions are theorized, and then campus leaders ask for information that can prove or disprove the proposed solution.

At many of the institutions we visit, we hear tales of endless debates that ultimately become circular. "We want to grow. However, if we grow, we will have to pay for expansion costs. Those expansion costs might be more than the revenues from growth. Therefore, we should not grow." Left as speculation, each point in the circular argument holds water. However, this leaves the institution deadlocked and unable to make a clear decision. Only when each element is quantified can the institution move beyond speculation and begin to make informed decisions. (What is the opportunity for growth? What are the costs of expansion? What is the cost of no-growth relative to peers?)

A data-informed culture, therefore, seeks to define the problems and opportunities it is facing using a rich mixture of both narratives and quantified data. All directors or department heads are free to define problems and propose solutions, but such propositions will be held suspect until there is a quantifiable impact substantiated by research that, in many cases, should be subject to peer review.

Second, institutions need to identify and learn to maximize relevant data from internal and external sources. The most basic division of data sources is internal and external. Each requires separate treatment due to constraints on the ability to control data presentation and quality. A common challenge to accurately constructing an institution's context is to rely purely on one or the other.

- *Internal data* comes primarily from an institution's internal databases such as the student information system, finance system, human resources system, course enrollment and classroom utilization databases, and collections of spreadsheets that individual departments may maintain for their departmental operations. Internal data is the most malleable, and therefore is often the most susceptible to error. Internal data primarily indicates your institution's historical and current performance. Extra care must be taken to precisely define which sets of internal data are presented in individual reports, what that data means, and how it should be presented. Departments that work with each section of data should be asked to review the reports and authenticate the accuracy of data presented prior to allowing the full SEP committee to see reports and begin analysis (lest the data be "shaped" to fit one's proposition).

- *External data,* by definition, comes from sources outside of the institution (e.g., IPEDS, National Student Clearinghouse, State Department of Education K-12 enrollment statistics, Delaware Cost Study, CUPA-HR, Bureau of Labor Statistics). External data is less malleable, as an outside entity has defined what each data point means, and institutions are restricted to the reports and delivery forms the outside entity has defined. Generally, while external reports should provide vetted data, institutions are also encouraged to estimate what level of accuracy to assume for each source. Sometimes, trends are more important than the measures themselves. External data also allow you to compare your institution's performance against other institutions.

It is important that data collection be purpose-driven and within a specific context. Later in this chapter we will discuss the use of strategy frameworks to help the SEP council narrow the body of data that could be collected to focus on factors that are under consideration in the SEP.

It is worth noting that institutional research and information technology departments should be central players in any SEP project. Personnel in these departments should be data experts and understand where to find the needed information. Being a part of the SEP council will help them understand the context of report requests. If not, the SEP council will ask for reports and data, but devoid of context, the IR or IT resource developing the report may present imprecisely defined data that answers the wrong question.

Third, present data in a historical-comparative context to facilitate true understanding. Say, for example, that an institution reports an 80 percent retention rate. Is that good or bad? If that institution has historically maintained an 85 percent retention rate and its peers have an 88 percent retention rate, then one would conclude there is a serious problem that ought to be addressed. However, if the institution historically maintained a 70 percent retention rate and its peers remain in the low 70's, then there is cause for much celebration and for planning to maintain those rates.

The example above makes clear that a historical-comparative context needs to be provided to interpret each specific data point. Data is most informative when presented in a combination of tables and graphs that display both history (typically the last five years) and comparison against other benchmark norms. Intuitively, most people understand how to make historical comparisons of institutional data, and are able to see if their institution is doing better or worse than in prior years. However, creating the right comparison groups with which an institution can benchmark its performance requires a little sophistication. While the intent of each of these groups must remain distinct, it is possible for certain institutions to be listed in multiple groups. Colleges and universities should consistently monitor the following benchmark comparison groups (which may or may not be mutually exclusive):

- *Peer institutions*—Peer institutions are those that represent the type of school with which your institution identifies. They might relate to the institution's size, control type, consortium relationship, or other commonly understood criteria that helps to broadly answer the question: "Who are your peers?" Peer institutions may compare favorably or unfavorably to your institution in terms of one or more specifically defined attributes.

- *Aspirant institutions*—Aspirant institutions represent the type of institution you hope to be like in five to 10 years on one or more specific attribute. It is important, when selecting aspirant institutions, to set your sights high enough to challenge your institution to make improvements, but not so high that the improvement seems impossible and exasperating to the SEP council.

- *Competitor institutions*—Unlike peer and aspirant comparison groups, the market defines an institution's competitors. This is a key point. Competitor institutions are observed as a function of the market as students move through the enrollment process. They are not chosen by the institution. Competitor lists can usually be identified through the following: ACT and SAT overlap, FAFSA overlap (though that resource will soon be going away), cross applications, and National Student Clearinghouse lost-admit research.

By agreeing to present an institution's data in these comparative-historical contexts, all members of the institution's SEP council should feel prepared to begin discussing what measures are truly important for driving future success. Tables will appeal to the numerically inclined, but graphs will appeal to more visual members of the SEP council; both are required to engage all members, see an example in Figure 4-2.

Figure 4-2: Comparative-Historical Data: Percent of Admits That Enroll

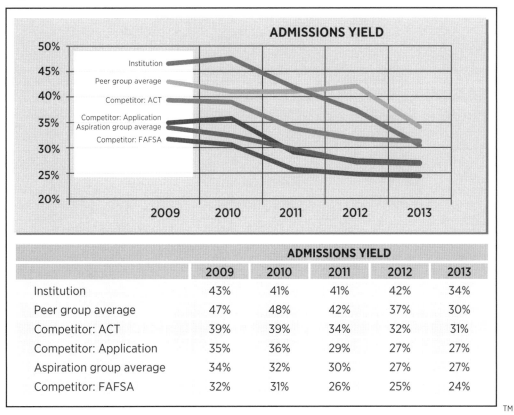

ADMISSIONS YIELD	2009	2010	2011	2012	2013
Institution	43%	41%	41%	42%	34%
Peer group average	47%	48%	42%	37%	30%
Competitor: ACT	39%	39%	34%	32%	31%
Competitor: Application	35%	36%	29%	27%	27%
Aspiration group average	34%	32%	30%	27%	27%
Competitor: FAFSA	32%	31%	26%	25%	24%

TM

Such renderings take more effort to produce, but often profoundly shape discussions of institutional context. The SEP members can now plainly see what is unique to an institution and what is common to the industry. Issues such as what are (or are not) realistic goals can now be debated in light of the performance of both aspirational and peer benchmarks.

Fourth—and potentially most important—data-informed cultures use metrics and data to _engineer_ success. By defining, early in the planning process, the institutional metrics upon which the success of the plan will be determined, the SEP council is able to identify and implement strategies designed to make the right contributions. If the contributions are not realized, corrective actions may be taken accordingly.

Metrics pertain to what is measured and _goals_ pertain to the level of a metric that is desired. During the first phase of planning, the strategic enrollment planning council must take the time to discuss how success will be assessed at the end of the plan. What metrics must change for success to be achieved? Is the institution seeking higher enrollment? Or does it want to have the same number of students, but with a higher academic profile? Is the primary outcome a more diversified set of enrollment and revenue streams? This goal discussion must include the president and senior leadership to ensure that relevant metrics will be used to determine the success of the project. The importance of this conversation cannot be overstated. Early in the SEP process, we are intentionally not determining the goals (e.g., the exact number of students we are after or a precise test score range), but knowing the metrics of the plan (e.g., enrollment and academic profile) is important in itself. Now the SEP council has a basis for focusing on developing the right strategies— or processes—that will impact these metrics and estimating what the impact of those strategies can be.

Key Performance Indicators

A strategic enrollment plan should contain a set of clearly defined metrics stated in the form of Key Performance Indicators (KPI). Any outcome that an institution wishes to emphasize as an important outcome of the strategic enrollment plan is a valid potential KPI.

In order to accomplish each outcome, the strategic enrollment planning team will want measures to assess whether or not they are on track; such measures are called Performance Indicators (PI). If a larger headcount is the desired outcome (a KPI), the SEP council might consider looking at the yield rates of new student applicants (one leading indicator of overall enrollment) and retention rates (another leading indicator of overall headcount) to see if they are on track to reach the desired outcome. By understanding how each Performance Indicator contributes to Key Performance Indicators, the impact of variances can be estimated and corrective actions can be determined.

In short, KPIs are commonly acknowledged measurements critical to the mission and fiscal health of the institution. As a rule, they:

- Are institution-specific, data-derived measurements that provide the foundation for determining the current state of the institution and, when matched with historical comparisons, are relevant for the creation of the situation analysis (often in the form of a strengths, weaknesses, opportunities, and threats—or SWOT—exercise) and overall strategic planning;
- Reflect the effectiveness of broad, cross-departmental cooperation;
- Provide points of comparison in relation to KPIs of peer, competitor, and/or aspirant institutions;
- Are often complex and expected to improve over a long period of time, as action items may take three to five years before delivering return on investment; and
- Are supported by and dependent on multiple performance indicators.

Typical KPIs

KPIs are enrollment, performance, quality, and fiscal indicators and other outcomes that institutional leadership uses to measure the fulfillment of the institution's mission and vision. Typical KPIs include the following:

1. Enrollment (headcount and full-time enrollment for overall, off-site, online, undergraduate, graduate, in-state, and out-of-state);
2. Student quality (average SAT/ACT, 25th and 75th percentile SAT/ACT, and average high school GPA);
3. Student progress (new freshman first-to-second-year and first-to-third-year retention, and four-, five-, and six-year graduation rates);
4. Program quality (student-faculty engagement [NSSE/CCSSE scores], student-faculty ratio, class size, profile, undergraduate research, and graduate research);
5. Diversity enrollment and cohort profile (numbers enrolling and percentage of students from diverse backgrounds or under-represented groups and their success rates, gender balance, full- and part-time ratios); and
6. Fiscal health (enrollment-related revenues and operating expenses).

Performance Indicators

It takes improvement in multiple PIs to impact any one or more KPIs. Often, PIs can be addressed more readily than KPIs. PIs are often a part of the work done among two or more functional areas. Through the planning process, institutions should create a list of PIs to support the achievement of each KPI target.

The examples below illustrate the relationship between common KPIs and PIs. Note that these are not exhaustive lists, but campuses engaged in SEP often track many of these KPIs and PIs.

Typical Performance Indicators

To support enrollment KPIs

1. Undergraduate enrollment by term;
2. New freshman enrollment, admits, applications, and inquiries by term;
3. Transfer enrollment, admits, applications, and inquiries by term;
4. Undergraduate second-to-third-year retention rate, third-to-fourth-year retention rate, and beyond fourth-year graduation rate;
5. Graduate enrollment, admits, applications, and inquiries by term;
6. Graduate retention rate; and
7. Graduate graduation rate.

To support enrollment profile (diversity, academic) KPIs

1. Inquiry profiles;
2. Applicant profiles; and
3. ACT and SAT market share profiles.

To support retention and graduation KPIs

1. Student satisfaction indicators;
2. Student engagement indicators;
3. First-to-second term persistence;
4. Grade point distributions by student cohort and by course;
5. Number and percentage of students not able to enroll in desired major;
6. Number and percentage of students not able to enroll in desired courses;
7. Student debt burden and profile; and
8. Award gaps between student need and actual financial aid awards.

To support fiscal health KPIs

1. Net tuition revenues;
2. Auxiliary (housing, dining, and bookstore) total revenues and net revenues;
3. Education and general costs by student subgroups (by program, ability level);
4. Net tuition revenue and scholarship costs by student subgroups (ability level and resident/non-resident); and
5. Net tuition revenue and financial aid cost by needy student subgroup.

Clearly defining the PIs and how they are associated with KPIs offers the strategic enrollment council a few advantages:

- The SEP council will know more clearly which processes will impact which outcomes. Some of these relationships are not always clearly understood by all members of the institution. Seeing these relationships can be a powerful communication tool.

- As the SEP is rolled into implementation, an SEP dashboard (see Chapter 8) can be developed. PIs will help the team to see if it is on track for reaching its goals. This creates opportunities to implement corrective actions to accomplish outcomes (i.e., if deposits are down, the SEP team will realize they may need to do an application generation or completion initiative in order to help meet the overall enrollment goal).

Strategic enrollment planning councils are encouraged to review lists of KPIs and PIs from other institutions in addition to the list above. In so doing, however, it is critical that they carefully think through the reasoning of how the PIs should relate to the KPIs. The best PIs will be leading indicators that an institution is on track (or not) in achieving the overall KPI.

Using strategy frameworks to see *through* the data: moving from data collection to the situation analysis

How does an organization know where to begin to define KPIs? As data collection proceeds, it is easy to feel overwhelmed by the amount of data that can be collected, resulting in "analysis paralysis." Strategic analysis frameworks provide scaffolding upon which institutions give form to the key issues confronting an organization. Two examples—and there are many others—include the "Big Three" and the SWOT analysis.

The "Big Three" framework helps institutions identify possibilities where a sustainable competitive advantage can be cultivated. Institutions collect data about their programs to identify strengths, market demand for current or future programs, and offerings by current competitors. As this data is reviewed, the SEP council searches for the convergence of authenticity, differentiation and relevance; the sweet spot where a competitive advantage can be leveraged, as illustrated in Figure 4-3.

- *Authenticity:* In which areas does an institution perform well and produce demonstrably better results than its competition? Which areas stoke the passions of faculty and staff? With a little more effort, can the institution make substantial gains from the relative strength of these areas?

- *Differentiation:* What are the areas where an institution provides a unique program or experience relative to the competition? Are there any unique offerings that are not provided by other institutions? What makes an offering unique may be a result of its category or type, volume, a specific characteristic, its nature, its geography, or any combination thereof.

- *Relevance:* What is the market demand for an institution's programs? What are its prospective students looking for? What kind of graduates are regional employers looking for? Unique characteristics become important when they are attractive to potential students. Assessments of market demand should provide evidence of demand volume (how many students are willing to enroll, and what is the placement rate of graduates?), levels of price consciousness/sensitivity (are they willing to pay or pay more?), and sustainability (will student demand and relevant jobs continue to exist 10 to 15 years from now?).

Figure 4-3: Convergence of Authenticity, Relevance, and Differentiation

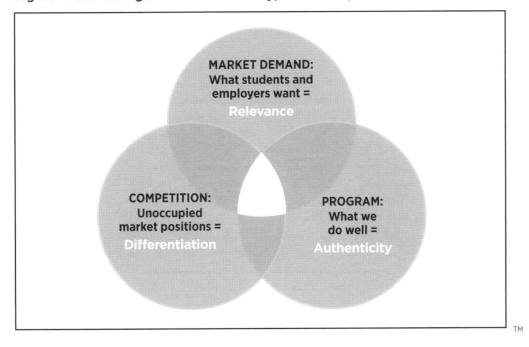

The SWOT analysis, as illustrated in Figure 4-4, provides a strong sense for how an organization's overall competitive context can be framed. Most executives are familiar with the traditional SWOT analysis wherein the planning team enumerates strengths and weaknesses (internal to the institution), as well as opportunities and threats (arising from external conditions).

- **Strengths:** Existing characteristics (programmatic, physical, and financial) that clearly contribute to institutional success and the achievement of enrollment goals and that are measurably better than those of the competition.

- **Weaknesses:** Existing characteristics that detract from institutional success and the achievement of enrollment goals and that are measurably worse than those of the competition.

- **Opportunities:** External conditions that allow for opening new markets, launching new programs, strengthening a market position, or increasing organizational strength due to the ability to realize new efficiencies.

- **Threats:** Potential external conditions that could become obstacles to institutional success and achievement of enrollment goals, or that threaten to close existing markets or programs, or reduce organizational strength.

Figure 4-4: SWOT Analysis

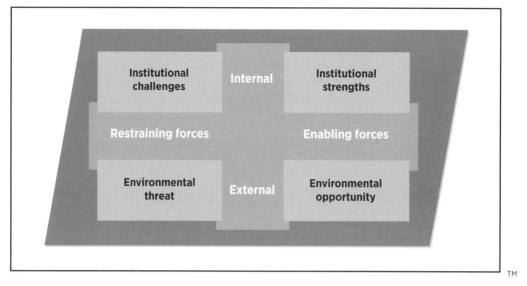

TM

The high level of familiarity with SWOT may be considered a strength or a weakness of this framework. It is a strength, as members of the planning team have likely used it before and will be able to become involved quickly. However, this also may be a weakness, as members may have had poor experiences in the past with this framework and may come to feel jaded.

While each strategic analysis framework will emphasize different aspects of the competitive context, the key point is that this analysis requires both a qualitative and quantitative approach. Claims made for each of the elements in each framework need to be substantiated using real data, lest they be held suspect. Data that does not serve to substantiate a claim within the framework is extraneous.

To do a SWOT analysis well, not only must the planning team enumerate each of these elements, but it must also quantify the impact to provide proper perspective. For example, many institutions claim that their faculty is a strength, and frankly, who would want to argue that they don't hire a strong faculty? But what is more helpful to identify strategic opportunities is to define how faculty members are a strength relative to the competition—and then measure it. For example, one institution's faculty may be a strength because they mentor students in their programs (measured by field experience placement, job placement, timely completion, and satisfaction with advising rates), while another institution's faculty may be a strength because they do more research (measured by research grant dollars per faculty member, a higher percentage of terminal degrees). Therefore, completing a SWOT analysis requires not only identifying these elements, but also constructing arguments using data to prove why elements cited are to be considered strengths, weaknesses, opportunities, or threats. Such arguments are best displayed in the form of historical comparisons with institutional data benchmarked to aspirant, peer, and competitor institutions.

Frequently, the process of measuring elements in the SWOT analysis *changes* "the story." An institution may claim it has an opportunity to capture more Hispanic students because it is aware of demographic changes. But to really plan effective strategies, the institution should know how many Hispanic families are in its recruitment territories and whether or not they are likely to enroll. The actual market opportunity may be greater or lesser than first suspected. As institutions learn to use data as a part of their SWOT processes, certain myths are debunked and claims previously made become suspect, are discarded, or are re-categorized (e.g., a perceived strength is discovered to be a weakness after examination).

When the SWOT analysis is completed—and there is agreement in the story and the facts—the SEP council will have a compelling and realistic vision of their institution's competitive context from which strategy ideation can proceed. For SEP, the situation analysis should become a narrative that communicates the current state and the challenges to reach the desired future state, thereby illuminating the need for change, priorities for action, and current activities to be continued or further enhanced.

Creating a data-informed narrative situation analysis

Stories worth telling—the best stories—inspire us to improve because we see how the hero overcomes great challenges. Perhaps the hero emerges victorious over some overwhelming challenge against the odds through a great strength or is able to take advantage of some opportunity. Such narratives offer a blueprint for how the SEP not only inspires the right actions an organization needs to take, but also the kind of analysis required to identify the situations and characteristics from which institutional success can emerge.

Strategy frameworks as described are not only scaffolding, but they are also the lens through which the institution's narrative can begin to be seen. As the SEP council moves through the process of adding and testing claims in a strategic analysis framework, they should be asking many questions:

- What are the big stories and themes that we see in our current situation?
- Which of our debates seem to run into endless loops? How can we quantify each point and counterpoint in order to test scenarios of which way to go?
- What are we really passionate about? How aligned is that with our institution's mission and vision?
- Given the KPIs that have been identified to measure our success, what do we think will be the most important strategies to get us there? Can we test them to see if they are realistic?

By asking these kinds of big questions and using strategic analysis frameworks to test claims with data, the SEP council will come to discover a data-informed situation analysis that conveys a compelling institutional narrative. The SEP council should actively debate which claims are supported by the data and which claims may need to be reconsidered. When the SEP council is satisfied that they have the right claims supported by the best available data in a reasonable way, they will find that they are also able to tell their institution's story by describing how varied strategy framework elements are interrelated and can offer stories from the institution's history to illustrate these interconnections.

Dialogue: Next steps in becoming a data-informed champion

- Take a thorough inventory of data you have and the gaps that exist related to the identified KPIs;
- Establish reports that clearly capture key data findings; and
- Share the results of initial data findings.

Themes drawn from the data review may lead to changes in communications and resource distribution, including staffing and budgeting. Those themes may also lead to a better understanding of the amount of time required to respond and proactively move forward.

The SEP process can also demonstrate how data can be used throughout the campus, regardless of its connection to enrollment, to inform priorities and prompt action. Data collected through the planning process should be stored and shared in open sites (both during and after the planning process) to ensure transparency.

When identifying data elements and ensuring that the review of data becomes an ongoing process, institutional leaders should consider the following:

- Does the current SEP planning team understand the importance and value of KPI identification, monitoring, and annual/biannual updates?
- Who will be responsible for collecting and collating the data as well as monitoring the data on at least a semesterly basis?
- What types of data are needed to support the planning process and foster a better understanding of opportunities or threats in meeting institutional strategic plan goals?
- How will these measures be linked to the long-term planning and plan monitoring process?
- How widely are data currently shared among important campus units? How will data need to be shared in the future?
- How will KPIs link to academic programs as they are evaluated and reviewed?
- Who will be responsible for an ongoing review of external data that will affect KPIs?
- How will the KPI review and the work of the strategic enrollment management (SEM) council be linked to the institution's financial condition?
- How will the review and the work of the SEM council be linked to the institution's marketing efforts to showcase campus points of pride and accomplishment?

This is hardly a comprehensive list of discussion points, but it is meant to spur campus dialogue about the importance of data usage, particularly during the SEP process. For example, an institution may not be at a point where academic program evaluation and restructuring can be incorporated into the planning process; however, the campus can use internal and external data to understand program trends and expected future demand. If a campus has a distinctive computer information program that is small but expected to see increased demand due to increased employment opportunities, the planning process might identify this and result in the designation of specific marketing or recruitment efforts to expand interest and increase enrollment. In this same example, if the data show a large gap in the interests of entering students and degree completion, strategies can be developed to help support program outcomes and increase completion rates. These strategies would support the academic program, but not necessarily move into an in-depth analysis that would be considered a detailed program review. Regardless of current academic program offerings, it is essential that the data provide information and insight about student interest (by subpopulation) and current or potential market share.

To be truly strategic, campuses must use data to inform SEP strategies and goals. Failure to incorporate relevant data throughout the process can limit success.

CHAPTER 5

Integrating Academic and Co-curricular Programs

By Evelyn (Bonnie) Lynch and James Mager

In studies conducted by Ruffalo Noel Levitz, OmniUpdate, CollegeWeekLive, and NRCCUA, a majority of prospective students indicated that they looked at webpages related to an academic program offering before any other information. While there certainly are many factors leading to a student's selection of a college or university, student satisfaction data also indicates that academic reputation is important when comparing other institutional factors (Ruffalo Noel Levitz, 2016). Therefore, the need for institutions to connect and align academic and co-curricular programs with their strategic enrollment efforts is paramount. From a broader perspective, connecting students (even undeclared majors) with academic programs, and deepening that connection through co-curricular and support services, is critical to strong enrollment planning outcomes.

> **CHAPTER HIGHLIGHTS**
>
> ■ **Academic and co-curricular programs are at the forefront of planning**
>
> ■ **High-quality situation analyses lead to high-quality strategy development**
>
> ■ **SEP leaders must understand how programs, current and projected demand, competition, student success, and ROI intersect**

Unfortunately, few institutions build their strategic enrollment planning (SEP) and their enrollment management programs with academic and co-curricular program planning as the focus. Instead, most institutions put marketing, recruiting, financial aid, scholarships, and retention strategies at the forefront of their enrollment planning with relatively little or no emphasis on program development and enhancement during the planning horizon. This approach is inefficient and does not consider all that the institution should be doing to optimize its Key Performance Indicators for enrollment, student success, and fiscal health.

The SEP process facilitates a balanced approach to the strategies mentioned here, but most importantly, places academic and co-curricular programs at the forefront of planning. This chapter explores important considerations in aligning the SEP process with academic and co-curricular programs. Here, the term "program" refers to an academic major, minor, graduate degree, certificate, or student service, and is not synonymous with the department in which it is housed. This chapter builds on the framework and concepts of the previous chapters to describe the alignment with and inter-relationships among academic programs, co-curricular services, and the other elements of the strategic enrollment plan.

Current state of most academic and co-curricular planning

The academic enterprise is both the heart of an institution and its major cost center (Leslie and Fretwell, 1996). Yet academic programs have seen little additional investment as fiscal resources have been directed toward institutional recruitment/marketing strategies, better-quality service (more staff), advanced athletic or recreational facilities, and/or dynamic and diversified student centers (Astin, 2003). In order to compete in today's markets, institutions have allocated resources for purposes that foster advancement of all programs. Fewer resources have been focused on ways to improve faculty performance in the classroom or provide them with the professional development needed to integrate technology as a supplemental tool to further engage students and improve course outcomes.

While academic programs and departments have seen few boosts in funding, they have also been insulated from short-term cost-cutting during times of financial turbulence. Reductions are often made in nonacademic areas, particularly in student affairs, marketing, and physical plant/operations, as these areas are sometimes considered discretionary and their work viewed as peripheral to the mission of the institution (Ehernberg and Webber, 2010). If academic programs are included in an across-the-board cut, funding is usually returned to its prior level once the situation has stabilized. Moreover, on many campuses, the annual budgeting process does not include academic program/department revenues, operating costs, or academic productivity measures (e.g., credit hour production, degrees/certificates awarded) as part of the process. The direct and indirect costs to operate academic programs are assumed as baseline expenses in each budget cycle.

At the outset of most institutional strategic planning processes, academic programs are assumed to be equally aligned, integral to the mission, and therefore beyond re-allocation or termination considerations (Leslie and Fretwell, 1996). Dickeson (2010) suggested that institutional planning efforts were usually additive, resulting in new resources, new faculty in existing programs, and new programs, with little consideration of future employment or graduate school opportunities, or of initial start-up recruitment and marketing costs to generate students for new academic programs. In addition, decision making occurred at all levels and across all units of an institution, often in isolation from other units and departments within the organizational sphere. Although it is obvious that the larger and more complex an institution, the greater the challenges of sharing information and collaboration, even smaller institutions are not immune to silo-style decision making.

Senior leadership, deans, department heads, and academic and student affairs program coordinators generally do not stop to question how each decision impacts the institution's overall budget, effectiveness, or efficiency. The longer-term effects of repeated independent decision making across all units may not be evident in conventional planning.

Planning for student affairs generally occurs within the broad context of institutional planning, with mixed fiscal and resource outcomes. Such planning efforts may result in internal personnel efficiencies and/or changes to existing in-house programs or activities, but most often, these actions are not aligned with the institution's overall vision for the future or with academic affairs (Atkins, 2010). Recently, student affairs leaders have advocated for the use of traditional planning models as a strategy to position co-curricular units and demonstrate relevance to mission, student outcomes, and the external and internal future (Ellis, 2010). In his discussion of academic and student affairs collaboration in strategic planning, Whitney (2010) noted that, "Student affairs and the faculty have a stake in working together," and identified retention and persistence as areas for collaborative planning. Yet too few institutions plan collaboratively, and, when they do, it is generally at the department level rather than institutionwide.

Co-curricular programs within the educational experience

Along with academic programs and reputation, students are also attracted to institutions because of the range and types of co-curricular programs available. Such co-curricular experiences take many forms, depending upon the types of students, institutional mission, personnel, and fiscal resources allocated to them. For student-centric institutions, co-curricular experiences are no longer viewed as ancillary or peripheral but are seen as integral to student success.

Data suggest that well-planned, large-impact experiences inside and outside of the classroom contribute to retention, persistence, and graduation (Kuh, 2008; Newton and Smith, 2008; Terenzini, Pascarella, and Blimling, 1996; Zlotkowski, 1998). Collaborative, high-impact practices shown to correlate with student success include, but are not limited to:

- Living-learning communities;
- First-year seminar/course linking;
- Early-alert systems;
- Supplemental instruction;
- Athletics/intramurals; and
- Service learning.

In his discussion of faculty perspectives on undergraduate education and curriculum, Bok (2006) stated that the "extra curriculum" was most often overlooked as a valuable component of a student's educational experience. While acknowledging that the overall impact varied based on the type of student and the nature of the institution, he suggested that such experiences may have a more lasting impression than classroom experiences. He concluded that what students study in class often affects the value of their extracurricular experience, which, in turn, can enhance what they learn in class.

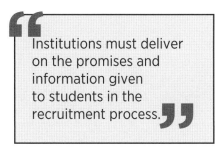

Institutions must deliver on the promises and information given to students in the recruitment process.

Collaborative endeavors between the academic and student affairs spheres may result in conflicts over turf, resources, and expertise. Schroeder (1999) identified obstacles and constraints that contribute to the separation of the formal and informal curriculum and how such impediments differ by institution type. Whitney (2010) compared the faculty and student affairs divide to a clash of cultures based largely on a lack of understanding about how each unit contributes to the mission and vision. He concluded that collaboration between academic and student affairs is now essential, and institutions must deliver on the promises and information given to students in the recruitment process.

Figure 5-1 contrasts the prevailing silo perspective of segmented academic and co-curricular programs with the desired alignment of these two areas.

Figure 5-1: Strategic Enrollment Planning Academic and Co-curricular Alignment

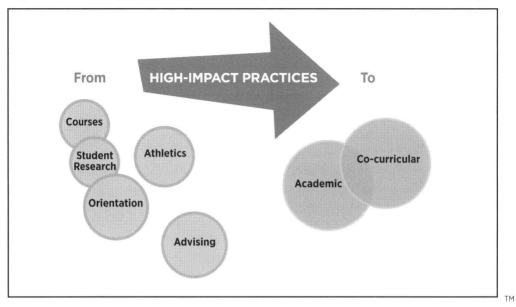

The SEP process seeks to create a future state of studying all of the aforementioned considerations (and a number of additional ones) before announcing or approving a new academic or co-curricular program. Similar to program review, the SEP process ensures that the campus explores market demand and the ability to penetrate existing markets to determine if program offerings are minimally sustainable, ultimately financially viable, and aligned with a desired future institutional state.

Aligning academic and co-curricular program planning with SEP

SEP is a complex and organized effort to connect mission, current state, and changing environment to foster planned long-term enrollment and fiscal health. It aligns and integrates academic and co-curricular planning with marketing, recruitment, retention/ completion, and financial aid strategies, with an eye toward future demands and trends. It also aligns with physical facility, technology, and fiscal development planning.

SEP begins with data collection related to the institution's Key Performance Indicators, and aligns that data with a situation analysis. The institution's strengths, weaknesses, opportunities, and threats form the basis for the strategy development and prioritization.

How do academic and co-curricular program analyses and strategy development align with the other types of SEP analyses and strategy developments?

The mission of the institution and the academic and co-curricular programs are the essence of the institution. Therefore, planners need to understand the scenarios for how much, if any, the essence of the institution could change during the planning horizon before proceeding with in-depth strategic planning in the other components of SEP. The institution's planners and leaders must acknowledge the following throughout the entire SEP process: The mission of the institution and academic and co-curricular program planning are at the forefront of SEP.

Strategies for marketing, recruitment, retention/completion, pricing, financial aid/scholarship, physical facilities, and technology cannot be fully developed or implemented without first developing and committing to strategies for academic and co-curricular programs.

Successful long-range SEP strategies should include the following characteristics:

- Marketing and recruitment strategies should be based on the academic and co-curricular programs that they will promote and feature during the planning horizon and the potential student markets that these programs will attract.

- Pricing and financial aid/scholarship strategy development should support the prospective and current students in the programs that the institution will develop, enhance, and maintain during the planning timeframe.

- Student success and retention strategies can only be developed within the context of programs the institution will develop, enhance, or reduce in upcoming years.

- Physical facility, learning technology, and fiscal development planning cannot occur without strong integration with the programs that will emerge during the planning horizon and the number of students they will attract.

One of the complexities of SEP is that it is not a linear planning process. Typically, there are numerous interactions and feedback loops in the planning process. Certainly, the SEP subcommittees that are working on marketing, recruiting, retention, pricing, and financial aid/scholarships should not wait until all the program strategies have been developed, evaluated, and approved before beginning their work. However, to help ensure both an effective and efficient SEP process, strong emphasis should be placed on continuous subcommittee interaction and collaboration.

Situation analyses for academic and co-curricular program planning

The foundation of effective, strategic academic and co-curricular planning is a situation analysis that includes recent trends and future projections regarding the internal and external environments of the institution. The information that is collected for the situation analysis comes from a variety of data sources outlined below, as well as from as the qualitative observations and opinions of those with significant experience in a relevant topic (e.g., adult education) and those important perspectives (e.g., students). High-quality situation analyses lead to high-quality strategy development and to outcomes with higher probability of success.

The main objective of a strong situation analysis for high-quality strategy development is to identify strengths, weaknesses, opportunities, and threats that emerge from the following:

- **Internal environment analyses,** involving effectiveness measures such as student persistence, retention and graduation rates, current enrollment demands and capacities, and fiscal considerations for each existing program;

- **Market demand analyses** of trends and projections of prospective student interests and occupation skills; and

- **Competition analyses,** involving competitor program strengths, weaknesses, and voids in order to identify institutional strategic program opportunities and threats.

These analyses support the "Big Three," program, market demand, and competition, that are mentioned in the situation analysis section and Figure 4-3 of Chapter 4, as well as the search for the sweet spot that is mentioned in that chapter.

Internal environment analyses

For periodic institutional program reviews, institutions have developed a number of ways to organize internal environment analyses of academic and co-curricular programs. The organization of these analyses is secondary; however, the essential questions that need to be answered are very important to strong program reviews and strategy development. For this chapter, the internal environment questions and components are presented in two categories:

- Program effectiveness analyses; and
- Program enrollment, capacity, and net operating income studies.

For **program effectiveness studies**, program strategy development is dependent on the answers to fundamental questions such as:

- How does each program align with institutional mission, vision, KPIs, and goals?
- How does the program align with future-oriented knowledge and skills?
- What are the strengths and passions of the faculty and staff in each program, and are there attractions for potential students now and in the future?
- How does the program document student success outcomes, and what are these outcomes?
- How does the program measure student expectations, satisfaction, and engagement?
- How does the program measure expectations, satisfaction, and outcomes of alumni of the program and employers of these alumni?
- What are the co-curricular program outcomes (e.g., living-learning wing of residence hall, athletic teams, or support programs for developmental learners)?

In determining student progression and graduation rates, strategic planners need to be careful how to interpret these rates for each program. If a program's retention rates are relatively low, are the students who are leaving the program going to other programs, or are they leaving the institution? Program retention rates are also affected by the incoming flows of students from other programs. Without this effectiveness analysis, institutional behavior patterns over time lead to an attitude of "this is how we do it" without regard to the potential negative consequences or the connections among recruitment, program delivery, and student progression, or the interconnections among campus experiences, services, and completion.

Responses to the above questions will position specific academic and co-curricular programs in relation to the current institutional environment. Typically, the more data-informed the responses to these questions, the more likely it is they will lead to sound program strategies that will gain the confidence of both strategy decision makers and also the individuals who will implement the resultant strategies and tactics. As will become evident, these program effectiveness responses, in combination with the other analyses mentioned below, will also guide short- and long-term SEP priority determination.

Another very important type of analysis that informs SEP program priority determinations is the collection of **studies of the enrollment, capacity, and net operating income of each academic and co-curricular program**. These studies are quantitative and typically require the enrollment and accounting expertise of individuals from the office of institutional research, the fiscal office, the office of academic affairs, and the office of student affairs. The studies can be time-consuming, but they are also extremely valuable for ensuring the fiscal health of the institution and for addressing the student demands for its programs. These studies answer the following questions:

- How does each program contribute to the fiscal health of the institution? Chapter 7 provides a thorough discussion of fiscal considerations, the costs of educational capacity, and demand.

- Which programs are at or near capacity? What are the demands and costs for expansion of these programs?

- Which programs have little demand or are operating significantly below capacity? Should the capacity and operating expenses be reduced for these programs?

- What are the top programs for positive net operating income? Can we increase the external market share of students interested in these programs?

- What are the programs that have negative net operating income? Are these programs critical to fulfilling student educational needs, student demand, or institutional mission?

Capacity and demand may be influenced by the days and times of course offerings, scheduling of corequisites, time between classes and distance between buildings, and ease of the scheduling process. These are obvious but frequently overlooked variables that may indirectly influence retention, progression, and course and program decisions.

Figure 5-2: Evaluating the Economics of Programs—Strategic Options

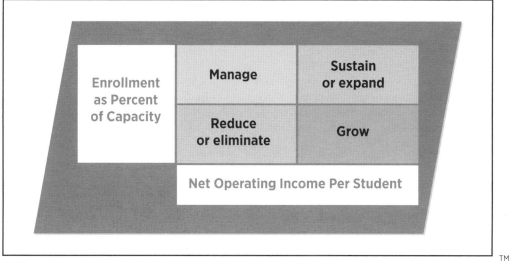

Figure 5-2 depicts four categories of programs as a function of current demand, capacity, and net operating income. This figure indicates the types of departments that are *candidates* to grow, manage, reduce, eliminate, or start. In using the results of these studies, strategists and institutional leaders must keep in mind at all times that SEP is a data-informed process and not a data-driven process, and, therefore, no academic or co-curricular program strategies should be developed solely on where the programs land in this grid. Certainly many other factors, including the results of the other analyses mentioned in this chapter, must be considered in program strategy development.

As an emerging component of SEP, academic and co-curricular programs are subject to cost analysis not only by program area, but also by student population (e.g., undecided, transfer, athlete). However, students do not segment their college experiences or choices by cost centers or organizational structures. Institutional leaders who understand students' perspectives and the value of academic and co-curricular collaboration will reap the benefits in retention, progression, and graduation. Although difficult to determine, the cost-per-student implications of these success initiatives may prove to be investments in long-term institutional success.

Market demand analyses

An important component of data-informed strategic academic and program planning is market demand analyses to identify program development opportunities and threats. Strategists and institutional leaders should ask the following questions before developing program strategies for the planning horizon:

- What are the recent trends for student academic and co-curricular interests in the institution's primary and secondary markets?

- What are the future occupation and occupation skill projections in the institution's primary and secondary geographic markets?

- How do student interests and the occupations that are increasing and decreasing match with the programs that the institution is currently offering or could offer in the future?

- What is the current market penetration of program offerings compared to the expected level of interest?

- What are the demographic trends and projections of the institution's primary and secondary markets?

- What are the prices that students pay and the price sensitivities of prospective students for the programs that the institution currently offers or could potentially offer?

In order to answer these external market demand questions, the strategic planning team typically needs to use data sources such as U.S. Department of Labor occupation projections, SAT/ACT academic and extracurricular interest trends, GRE/GMAT academic interest trends, competitor enrollments by program, Western Interstate Commission for Higher Education (WICHE) high school senior projections, and workforce readiness data, and compare these data to institutional offerings, adult learner trends, and regional accreditation information.

The findings from these market demand studies should be a significant catalyst for more detailed discussion of scenarios for program development, expansion, reduction, and elimination. However, decisions should not be based solely on external information. National databases, public policy documents, and large-scale research and evaluation reports are of limited value when considered in isolation from the institutional data and qualitative information collected in the internal environment analyses mentioned earlier. For example, demographic trends and occupational projections may influence an institutional leadership council to urge the initiation of a new program in response to reported enrollment increases at competitor institutions, but that program may be well beyond the institution's current core competencies as determined within the internal analyses.

Competition analyses

In addition to the internal environment and market demand analyses, the strategic academic and co-curricular program planning process should include competition analyses to determine strategic opportunities and threats for each current and potential program. Strategists and institutional leaders should ask the following questions during this program planning process:

- What are the competitor program enrollment and quality strengths, weaknesses, and voids? Are there any program opportunities to be derived from the competitor weaknesses or voids? Are there any program threats to be derived from the competitor strengths?

- What are the areas where the home institution performs well and produces demonstrably better results than its competition?

- What is the home institution's market share for each program, and how does this compare to competitors' market share by state/county/region?

- What are the areas where the home institution provides a unique program or experience relative to the competition?

- Are there any offerings that are not provided by other institutions or are provided by few institutions in the state or region?

- What competitor programs are strong or weak for program delivery, and what program delivery voids can we fill?

Data sources to answer these types of questions typically include state higher education sources, individual institutional and consortium data sources, National Student Clearinghouse data, and ACT enrollment information services for incoming new freshmen who took the ACT. The answers to these questions will determine another set of strategic opportunities and threats to be integrated with the other program strengths, weaknesses, opportunities, and threats that were identified in the internal environment and market demand analyses.

Place and program delivery analyses

Internal environment, market demand, and competition analyses should be performed not only for academic and co-curricular programs, but also for each place the programs are offered (campuses, learning centers, remote sites, corporate settings) and for each mode of program delivery (traditional, online, executive format, weekend, evening). These analyses should be conducted because student demands, program effectiveness measures, and delivery costs can vary significantly for each combination of place and mode of delivery of the same academic major and co-curricular program.

Program strategy development and prioritization

The situation analyses described here provide the foundation for determining and prioritizing the key strategies needed to attain realistic enrollment goals. This sets the stage for academic program and co-curricular strategy development. Ultimately, the planning process should seek to align curricular, co-curricular, and support services with new student and enrollment processes that connect through each stage of the student engagement stream: prospect to enrolled to completed to engaged alumni, and all of the segments in between.

Whether the overarching enrollment KPIs are focused on increasing, maintaining, or decreasing enrollments, it is essential that SEP leaders understand how programs, current and projected demand, competition, student success, and ROI intersect. For institutions that have KPIs for increasing enrollment, SEP leaders will search for the convergence of authenticity, differentiation, and relevance—the sweet spot where a competitive advantage can be leveraged, as described previously and in Chapter 4.

Dickeson (2010) provides a similar approach to strategy development and prioritization by suggesting 10 criteria and related applications for academic programs:

1. History, development, and expectations for the program.
2. External demand for the program.
3. Internal demand for the program.
4. Quality of program inputs and processes.
5. Quality of program outcomes.
6. Size, scope, and productivity of the program.
7. Revenue and other resources generated by the program.
8. Costs and other expenses associated with the program.
9. Impact, justification, and overall significance of the program.
10. Opportunity analysis of the program.

The analyses described in this chapter provide the information needed to support these criteria for program prioritization.

Though Dickeson's focus is on academic programs and services, the same criteria can and should apply to nonacademic and co-curricular areas. For example, some campuses have a rich and robust Greek tradition. Over the years, these programs may have evolved into strong, positive organizations that provide significant community service to the local area, generate more graduates, and/or develop major alumni contributors. The size, scope, and productivity of Greek programs may justify additional staffing and other resources to further enhance these programs, while the reverse may justify a decrease in support.

For academic and co-curricular program strategy development, SEP leaders should combine the analyses outlined in this chapter to be certain that all available data and information is considered. More information regarding strategy identification is provided in Chapter 6.

After the strategy development and prioritization phases are completed, an institution can pursue one of the following seven options for academic program planning:

1. Do nothing.
2. Modify/enhance what already exists.
3. Create new or multidisciplinary programs out of the existing curriculum.
4. Create entirely new programs.
5. Adopt alternative delivery formats for nontraditional markets or within traditional markets if there is growing demand for these formats.
6. Connect undergraduate majors to complementary graduate offerings, or link non-credit offerings to credit-bearing programs.
7. Close/downsize underperforming programs or programs that data suggest will no longer align with future market interests.

Purpose and identity strategy development

As an institution reviews its curricular and co-curricular programs to ensure it has a quality product and is producing graduates well-prepared for careers or the achievement of higher credentials, it must also consider whether its current mission aligns with the anticipated future state of higher education. The College Board *Trends in Higher Education* series has reported numerous positive outcomes linked to degree completion, particularly at the bachelor's level. Institutions must continue to review their true market niche and market potential, connecting their current mission with a vision for a future that understands market demand, competition, and program strengths. In considering what it does best, an institution must also understand the market demand for or relevance of its program offerings (both curricular and co-curricular).

Conclusion and dialogue

"The future ain't what it used to be." Yogi Berra's words serve to remind institutional leaders of their responsibilities in guiding colleges and universities toward the future. At its most basic level, SEP invites institutions to envision their future and determine the scope and magnitude of change required to spur progress toward the desired state. As an institutionwide process, SEP includes all facets of the institution, including academic programs, and presents an opportunity to align academic and co-curricular programs with institutional mission. Equally important, it provides a pathway to foster links between academic and co-curricular initiatives, and with the enrollment functions of the institution.

This chapter provides a number of questions that should be answered as part of the situation analysis phase of strategic academic and co-curricular program planning. Some additional questions the campus community should consider include:

1. How does the campus integrate curricular, co-curricular, and support service functions to yield a dynamic and seamless learning experience with positive outcomes?

2. What are the resources needed to ensure that academic majors, linked to employment demand, are being delivered in contemporary ways that teach the skills needed for future professionals in these areas?

3. Based on recent employment trends and the latest occupation projections, how do the skills acquired by students in each academic program relate to the skills required for existing and emerging occupations?

4. How do co-curricular and support programs help to engage students, make them more well-rounded, and prepare them for the future (i.e., employment or graduate school)?

5. For programs with low or no student graduation rates, is this due to lack of student interest, lack of targeted new student enrollment efforts, or lack of up-to-date curricula that engage the students and link the degrees to skills for the 21st century?

6. How many students complete gateway or prerequisite courses successfully (i.e., with the thorough understanding of course outcomes) to prepare them for advanced-level courses?

Remember that exploration of change and opportunity in the academic arena is not for the faint of heart, and communication and transparency are essential to successful planning. For those who persist, however, the long-term institutional benefits are well worth the investment of time and resources.

Strategy Identification

By Brian Ralph

The process of strategy identification and development is arguably the most pivotal component of strategic enrollment planning (SEP). This stage connects the current state to the desired state. The migration from current state to desired state requires strategic thinking and strategic behavior, both of which flow out of critical analysis of the environment to develop and implement creative, impactful strategies.

CHAPTER HIGHLIGHTS

■ **Form work groups around key areas of focus**

■ **Tap group leaders who are skilled facilitators**

■ **Develop goals after strategies are identified**

It is helpful to think of SEP as a continuum that resembles a teeter-totter, as illustrated in Figure 6-1. The early stages all sit to the left of the fulcrum. Climbing up that ramp is hard work; it requires tenacity, focus, and courage to keep asking questions and seeking data to answer those questions. However, as an institution identifies and develops strategies, actions, and tactics, the teeter-totter begins to tip to the right, moving the campus to action. Most campuses find this part of the process, tipping to the right, to be an exciting time, as all of the knowledge and research begins to bear fruit and provide direction.

Figure 6-1: Migration From Current to Desired State

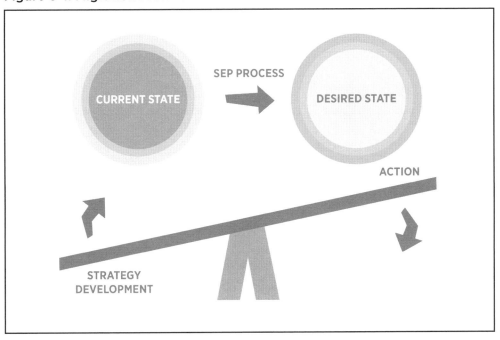

The beauty of SEP is that the desired state evolves from research and a clear (or perhaps slightly less foggy) view of the direction an institution can head, taking into account the current and anticipated future environment in which it will have to operate. As we learned in Chapter 4, the current state is most accurately understood through a thorough and robust assessment of an institution's strengths and weaknesses, as well as a close look at what is going on in the external environment. The opportunities and threats that are all around an institution must be monitored. According to Kotler and Fox (1985), "The first step in strategic planning is to analyze the environment, because changes in the environment usually call for new institutional strategies." The quality of strategy development to create a stronger future state will correlate directly with the quality of the environmental assessment and the depth of understanding of the current state.

SEP enables a campus to develop a plan that is grounded in information and research, not in anecdotes and hope. Connecting the data and information from the environmental assessment to strategy development is critical to the success of the process. Too often, planning starts with setting arbitrary and uninformed goals with little or no understanding of an institution's strengths and weaknesses, the external environment, or what steps may be needed to achieve those goals. We have all been part of (and probably contributed to) discussions in which stories of a single student from six years ago drove the development of six strategies about how to improve the ventilation on the sixth floor of the residence hall because the student called six times to complain that the air was stagnant. Of course, we learn later that there wasn't a ventilation issue, but rather the student forgot to breathe. In all seriousness, way too many strategies and goals are developed and executed based on anecdotes, legends, and opinions with no reference to research and information collected through an exhaustive environmental assessment.

We will discuss strategy development in detail throughout this chapter, with the topic of goal setting addressed more fully in Chapter 7. True goal development comes from an understanding of the likely enrollment impact of each strategy and which strategies are ultimately selected and funded in the SEP.

Using the situation analysis

As participants in the SEP process dig deeply into the results of the situational analysis, the entire group will gain clarity about the areas that need work, as well as the opportunities for success. An important component of strategy development is a clear understanding of the need for two distinct levels of strategic thought: top-level and second-level. Top-level strategies are broad statements about what we are going to do. Second-level strategies bring focus and accountability to our needed actions.

Top-level strategies are general statements relating to the categories outlined in Chapter 3 (the Six P's: Program, Place, Price, Promotion, Purpose, Process) that highlight what the institution will do to move toward its desired state. For example, a top-level strategy statement could be, "Ruffalo Noel Levitz University will provide co-curricular programs that will attract new students to the university and increase the retention of currently enrolled students." Top-level strategies are an outflow of the Six P's and are generally crafted by the leadership group of the SEP process.

Figure 6-2: Strategic Enrollment Growth Matrix

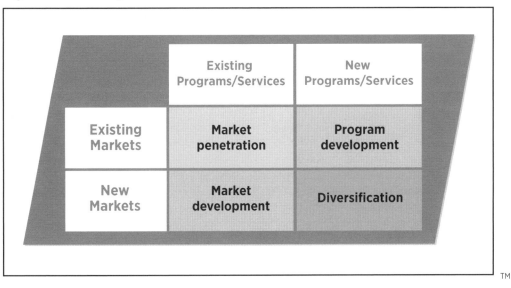

Top-level strategies may also relate to quadrants of the Strategic Enrollment Growth Matrix (Figure 6-2). This two-by-two matrix describes four ways to grow: enroll more students from existing markets in existing programs (market penetration); find new student markets to enroll in existing programs (market development); add new programs to enroll more students from existing markets (program development); or build new programs to enroll students in new markets (diversification). For example, a top-level strategy statement for market development could be, "Ruffalo Noel Levitz University will expand delivery of its existing programs in health and business into a currently underserved region of our state." Ultimately, well-balanced strategic enrollment plans will include strategies that address both the Six P's and, typically, three of the quadrants in the strategic enrollment growth matrix: market penetration, market development, and program development. (Few institutions jump directly to diversification in the first phase of SEP.)

Second-level strategies are specific actions that will enable the institution to fulfill the top-level strategies. A corresponding follow-up example would be, "Develop weekend programming and events that engage students." The quality of second-level strategies is directly related to the level of engagement by faculty and staff in the strategy development process. The strategies and commensurate action plans not only identify a specific tactic, but who is responsible, when it will be executed, how much it will cost, and a measurement tool that will make it possible to know when a plan has been successfully completed.

The best way to start developing strategies based on the situational analysis is to form working groups aligned with key areas of focus. Examples include external environment, competition, enrollment, selectivity, capacity and demand, quality of the educational experience, marketing, student engagement/satisfaction and outcomes, quality of faculty and staff, persistence and graduation, diversity, finances, and financial aid, as well as specific subgroups in areas where data indicate a large gap between institutional practice and the desired reality. Few campuses will have this many working groups, but this list should give you a flavor of the kinds of working groups to consider. The situation analysis should determine the areas of priority and the working groups needed to address them.

The working group process is extremely important to the success of SEP. For perhaps the first time, these groups will be "confronting the brutal facts" that Collins so powerfully addresses in Chapter 4 of his book *Good to Great* (2001). In particular, the working groups will "lead with questions, not answers." The answers come much later in the process.

One of the most compelling aspects of the working group process is that it often leads to strategies that diverge from an institution's current path. Strategies evolve in this manner for two reasons. First, the SEP process pulls people together who, in many cases, have not worked together before. This alone creates an exciting dynamic of new ideas and approaches to the development of strategies based on the data collected in the situational analysis phase. Secondly, the data often bring to life a completely different approach or way of thinking because it is either new data or data that contradict the current worldview held by some (or many) on campus. It is critically important that the working groups embrace the challenge of grappling with different points of view and conflicting data so that the institution will be in the most knowledgeable position possible when it considers strategic next steps. There is an opportunity here for faculty and staff to emulate the very heartbeat of an academic institution by engaging in its defining discipline—critical analysis.

Working groups diverge, converge, and act

The working groups will develop such divergent paths at times that they may, in fact, leave old thinking behind to follow a completely new path that is sprinkled with breadcrumbs from fresh data and the environmental assessment. The divergent thoughts will eventually converge through analysis of the information, and with that comes clarity and the development of potential strategies that would not have evolved without insightful critical thinking by members of diverse working groups. The journey also equips the group to be thoroughly informed and prepared to prioritize strategies at the appropriate time. Lastly, this approach enables the institution to move incrementally toward what Peters and Waterman call a "bias for action" and willingness to experiment (1982). The participants naturally challenge the status quo because they are immersed in an environment that forces them to ask deeper questions.

The working groups should thoroughly review the research and data from the institutional situational analysis and develop their own focused situation analyses, or at the very least, an executive summary of the information that pertains to their group. This step is critical, as it represents the first interaction between the data and the members of the SEP working groups. These groups are typically composed of faculty and staff from across the campus with experience and/or expertise in the themed areas. It cannot be stressed enough that the broader the representation, the more powerful the outcomes. The temptation will be to pick the usual people from a small group of departments that seem to be the "logical" participants. This attitude will short-circuit the power of the SEP process.

Getting diverse input isn't the only benefit of broad campus representation in the process. The working groups will form relationships that will be essential for establishing partnerships on strategies and initiatives that evolve through the journey. Some members of the working groups may be part of the SEP council, and many others may contribute to the SEP process exclusively through the working group structure. The role of the SEP council is to ensure the various strategies converge into a comprehensive and realistic plan.

Potential working group tasks and responsibilities

As stated above, working groups are formed around key areas of focus. Below is a sample of potential working groups and their foci. (Note: No campus should have this many working groups. The institution will determine which working groups are needed based on data review, institutional priorities, and the identification of possible strategies.) In order to remain strategic, there must be a central focus on the interconnections between the academic and co-curricular areas (i.e., programs and the educational product).

- The **external group** will evaluate data and information that is outside of the institution, such as demographics, population trends, and employment statistics. This is a very important task, as many institutions are painfully insular and unaware of the environment in which they operate. The results of this group's work will likely be highly instructional for the rest of the campus community.

- The **competition group** will evaluate the competitive landscape. It will assess the different types of competition in their market and how the institution will need to address and adapt to a changing environment. Developing the definition of competitors is always an entertaining exercise. It will be important for the group to develop agreed-upon assumptions regarding competition so that the work conducted is valuable to all. Typically, a discussion of competition focuses on topics such as cross-admits, geographic proximity, athletics, competing institutions, peer institutions, aspirant institutions, and program offerings.

- The **enrollment group** will take an intensive look at enrollment-related data and trends, addressing questions about the composition and behavior of prospective and enrolled students, including demographic trends, student engagement stream and funnel metrics, performance, and persistence.

- The **marketing group** can take on a variety of tasks depending upon the institution's level of maturity related to marketing functions. Some working groups will focus on social media, sophisticated marketing and communication messages, and strategies guiding students to specific next steps in the enrollment process.

- The **student composition group** will tackle data and issues related to admission rate, academic profile, institutional profile, cohort shaping, etc. For four-year institutions, this group may focus on selectivity, a complex issue because of the number of variables that must be taken into consideration, and one that is changing with increasing numbers of institutions moving away from standardized testing requirements. For two-year schools, this group may focus on the proportion of adult or re-entry students, or the proportion of students in non-credit, certificate, or degree programs. It is important to designate members of this group who are well-versed in the intricacies of admissions stages and processes and who understand demography and competitive market forces.

- **Capacity and demand** is a multifaceted topic that a group will address by assessing such matters as classroom space, faculty load, program demand, and curricular requirements. It will be important to have academic leadership in this group, as capacity incorporates issues such as classroom size, faculty-to-student ratios, pedagogical approaches (e.g., hybrid courses), course demand, and related areas.

- Another working group will assess the **quality of the educational experience** through the analysis of learning outcomes and quality of instruction data. Academic leadership is also critical for this group, as concepts of learning outcomes and instructional quality are highly complex, often contested, and not easily measured.

Furthermore, regional accreditation bodies have been placing more and more emphasis on these issues, with a resulting need for substantial expertise.

■ The **student engagement/satisfaction group** will focus on data related to student surveys (e.g., National Survey for Student Engagement [NSSE], Community College Survey of Student Engagement [CSSE] and Student Satisfaction Inventory™ [SSI]) along with other measurement tools utilized by the institution to identify potential ways to bring about improvement. Understanding the level of student engagement and satisfaction is important to predicting student success and building institutional awareness of issues that impact a student's journey (Kuh, Kinzie, Schuh, and Whitt, 2005).

■ The **quality of faculty and staff** has a significant impact on enrollment success. Therefore, another working group will wrestle with data ranging from customer service to adjunct faculty counts. This group may need to grapple with the definition of quality; I encourage you to explore the best ways to measure it on your campus, comparing your tools with the wide range of indicators that are utilized by other colleges and universities.

■ The **persistence and graduation group** will use data to develop strategies that address student success. Issues can range from admissions practices and course scheduling to academic support and student life. This group needs to have broad representation from numerous areas of campus because of the breadth and depth of persistence issues.

■ The **diversity group** will focus on ethnicity, religious backgrounds, age, prior educational experiences, and other characteristics of enrolled and prospective students, as well as faculty and staff diversity, and how these issues impact the institution as a whole. It will be important for this group to develop a working definition of diversity so that the analysis and strategies are aligned and the group's work will be supported. Clarity and agreement about the definition of diversity are essential to success, as each institution may define it differently.

■ The **financial group** will evaluate resource utilization and allocation and develop strategies to enhance the financial health of the institution. This group may navigate some delicate questions, as the costs of programs and services are assessed in order to help prioritize work. "The inescapable truth is that not all programs are equal," as Robert Dickeson points out (2010). Dickeson's book, *Prioritizing Academic Programs and Services*, provides methodology and considerations for campuses to rethink their academic offerings and align those offerings with enrollment-related strategies.

■ Obviously, the **financial aid group** (sometimes a part of the previously mentioned financial group) will review the research to determine appropriate strategies for policies regarding scholarships, grants, discounting, etc. As financial aid and pricing continue their ascent as key policy concerns in higher education, this group will need to understand both the internal and external issues at play.

Working group responsibilities

Once these groups have been formed and the scope of their work defined, the participants will begin to develop second-level strategies that the institution might undertake to build on its strengths, address weaknesses, take advantage of opportunities, or prepare for threats. As mentioned earlier, these groups are charged with evaluating all available data relating to their area. "Strategies need to be detailed enough to provide direction, but they do not have to describe every step in the process" (Black, 2001).

Once the working groups have developed a list of potential strategies through a brainstorming process, they must estimate the cost of execution and the potential impact of implementation for each strategy. To keep from getting bogged down at this point, the group may use general ranges of cost (high, medium, and low) and impact (high, medium, and low) to create a matrix of potential strategies. Cost and impact will be relative for each institution ($25,000 may be a lot of money on some campuses, but the equivalent of a departmental supplies budget at another). It is important to set general parameters so that everyone is operating under the same assumptions. It may be best to use dollar ranges (e.g., low cost is $0 to $2,500).

Because SEP is a fluid process, members of a group will often look around the room at the end of a brainstorming session and say, "Why in the world would we wait to execute X strategy? We can do it with existing resources, it is high impact, and we can do it now," and off that strategy goes into implementation without waiting for the creation of the SEP plan. While some might argue that the plan should be completed and approved before starting implementation, this example suggests that some action items may be so easily implemented and demonstrate such a high return on investment that waiting is a mistake. Needless to say, the credibility of the process and those involved will be substantially undermined if the vast majority of strategies and action plans require significant financial resources. Every campus should be able to identify some low- or no-cost strategy and action plan options. Failure to do so demonstrates a lack of creativity and authenticity in the assessment of the research and current practices.

Regarding the fluid nature of SEP (Figure 6-3), some planning processes have a pour-lather-rinse-repeat cycle to them, a tidy start and finish. However, this is not the case with SEP. The SEP process requires flexibility, adaptability, and willingness to try things midstream while keeping an eye on the future state, the realities of the current state, and quickly changing economic or demographic variables that may affect the long-term plan.

Figure 6-3: Fluid Nature of SEP

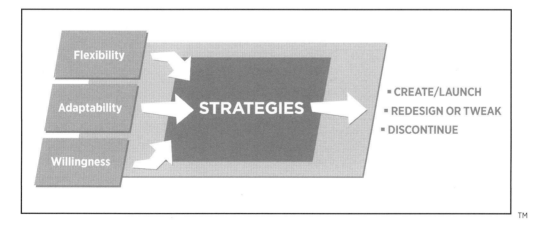

After the group has assessed costs and impact, it will identify which strategies should be at the top of the list and which ones should be at the bottom, thereby helping the council to determine priorities. There is an important point to consider here: prioritization allows the entire group to build consensus (most of the time) not only on what is important, but on which strategies will get the best results and which will require new or reallocated resources. The exercise of assembling preliminary strategies and prioritizing them allows the group to realize that not all great ideas cost a lot of money and, if they do, their priority indicates that the desired action has the potential to make a significant difference and is therefore worth the investment. Once preliminary prioritization is complete, the group should create action plans for strategies with the most promise and finally move to a more detailed analysis of cost and enrollment impact, with estimated returns on investment (ROI). When this is done well, the next level of prioritization is relatively easy because the high ROI strategies quickly move to the top of the working group's list of recommended strategies for inclusion in the larger SEP plan. (We will look more closely at ROI in Chapter 7.)

Action plans are documents that outline each step required for the execution of a second-level strategy, the timeline to complete each task, the person(s) responsible for each step, other campus areas that need to be involved and/or are affected by the plan, the budget and/or resources needed, the estimated enrollment impact, and an evaluation component that will guide the institution in determining the impact of the action plan and measuring its effectiveness. We will look at a specific example later in this chapter.

Strategies before goals

Once the group members have fleshed out the second-level strategies, they will explore setting quantifiable goals. Given the tendency to stumble around the concept of goal setting at this point, it is important to clarify what is meant by the goal-setting process. Many leaders and organizations set arbitrary quantitative goals prior to research and strategy development, an unwise practice that often misaligns an institution with the evolving environment as well as the institution's own strengths and weaknesses (Sevier, 2000).

> **Goals developed after strategies are identified will be far more accurate.**

It is critical that an institution understands its context and develops strategies in light of the environment first, and then sets quantifiable goals that are realistic and in line with the institutional vision. For example, it is not unheard of for a campus to set an arbitrary goal to increase enrollment by 15 percent over the next two years. However, what if the institution finds itself in a situation that makes this fundamentally impossible? What if the institution's core market is going to decrease by 5 percent over that same time period? What if its budget is running a deficit and perhaps carrying an unhealthy, unfunded discount rate? And how does an institution even wager a guess at a goal if it doesn't know what strategies it is able to employ, taking into account talent, resources, and the like? Furthermore, what if increasing enrollment is not the most effective way for the institution to solve the revenue problem? Quantitative goal setting is obviously very important, but it must follow a comprehensive situational analysis, strategy identification and development process, and projections about return on investment in order for the goals to be based in reality. Goals developed after strategies are identified will be far more accurate, because organizational leaders will be able to envision the execution of a specific strategy and the potential impact on the campus.

A final critical point to consider during the planning process is the need to make prioritization extend beyond potential new ideas to an honest review of current practices. As we have learned, successful implementation of the SEP process requires the prioritization of many possible new strategies in order for the institution to properly align its resources. We can agree that a day is 24 hours long, and even the most enthusiastic SEP participants will not be able to change that. Therefore, the organization must review its current practices and strategies to decide what it should continue doing and what it should stop doing, especially in light of the creation of dozens of new strategies. Many of these will be started immediately, and others will be scheduled over a two- to five-year period. During that period, it is essential that the various departments assess the effectiveness of existing strategies and eliminate ineffective practices, allowing them to deploy human and financial resources in a way that allows the institution to maximize its effectiveness. If the groups continue to do what they have already been doing by simply adding several new and vital strategies, they will fail to implement and execute any of them successfully. The campus must engage in a disciplined approach to assessing strategies with a faithfully executed stop-start-continue evaluation loop.

Working group action planning development

To understand how this process comes to life, consider the example of a working group that was focused on the topic of student engagement and satisfaction. As you would expect, the group first considered the various forms of information available from the NSSE, the SSI, and metrics collected by the office of student life listing the number of clubs and organizations, membership counts, number and types of student events, and so forth. Once the group reviewed all of the available information, they drafted a one-page executive summary of the key observations made by the group. This is an important step, because it forced the group to discuss the research in detail and agree on the most important components and issues.

After summarizing their findings, they moved to the strategy development phase in order to identify and create suggested steps to address the issues and opportunities presented by the research. They produced a list of potential strategies that addressed strengths, weaknesses, opportunities, and threats identified through the research process. At this stage of the process, it was critical that the group not be encumbered by historical or current constraints (real or perceived). In order for the group (and the institution) to move forward, it needed to think about the potential/desired state instead of being held back by current and past strategies. In other words, this stage enabled the group members to think big and creatively about how the institution could tackle the issues that had been identified.

The working group in this example developed numerous strategies, many of which, after being subjected to budget assessment and prioritization, were eliminated. Let's examine their second-level strategy to improve student engagement on weekends, as significant findings showed that students were feeling disconnected from the campus during weekends and going home.

Second-level strategy example
Develop weekend programming through the office of student life that will engage residential and commuter students.

What issue are we trying to solve?
The research shows that our students believe the quality and quantity of weekend programming is poor. Furthermore, students are not staying on campus over the weekend

and tell us they leave because "there is nothing to do." Strategies aimed toward solving this issue will impact student satisfaction and improve our first- to second-year retention rate (Key Performance Indicator number three for Ruffalo Noel Levitz University).

Tasks

- Develop a Saturday Night Program Series, providing a large-scale programming event (concert, comedian, coffee house, game show) every Saturday night for the fall and spring semesters.

- Develop a Weekend Spirit Program that links specialized giveaways or entertainment with home athletic events on Friday, Saturday, or Sunday. In the program, include special seating and T-shirts or sweatshirts for students who attend three or more athletic events each month.

- Upgrade to a more upscale Sunday brunch menu, and cook on-demand selections such as a waffle bar, omelet bar, etc.

- Require residence halls to provide one weekend activity per semester to engage residential students.

Budget

Reallocate student programming fee dollars—add $50,000 for additional programming and $2,500 for the athletic spirit program. Additional programs can be absorbed into existing budgets.

Evaluation

Satisfaction scores and participation at events will be the metrics used to gauge the success of new programs.

The above action plan is obviously rather simple and makes certain assumptions, but it serves as a good example of how the situational analysis feeds strategy development. The action plan is a direct next step to accomplish a strategy that was created to address a weakness and hopefully improve student satisfaction and, therefore, retention.

Selecting strategy priorities

Usually, individual working groups each create 15 to 25 strategies and action items that are forwarded to the larger group. No campus can implement 100-plus strategies and action items effectively. One method to bring a large group to consensus on a list of potential ideas is to rank all of the items by impact, effort, and cost. Each item is brought before the group and evaluated on each criterion, one at a time. Once each item is ranked, the entire list can be sorted with ease.

Ranking is done by assigning an A, B, or C to the three categories of impact, effort, and cost: A for the highest positive value (high impact, low effort, low cost), B for medium or moderate in each category, and C for the lowest value (low impact, high effort, high cost). For instance, moving from paper registration to online registration would be a long, complex process that would likely require expensive software. However, students would perceive this as having a high value. The ranking evaluation would look as follows:

- A-Impact
- C-Effort
- C-Cost

Therefore, online registration would be ranked an ACC.

Another idea might include re-landscaping the campus and creating a new front entrance. This might be one team member's favorite idea, but the rest of the team may feel that it would not make enough impact. The evaluation would look as follows:

- C-Impact
- C-Effort
- C-Cost

In this case, the landscaping project would be a CCC.

Once the entire list has been ranked, it is important to open the discussion to ensure that the group is confident with the rankings. Next, sort the items with all of the AAAs at the top, all of the CCCs at the bottom, and each of the combinations and permutations in between.

This exercise allows the SEP team to identify "low-hanging fruit" (i.e., AAA— high impact, easily implemented, low cost). Low-hanging fruit could be acted upon right away while the teams identify other high-impact, lower-cost ideas over the course of the planning process. In this manner, there can be some immediate "quick hits" during the actual strategic planning process.

Dialogue

We have learned that strategy development and identification involve a fluid process requiring faculty and staff to be courageous and bold in their thinking in order to bring about the best results. It starts with a high-quality environmental assessment and ends with detailed action plans. It is critical that the institution spends time developing the working groups and encouraging a climate of inquiry throughout the environmental assessment and strategy development process. A failure to be thoughtful about group composition will weaken the effectiveness of the process.

What can you do to ensure unencumbered and productive brainstorming and strategy identification on your campus?

- Take a minute to think about the organizational culture and institutional assumptions that might be keeping your campus from maximizing its potential. As I mentioned at the opening of the chapter, the quality of strategy development correlates with the quality of the situational analysis; do everything you can to make sure the analysis is thorough, honest, and as unencumbered as possible.

- Embrace the value of divergent thinking. Be sure to include faculty and staff from various parts of campus. Be intentional about including smart but independent-minded individuals who seem to elevate the level of thinking. The SEP planning process is not a time to try and convert the non-believer or less-motivated campus employee. This process should engage the most innovative, creative campus minds that, together, can create a stronger future state for the institution. Be a champion for facing the music regarding the dramatic changes occurring in higher education. The environment in which colleges and universities are operating is challenging and becoming increasingly scrutinized. Furthermore, demographic, economic, and social dynamics are changing in significant ways—ignoring those issues will place the future of the institution at risk.

Infuse the process with patience and persistence. The data analysis, creation of potential strategies, prioritization of strategies, and action plan development take time and focus. SEP can be exhilarating and exhausting. Be sure to tap working group leaders who are skilled facilitators and develop working assumptions that enable participants to be on the same page.

CHAPTER 7

Establishing Enrollment Goals and Identifying Return on Investments

By Marilyn Crone

This is where the rubber meets the road. A comprehensive situational analysis is complete, including agreement on the fundamental planning assumptions. The campus is engaged to identify, develop, and prioritize numerous long- and short-term enrollment-related strategies that support the mission, values, and overall goals of the institution. Action plans have been developed that reflect the tactical steps it will take to accomplish these strategies, delineate the order of those steps, identify the "ringleader" to complete each step, estimate how much time each will take, and document additional resources (particularly budget dollars) that will be required.

CHAPTER HIGHLIGHTS

- ■ **Enrollment goals need clearer agreement with strategic planning goals**

- ■ **Strategies lead to clear goal setting**

- ■ **Return on investment analysis is critical to plan success**

External eyes on universities

In July 2015, Moody's Investors Service revised the outlook for U.S. four-year higher education...to stable from negative, the status it had since January 2013. While an encouraging sign, the outlook needle has not moved to "positive," and suggests mixed results. Among the report findings:

- ■ "Aggregate operating revenue growth for four-year colleges and universities will stabilize at a post-recession level of just above 3 percent over the next 12 to 18 months, providing some predictability in operating budgets for the first time since fiscal year 2009," author of the report and Moody's Vice President and Senior Analyst Eva Bogaty says;

- ■ "State funding for public universities should increase above 3 percent in fiscal year 2016, and a small uptick of 1 to 2 percent in federal research funding is expected;

- ■ "Pockets of stress will persist with roughly 20 percent of public and private universities experiencing weak or declining revenue growth owing to limited pricing flexibility and fundamentally challenged student demand; and

- ■ "Stress will be highest at smaller, regional public universities with less than $500 million in revenue, and at small, private universities and colleges with less than $200 million in revenue."

While this Moody's report is reasonably current as of the publication date of this book, the outlook will remain fluid, and American colleges and universities will continue to be affected by broader financial trends within and beyond their immediate spheres. Furthermore, 20 percent of institutions is no small slice of the higher education pie. In light of the variability in financial trends, it is incumbent upon colleges and universities to diversify their program offerings and revenue streams. As Newman, Couturier, and Scurry (2004) noted over a decade ago in *The Future of Higher Education: Rhetoric, Reality, and the Risks of the Market*, "One goal...should be development of diversified funding sources as a means of creating greater stability and facilitating response to new opportunities in a time of volatility. ... It is, however, critical that the nature of any new funding stream be compatible with the institution's mission and values."

Linking enrollment goals to the institutional strategic plan

An institution's strategic enrollment planning (SEP) council is charged with discerning and establishing enrollment priorities and goals. Setting realistic, quantifiable goals is essential. Surely these must take into account campus readiness and the likelihood of attractive returns on investment (ROI). In this context, we are grateful to George T. Doran for coining the term "S.M.A.R.T. Goals." In an article written for *Management Review* in 1981, Doran explained that "S.M.A.R.T." describes goals that are specific, measurable, assignable, realistic, and time-related.

An institution that has created a long-term institutional strategic plan (ISP) with broad campus support has a clear advantage over those that have not because they have direction, intentionality, and, hopefully, even momentum. For those without an ISP in place, undertaking the creation of an SEP will serve (in part) to provide institutional direction focused on enrollment management that aligns with curricular and co-curricular programs as well as budget and fiscal planning and management. Regardless, the strategies selected must serve to accomplish the goals the institution wants to achieve. These goals must be quantified and evaluated based on a host of criteria, not the least of which is the financial implication of these choices.

Goals and associated revenues and costs must be brought together in a coherent manner that allows the chief financial officer's team to build a multiyear financial model that will clarify and direct funding for the institution's operations and aspirations. Yes, we are talking about dollars and cents in addition to headcount. Whether or not the term "enrollment management" is used, the work of recruiting and retaining students is essential to a university's success. Like it or not, it is a business function that touches every other part of the college/university. Moreover, the results are of interest to both internal stakeholders (administration, faculty, staff, and students) and external stakeholders (board members, government officials, accrediting agencies, financial institutions, rating agencies, and alumni).

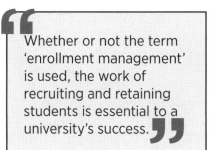

> Whether or not the term 'enrollment management' is used, the work of recruiting and retaining students is essential to a university's success.

How we implement enrollment management impacts:

- The **cost to recruit *and* retain students**, in the broadest sense, inclusive of institutional gift aid in addition to recruitment, student support, and other operational costs (not to be confused with the more narrowly focused cost to recruit).

- **Net revenue** produced by those students with diverse levels of academic ability/ preparedness who study in programs of varying:

  —Interest/demand. For example, business, engineering, and health science programs are generally easier to sell because of the clarity of career options.

  —Profitability. For example, cost of delivery (faculty, facilities, utilities, equipment, and special insurance) may be more expensive for some programs, and certain programs require lower student-to-faculty ratios. Some programs may be considered so mission-critical that an institution is willing to allow them to merely break even or, perhaps, even run at a deficit. Obviously, few institutions can afford many such financially challenging programs. As described in Chapter 2, the process of creating an SEP is as important as the plan itself because of the rich dialogue that occurs during the process that likely wouldn't occur otherwise. For colleges and universities that choose to run financially challenging programs, there is benefit in articulating such a choice and understanding the associated cost of resources to the institution.

—Requirements for flexibility, e.g., online courses, hybrid, evening and weekend offerings, multiple entry points, and services such as daycare.

—Persistence and graduation rates of different student segments, including student-athletes, transfers, or graduate students.

—Outcomes desired by students (successful transfer, job and graduate/professional school placement, average debt, and corresponding average starting salaries and lifetime earnings), which lead to future giving capacity as alumni.

- **Capacity in the system**, such as requiring the addition of new course sections, instructors, technology infrastructure and support, student life personnel, clinical placement or other internship sites, as well as classroom, office, lab, housing, and dining facilities.

- **Reputation** (rankings) of the college/university related to desired class quality (student profile) objectives, student-to-faculty ratios, and other indicators of interest, such as first-generation, race/ethnicity, gender, in-state/province, out-of-state/province, international, and enrollment at particular campuses in a system.

In their book, *Strategic Change in Colleges and Universities: Planning to Survive and Prosper* (1997), Rowley, Lujan, and Dolence provide an insightful perspective regarding the issue of quality vs. quantity in strategic enrollment planning: "Partially because many academics may resent reducing their work to numbers, and partially because of the difficulty in measuring quality issues and outcomes, it is probable that a discussion may begin about how strategic planning appears to be more interested in numbers than in quality. In the final analysis, however, it truly is quality that strategic planning is designed to achieve while it seeks to manage quantity. As external pressures on higher education continue to mount, those pressures are directed more at producing high-quality outcomes for the resources provided."

Prioritized strategies: An example

In conducting the situational analysis, an institution may have recognized that, in addition to being tuition-dependent, tuition revenues are largely generated by one or two principal populations. Let's assume undergraduate and graduate degree programs are offered by the institution, but the majority of enrollment is centered in a relatively small percentage of academic programs (some of which only operate at a break-even level because of the high cost of delivery), drawn from a narrow geographic region, and offered in a face-to-face classroom environment. The academic program analysis clarified demand trends, number of degrees granted annually, cost of delivery, and external endorsements of quality. Further, the institution has significant ISP aspirations and deferred maintenance obligations to fund; in other words, they need increased net operating revenues. This institution's strategy prioritization process bubbled up nine strategies:

1. Increase first-year enrollment in two specific business programs and hold enrollment constant in high-cost health science programs.

2. Increase enrollment in periods with high facility capacity (e.g., summer and intersession).

3. Increase enrollment of out-of-state and nonresident international students.

4. Increase enrollment in two graduate programs of distinction with interest from large regional employers.

5. Increase enrollment of transfer students with associate degrees (or equivalent hours from a four-year university).

6. Increase retention of second-to-third-year students.

7. Improve the student satisfaction and processes of the financial aid office.

8. Develop the capacity to offer some high-demand classes online.

9. Purchase and implement a constituent relationship management system for both recruitment and retention (and development) purposes.

Before setting goals

At the highest level of establishing enrollment goals, an institution must determine whether it wants to increase, maintain, or shrink enrollment. Below are a few examples for choosing a particular direction:

- **Increase** enrollment: The institution is focused on growing net tuition revenue, has capacity to grow, and has academic programs with growing demand.

- **Maintain** enrollment: The institution has little or no capacity to grow but may have other enrollment goals, such as improving academic quality, shaping the enrollment in specific academic programs, or improving the geographic and/or socioeconomic diversity of the student body.

- **Shrink** enrollment, either by design (maybe focusing on higher student academic quality and a narrowed set of academic offerings) or by necessity (e.g., catchment area is regional with declining high school graduates; there is declining employer support for students pursuing certificates or degrees; there is increasing competition from a lower-cost provider; there is declining demand for the academic programs historically offered).

An institution may offer courses at the undergraduate, master's, and doctoral levels, and make decisions about increasing, sustaining, or shrinking enrollment at each of these levels and in various colleges/schools and programs within the levels.

Let's address "capacity to grow." Like beauty, this critical determination is often in the eyes of the beholder. A dean may believe she can only grow enrollment in certain academic programs with four-year students; meanwhile, the enrollment staff sees significant demand for some of those programs, and much of it is from transfer students. The residential housing staff may believe they are operating over the preferred capacity and encourage reducing housing occupancy. When faculty offices are severely limited, faculty may uniformly express the opinion that the college/university is operating at capacity, even if enrollment demand exists and classroom and lab utilization is not optimized. There legitimately may be little or no growth opportunity for traditional, face-to-face instruction at the undergraduate level, but there may be opportunity at the master's level. There may be no opportunity for growth on the main campus, but there may be demand for academic offerings at satellite locations and/or delivery using hybrid methods.

As these examples illustrate, the issue of capacity is one that deserves a rigorous discussion and debate so that conventional assertions are not unintentionally accepted. For example, you may be at classroom capacity because (current) faculty members are unwilling to teach in the evenings or on weekends when there is student demand for a particular program. Addressing this demand may mean that such courses are taught by new faculty members.

Setting goals

Let's resume our look at the prioritized nine strategies in our example. At long last, the SEP council is given permission to establish enrollment goals for which there are capacity, campus readiness, and hopefully even a sense of energy focused on strategy development.

Figure 7-1: Strategic Enrollment Growth Matrix

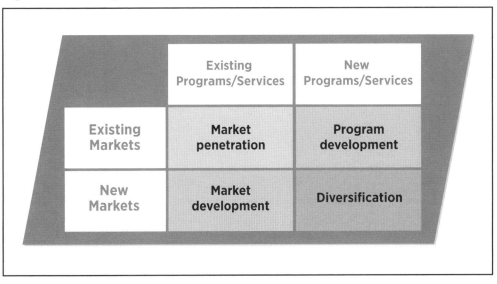

TM

Figure 7-1, which provided a helpful framework for strategy development in the previous chapter, also provides a reference for organizing goal creation. The first step is to create goals for each unique strategy. After determining which strategies will be implemented based on a data-informed situational analysis, the following goals might emerge from this process:

1. Increase enrollment of first-year students majoring in accounting and finance by 100 while holding constant the enrollment of first-year students majoring in nursing (market penetration).

2. Increase the number (from 20 to 40) and average class size (from 10 to 25) of high-demand summer and intersession undergraduate courses and offer them at competitive pricing (less than that of regular terms) to current and non-university students (market development).

3. Increase undergraduate, out-of-state enrollment from 20 to 30 percent and the international student enrollment from 3 to 10 percent over the next five years (market development).

4. Increase transfer enrollment by 125 students by actively recruiting students at community colleges and by developing partnerships with strong community college systems that recruit international students interested in transferring to a university upon completion of their associate degrees (market development).

5. Increase graduate enrollment by 45 off site by developing a business model to offer an (existing) engineering master's degree at a large employer and an (existing) education master's degree at a regional educational center (diversification).

6. Increase the second-to third-year retention rate from 85 to 90 percent over five years by:

   —Increasing the number of living-learning communities so that every first- and second-year student (including commuters) participates in a pilot program in which junior faculty members, living in two of the residence halls, each host a living-learning community; and

   —Increasing the number of professional advisors by one each of the next three years to achieve National Academic Advising Association (NACADA) student-to-advisor ratios (program development).

7. Increase the financial aid office student satisfaction ratings from 4.8 to 5.3 (per the Student Satisfaction Inventory™) by improving the self-serve information on the financial aid website, creating a more welcoming environment in the financial aid office, and implementing quality service training for all team members (program development).

8. Increase online course offerings to 15 in the next two years by recruiting a small group of faculty with interest in online course delivery to pilot courses or programs, principally at the graduate level. Begin studying possible partner organizations to assist with the design and delivery of online courses, recognizing that revenue will be shared for these courses (diversification).

9. In collaboration with the university development office, develop a request for proposal (RFP) for a constituent relationship management (CRM) system that will address the institution's recruitment and retention needs, as well as the communication/event management needs of the development office, and budget to purchase and implement the system in year two of the five-year SEP (program development and operational excellence initiative).

Quantifying the impact of goals on enrollment and revenues

In essence, overall goals for the SEP project should be based on the estimated cumulative impact of the identified strategies. Simply adding anticipated new enrollment to a particular baseline year, however, can be misleading. Projections for enrollment change based on demographic changes of primary student markets that were developed during the situation analysis should first be considered. For institutions in regions with declining markets, anticipated enrollment growth from SEP initiatives may actually result in a steady state or even a decline after demographic projections are factored into the estimates. Also be sure to phase in impact, and to use historical data to predict the cumulative impact of continuing student enrollment in subsequent years. Here, schools with bachelor's degrees have an advantage over certificate and two-year schools, because new students remain enrolled longer and will influence more out-years.

In addition to accounting for demographic projections in primary, secondary, and tertiary markets, enrollment projections and goals must also be tempered by the potential for overlapping impact among strategies. In our example above, it is entirely likely that students recruited through strategy one, targeting specific majors, may also be recruited through strategy three, out-of-state enrollment. If we simply sum the anticipated impact of these two strategies, we are likely to overestimate enrollment by a significant factor. Before enrollment impact is determined and expected expenses are totaled, the SEP council must engage in de-duplication of enrollment impact. This will lower enrollment and revenue expectations without lowering expenses, for the strategic initiatives will still require the same investments pre- and post-de-duplication.

Projection tools

It is essential for an institution to have an enrollment projection tool that allows the campus to see the impact of specific goals on headcount (and type of headcount) and net revenues. An effective tool will provide the ability to:

- Increase/decrease enrollment for targeted populations such as first-year, transfer, and graduate students;

- Increase/decrease direct cost to students, e.g., tuition, fees, room, and board;

- Increase/decrease residency by class, e.g., residency will increase as more out-of-state and international first-year students enroll;

- Increase/decrease retention by class, e.g., specific interventions for the newest cohort of first-year and transfer students have been implemented, which will likely result in improved year-to-year persistence, impacting net revenue and graduation rate;

- Annualize revenue—while the focus tends to be on the widely reported fall enrollment, institutions enroll new students each term while losing existing students to graduation and attrition. The impact of these enrollment changes is critical to a good estimate of annual revenue for budget-planning purposes;

- Identify institutional aid, discount rate, and net revenue by class and across all classes at the undergraduate level (graduate financial aid is likely much less prevalent, so estimating it is less onerous);

- Model the impact of changes in financial aid strategy across the timeline of the SEP and beyond; and

- Model the impact of demographic trends in primary, secondary, and tertiary markets.

Quantifying the cost of investments

At this point, the action plans take on particular significance. But let's be honest—the details within action plans should be considered more of a rough order of magnitude (ROM) than a return on investment (ROI). We want the plans to have the best ROM that time and expertise allow, because the timeline and costs articulated later in the action plans will allow constructing the cost-of-investment side of the ROI calculation. Institutions must strongly consider the ROI and ROM when setting final strategies and action plans to meet established goals.

For example, a direct marketing campaign working with the purchase of 100,000 high school names involves a few assumptions. An institution may decide to purchase pre-qualified NRCCUA (National Research Center for College and University Admissions) names in addition to College Board, ACT, and other name sources that are not pre-qualified.

This decision will necessitate the purchase of a predictive modeling service that may not have been included in the budget. There will be a fulfillment item of some kind as a part of the direct marketing effort. Once the proposals of direct marketing vendors have been evaluated and a selection is made, a fulfillment item that is more costly than was estimated at the level of prioritizing may be pursued. Again, numbers will firm up in the process of implementing action steps, but they should fall within a reasonable confidence interval in order to build confidence in the work underlying the SEP.

Let's look at the costs identified with the first five undergraduate enrollment-related goals noted in our example.

1. **Instructional costs** to increase the business course sections in response to the increase in first-year students will most likely begin in year two of the five-year SEP (when these students are sophomores). Realization of the incremental growth by 100 first-year students occurring over the five years of the SEP is estimated at 25 (year one), 50 (year two), 75 (year three), 100 (year four), and 100 (year five). Note that the enrollment projection tool will show an increase in first-year students in line with these estimates. With a student-to-faculty ratio of roughly 25:1, an additional faculty line can be added in years one and two for general education courses, then plan for the addition of a new faculty line in the business school in each of years three through five as the students recruited for business programs move into major courses in their junior and senior years. (Each institution may use larger or smaller student-to-faculty ratios for courses in the different class levels and for different academic programs, and may make greater or lesser use of part-time and adjunct faculty.) Be sure to add the fringe benefit amount to instructional costs.

2. To calculate **staff costs** to support the increase in undergraduate enrollment, a student-to-staff ratio, such as 50:1, can be used to account for the various support staff needs across the institution as enrollment grows.

3. In order to increase summer and intersession enrollments, consider hiring an existing faculty member known for creativity and active participation in achieving his/her department's enrollment goals. Costs are estimated to include an **administrative stipend, course replacement expenses, and marketing expenses** to promote these programs internally and externally.

4. To pursue out-of-state enrollment growth, estimate the cost of:

   —**Name purchases** from multiple sources;

   —**Predictive modeling services** to assist in rationalizing institutional resources appropriately, depending on the likelihood of a student enrolling based on certain characteristics, such as distance from campus, high school, and academic interest;

   —The selected **direct marketing vendor**, inclusive of printing and postage expenses; and

   —**On- and off-campus events** designed specifically for the target market, inclusive of promotion, travel, space rental, technology, and food expenses.

5. The increase in transfer students may not necessitate a new staff member in the enrollment division, but it may in student support services or transcript evaluators. This would likely include staff costs and expenses.

As the cost of investment in each of these areas is determined, note if the cost is:

- A base budget item, such as salary and fringe benefit costs;
- A one-time expense, such as market research and pricing research; or
- A capital expense, such as laptops, telecounseling equipment, and office furniture.

Account for costs in a manner consistent with the requirements of the institutional budgeting process.

Example of accounting for cost of investments for one year

To increase the market share of new students, the following costs may be incurred:

Table 7-1: Market Share Investment Example

Market share investments	Recurring	One-time
Enhanced telecounseling	$10,000	$10,000 (Capital)
Market research		$40,000
New faculty lines, including fringe benefits	$200,000	
New staff lines, including fringe benefits	$100,000	
Formalized predictive modeling	$25,000	
Constituent relationship module	$30,000	$150,000
Additional events and travel	$20,000	
Market share total	**$385,000**	**$200,000**

TM

To increase the retention of first-year students to the second year and beyond, the following investments are indicated by the SEP:

Table 7-2: Retention Investment Example

Retention investments	Recurring	One-time
Academic advisor, including fringe benefits	$48,000	
Predictive attrition modeling, early alert, and supplemental support program	$10,000	$30,000
Quality enhancement training	$5,000	$22,000
Other staffing, including fringe benefits ($50,000)*		
Other operating costs	$10,000	
Retention investment total	**$73,000**	**$52,000**

TM

* Funded by reallocation of existing position—not included in total

Quantifying revenue estimates

Estimated revenue for each potential strategy is the product of the annualized average net revenue per student times the number of new students anticipated to enroll, or continuing students anticipated to be retained above the historical average, less any factor for enrollment de-duplication. Determining average annual net revenue will be different based on both student and institutional types. Residential students will bring more revenue than commuters. Private institutions are more likely to have unfunded tuition discounts that must be factored into the estimates. Public institutions may have state appropriations based on enrollment. Graduate and undergraduate students may have differential tuition rates, and increasingly, higher-cost programs may have higher tuition rates.

One must also estimate the multiyear impact of strategies, so that enrollment increases in year one are carried into subsequent years depending on expected retention rates, the length of the program, and whether the program will attract first-time, transfer, adult degree completion, and/or graduate students.

Calculating the return on investment

We are principally using the concept of return on investment in the context of a financial investment. The calculation is relatively straightforward:

Expected Gain on Investment minus Expected Cost of Investment

---

Expected Cost of Investment

TM

However, the details of the calculations are important. While one does not need a finance background to calculate the ROI, it is essential to bring finance colleagues into this process to ensure everyone is on the same page. Below are a few comments that might prove valuable in this effort to determine the return on different investments.

1. SEP goals might prioritize a few investments that are discrete and best kept separate for calculating the ROI (for example, the ROI of different business lines, such as adult learners pursuing degree completion vs. adding new graduate programs).

2. SEP goals might lead to a couple of growth scenarios. Examples might include: a growth scenario that is pursued only through improved retention (at capacity for housing, classrooms, labs, and offices) and one that includes both growth in new students and improved retention. Investments for these two growth scenarios are likely quite different.

3. In considering growth scenarios, evaluate whether or not such growth will come at a greatly increased discount rate and require significant additions to fixed costs.

4. ROI should be calculated on the different scenarios or investments for each fiscal year and over the five-year horizon of the plan.

5. As important as it is to compare the ROI calculations, there are often valid reasons to prioritize investments with less glowing return rates. For example, when developing a new business line, the ROI in the first few years may be negative, but

this may be pursued with "eyes wide open" and with the expectation that it will not break even before year five but generate increasingly significant net revenue and net operating revenue streams after that. Further, *not* diversifying business lines may be considered a higher risk than continuing business as usual. Such decisions will be considered by the SEP council but, at the end of the day, fall under the purview of the senior administration and governing board of the institution.

6. The scenario of growth through improved retention may very well produce a much higher ROI rate than the scenario of growth in new students and improved retention. However, depending on the university's aspirations, need for greater net revenue, and apparent student demand, an institution may choose the scenario with the smaller ROI rate (maybe 5X as opposed to 15X) because it generates significantly greater net operating revenue. However, public institutions may bring different priorities to the planning exercise of comparing relative returns on investment, as their stakeholders may have different priorities, and mission imperatives to serve communities and regions may take precedence over revenue.

7. Often a campus will divide the net investment return by the number of full-time equivalent students gained from each initiative. This approach provides another filter through which to consider the net financial benefits from any given strategy within the context of like per-student revenues for competing initiatives.

8. Consider the difference in ROI between "do something" and "do nothing" scenarios. Since status quo is difficult to maintain, declining enrollment is most likely the result of a "do nothing" option, since competitors are not standing still. At best, this might mean maintaining the average enrollment picture from the past three to five years. Relatively few institutions have a brand or image effective enough to maintain strong enrollment demand regardless of changing economic times. The enduring excellence of these few institutions during a volatile economic era leads one to suspect that they have such a healthy brand because they regularly act to strengthen their offerings.

Concern about return on investment is not just the domain of the college/university chief financial officer. Increasingly, this underlying concept is at the heart of the college decision process for many families. In her article, "When the Price Is Right," in *NACUBO Business Officer Magazine* (2010), Margo Vanover Porter quotes Martin Van Der Werf, former director of Chronicle Research Services in Washington, D.C.: "Higher education needs to realize that people are beginning to see higher education as a consumer transaction," he explains. "The days when families were willing to pay whatever without any assurance of what they were getting are coming to an end. More than ever before, people are really looking for a return on investment." This is also true with the SEP process. Resources are limited. The SEP must articulate clear goals achieved through specific strategies, leading to projected returns on investment, in order to appropriately influence key stakeholders to fund these strategies.

Dialogue

It is hard to overemphasize the value of waiting to set enrollment-related goals until the situational analysis is concluded; the demand and economics of academic and co-curricular (and even extracurricular) programs, in light of institutional aspirations and mission, are analyzed; planning assumptions are agreed upon; the otherwise unwieldy list of short- and long-term strategies is prioritized; and campus readiness to implement final strategies is achieved. Setting goals earlier would undermine the effectiveness of the SEP process.

Which goals are most worthy of pursuit over the next five years?

- Those that assist an institution in moving toward its preferred future, as opposed to the future that "just happens";

- Those that represent the "sweet spot" among what is offered (or can be offered) in terms of a unique mix of academic and co-curricular programs, what is economically viable, and areas of strong student demand—all resulting in enrollment and related revenues that provide diversified revenue streams supporting institutional operations and aspirations;

- Those that have concern for the success of students at their very core;

- Those that provide adequate returns on investment, even if goals with higher expected ROI are dismissed because the net revenues are deemed inadequate;

- Those associated with clear key performance indicators, drawn from the enrollment projection process, that will serve as indicators that an institution is on course or needs to adjust the course toward goal achievement; and

- Those that can realistically be accomplished during the planning horizon of the SEP.

CHAPTER 8

Dashboards, Plan Evaluation, Modification, and Continuation

By Jim Hundrieser and Joyce Kinkead

For enrollment managers, setting a pathway for an institution's future and putting the wheels in motion to achieve this future state can be an immensely rewarding experience. A strategic enrollment plan (SEP) supports the future state of the institution using data and the campus strategic plan to establish a vision for the future. The SEP is a key element to drive the campus toward its goal.

CHAPTER HIGHLIGHTS

- **Dashboards help institutions measure performance and track progress**

- **Diverse campus community involvement ensures success**

- **SEM council manages next steps**

Reaching that overall objective requires achieving numerous goals along the way. However, the SEP process does not put goal setting first. Instead, as previous chapters have explained, SEP relies on a data-informed process that requires consistently analyzing important data points, using those points to guide planning, setting goals, measuring progress, and modifying behaviors and programs based on information gained through this feedback loop. After the plan is completed, an institution must establish a strategic enrollment management (SEM) council that shifts the institution from a planning mode to a management and action-oriented mode. The management council must continue to track and monitor the plan, monitor dashboards, and update the plan where needed, based on current market trends or other changes.

Dashboards

Campus dashboards bring multiple data points together in quick and easy visuals that provide all constituencies with a means to check the progress of campus efforts. Dashboards help an organization understand and make productive use of the data. They should drive prioritization and help identify areas of focus where actions are not making the projected impact.

In their simplest forms, dashboards document key performance indicators (KPIs) and performance indicators (PIs), discussed in Chapter 4, provide the means to set benchmarks, track progress, and fulfill demands for accountability and transparency.

Figure 8-1: Dashboard Example

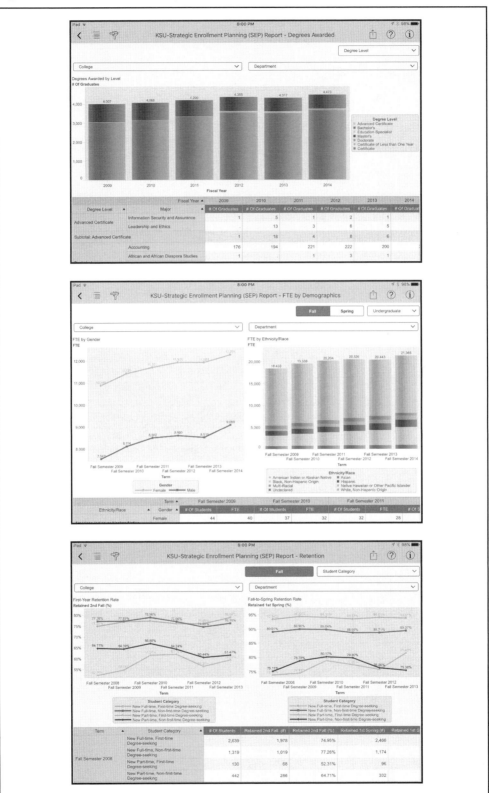

Source: Kennesaw State University, Enterprise Information Management and Institutional Research, used with permission.

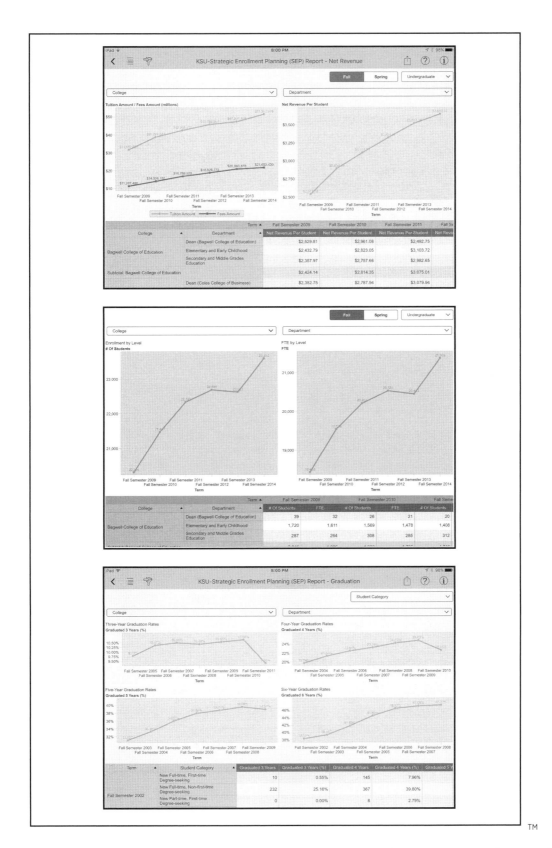

The dashboard examples in Figure 8-1 provide powerful views of organizational expectations and realities. What benefits do dashboards provide?

1. **Dashboards provide consistent data measurements and comparisons.** Each dashboard provides a quick and easy way to know what the institution has determined is a priority (enrollment, revenue, operating margin goals, academic program enrollment, persistence, and completion, for example). The dashboard supports campus conversations about what is important.

2. **Dashboards get everyone on the same page**—literally. When everyone is looking at the same set of numbers and the same key metrics, the organization can work together on a set of common goals, rather than being led in different directions by different sets of numbers (Tingley Advantage, 2014).

> " When everyone is looking at the same set of numbers and the same key metrics, the organization can work together on a set of common goals... "

3. **Dashboards track progress or areas for future focus.** A dashboard should be a tool that immediately points out to the entire campus community places where progress has been made, as well as places where no progress or, worse, decreased performance occurs.

Creating a dashboard

"Measure what you value, and value what you measure."

This universally stated motto across multiple topics also fits an essential part of the SEP process: creating a dashboard or scorecard that can track KPIs and PIs. This dashboard must be accessible, easy to read, and understandable so it can be used and discussed easily in important meetings by the SEM council and other stakeholders. Several authors have suggested approaches for constructing such a tracking system (Doerfel and Ruben, 2002; Stewart and Carpenter-Hubin, 2000).

The dashboard is a living document; some items may remain on it forever, while others may be deemed non-essential and dropped after a period of time. An institutional dashboard might resemble the example shown in Figure 8-1.

A data dashboard is an annual (or semesterly, or quarterly) snapshot; much of the information may be taken from the census data provided to the Integrated Postsecondary Education Data System (IPEDS). The institution decides which items are important to its success and gathers information on them. It is also important to monitor trends, comparing data for a minimum of three years (preferably five).

Notice how the dashboards in Figure 8-1 record metrics and also reveal trends to show whether the direction is positive, negative, or holding in the same pattern. This type of tracking allows the SEM council and institutional leadership to monitor these KPIs to ensure that changes are moving in the right direction. This is a data-*informed* gathering and review process.

When reviewing the data, the council should consider any extraordinary occurrences (e.g., economic situation, new state laws, significant state funding for financial aid, state appropriations, and changes in policy) that might affect the metrics.

Institutions just beginning the data collection process need to start somewhere. If the institution does not have three years worth of data, but the planning process revealed that certain data points are needed, the institution must start collecting and establishing the systems to collect those data to build a more robust dashboard over time. For some institutions, establishing a reliable and trusted dashboard may be a strategy or tactic identified as a part of the SEP process.

Another important aspect of a dashboard is comparing the institution to its peers, competitors, and aspirants. Dashboards take KPIs, such as retention and graduation rate, and quantifies them for comparison against an institution's peer group, as well as for its main competitors. Dashboards might also include comparisons to state data or regional data rather than national data. Specifically, SEM councils should look at employment trends, enrollment patterns, and demographic shifts (e.g., Western Interstate Commission for Higher Education [WICHE] data), price sensitivity, and federal and state funding formulas. These factors can have a tremendous impact on an institution and influence strategy development for achieving goals.

> **"Dashboards must include the most essential metrics needed by the institutional leadership and SEM council to measure institutional progress toward achieving enrollment and other strategic goals."**

While institutional dashboards provide an overarching view, they can be fed by unit- or program-specific dashboards. It is not uncommon for each institutional department or unit to establish a dashboard in order to measure its own valued metrics and evaluate its progress. This is a recommended outcome of the SEP process. An example might be showing how a first-year experience and student success office might measure valuable outcomes: retention of students who participate in a pre-semester orientation program, parental involvement, and success of students re-admitted to the institution.

Figure 8-2: Dashboard Example of First-Year Experience Program

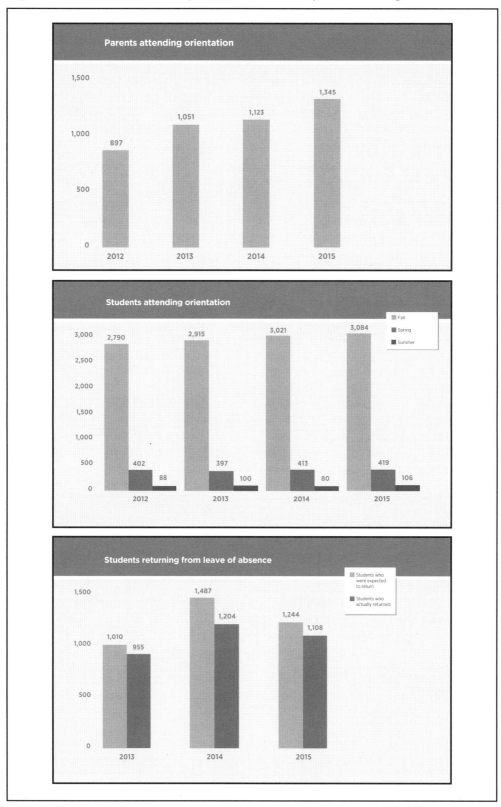

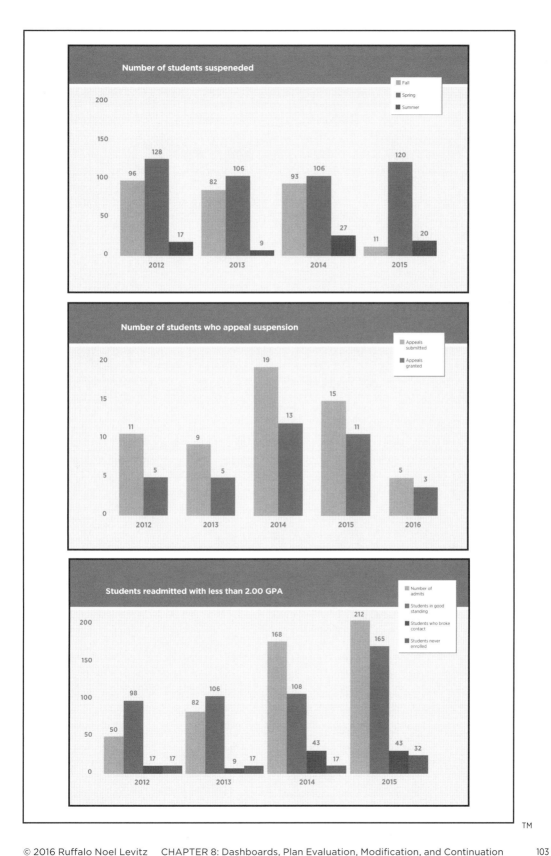

Dashboards must include the most essential metrics needed by the institutional leadership and SEM council to measure institutional progress toward achieving enrollment and other strategic goals. While all units within the institution play a role in achieving major institutional goals, some areas are particularly important to the overall effort. Recruitment, financial aid, and tuition pricing are key to both short- and long-term enrollment projections. These data should have primacy in the overall data dashboard.

Plan evaluation

Evaluation is often discussed in higher education, but rarely affects change when data is not integrated (and believed) by an institution. For some reason, higher education leaders dispute data more than they believe it, which can lead to misaligned decisions. Plan evaluation is an important exercise that requires discipline and a continued look at the realities of the organization's current state. Some of the most common misperceptions about evaluation include:

— The evaluation process will take too much time and effort;

— No change will come from evaluation; and

— Planning is important to the campus culture, but we can't measure what we do— we work with people.

Evaluation brings clarity to what has and has not been accomplished. It pushes the SEM council to ask tough questions and better understand current challenges and why action items are not accomplished. It also allows for the acknowledgement of accomplishment. If the plan was implemented successfully, evaluation should lead to celebrations and reinforce for the campus that planning is important and produces results that will be recognized.

Evaluation completes the planning loop

The strategic enrollment plan should establish how and when evaluation of the plan will be integrated into the institution's planning calendar. Evaluation is a key element of planning, as it completes the planning loop and identifies new priorities for action. As identified in Chapter 4, the KPIs and PIs should serve as guiding data points to lead the evaluation discussion and assess the institution's progress.

> Once a strategic enrollment plan has been created, attention will shift from planning to management.

While responsibility for overall plan evaluation rests with the SEM council, it does not have to build the evaluation plan from scratch. Well-written action plans (see Chapter 6) include evaluation plans. Action plan narratives should explicitly link particular tactics to relevant performance indicators. In some cases, evaluation of the strategic enrollment plan begins with a compiled evaluation checklist from the whole of the implemented action plans. In addition, an evaluation plan helps refine data collection and assessment practices so that the information is most useful for advancing the organization's mission and the objectives of the program under evaluation.

Evaluation is a key component of being a learning organization. Establishing a culture of evaluation within the organization is vital, so that people naturally take on the role of gathering the necessary information to improve programs (Tunis and Harrington, 2013). Evaluation results can also be extremely useful in marketing the institution's accomplishments to boards and donors, and establish credibility for future financial support as well as future planning efforts.

It is important to note that the entire institutional experience, from marketing and engagement to alumni relationships, impacts new student enrollment and, more importantly, student persistence, progression, completion, and learning outcomes. (For academic officers, Baer and Stace [1997] offer a good primer on enrollment, as does Barr [2002] on financial management. Kinkead [2011] provides information on marketing undergraduate research opportunities.) These factors make an institution a distinctive place of learning. While the SEM council cannot measure every factor, the SEP focuses the enrollment efforts and evaluation ensures that goals are obtained.

Shifting to strategic enrollment management (SEM)

Once a strategic enrollment plan has been created, attention will shift from planning to management. The institution must ensure that the plan is monitored, evaluated, and revised as needed. For this, either the planning council or a new team needs to be formed, potentially comprised of a mix of high-level administrators and director-level staff who can ensure the work is being accomplished. This SEM council may have a similar makeup to the SEP council described in Chapter 3. This team needs to continuously scan the environment and SEP datasets for emerging opportunities that can be added to the plan in future years. Ideally, the SEM council will exhibit exemplary collaboration with highly participatory decision making, engaged members, and representatives from across the campus. The SEM council also serves to educate the campus about the importance of the enrollment landscape, as well as how institutional and national trends and data affect enrollment. Additionally, the council looks at big-picture issues, KPIs, and enrollment strategy recommendations for the institution.

Offices that focus on gathering, collecting, and analyzing data are critical to ensuring the institution is meeting its plan objectives. Someone on the council needs to be charged with collecting and updating KPI and PI reports for the council's review.

The SEM council or ongoing planning committee needs to accomplish the following:

- Meet regularly (at least quarterly, but more commonly bimonthly) to evaluate the progress of the plan and identify actions that must take place during the next two months;
- Track KPIs identified in the plan;
- Track the effectiveness of each strategy and action plan identified in the plan;
- Track updated information related to new internal and external environmental assessments and projections;
- Propose changes or adjustments regarding implementation of the plan; and
- Identify new strategies to respond to the changing environmental and institutional contexts.

Depending on institution size, an additional subcommittee may be needed to review financials, review relevant fall and spring census data, and calculate actual return on investments from planned initiatives compared to planned budget estimates. This information helps the SEM council understand implications of enrollment figures and, in turn, allows them to determine any necessary changes in direction while providing updated enrollment projection and financial reports.

Modification

Organizations that are most effective at implementation continually revisit their strategic enrollment plans, viewing their strategies as anchors, not constraints, to what they can achieve (Hadley, Lanzerotti, Nathan, 2014). Planning, when done correctly, can be a meaningful and helpful process that garners campus buy-in and sets direction. During planning, sometimes great and bold initiatives are declared. Reality is what is lived on a campus daily. The reality is that models of shared governance, budget reprioritization, unexpected market changes, or other disruptors will occur that shift people, resources, or the organization's focus from "the plan" to "the reality of the current situation."

A living plan needs to be modified annually or biannually to ensure the SEP aligns with the desired future state of the institution, as well as the realities of the current state. An annual planning cycle that is led by the SEM council aligns the organization with core priorities.

As the SEM council reviews the plan's progress, timelines may not be met. Council members should ask themselves and those assigned responsibility for unmet action items the following:

1. Why wasn't the identified goal or action item achieved?
2. Does the goal remain a priority?
3. What data, if any, was inaccurate and precluded the action team from accomplishing the goal?
4. What infrastructure changes are needed, if any, to accomplish the goal?
5. If it remains a priority, what needs to be done to get the action team (or institution) back on track to accomplish the goal? Who will shepherd action items identified? How will the SEM council more closely monitor these activities to ensure the institution remains focused on accomplishing the goal?

As the plan is modified and updated, the action team focus needs to remain targeted at specific goals, yet sometimes new strategies are necessary. (Chapter 6 provides an outline for strategy identification and development.) The council will provide clear support for and definition of what needs to be accomplished. Additionally, the council identifies or updates tasks and determines people to accomplish these tasks. Budgets also need to be provided as well as dates and timelines for a clear path toward goal accomplishment.

It is essential that campus leaders not dismiss the entire plan because a key goal was not accomplished. Delays happen, and revisions to plans will reinforce to the campus community that planning is important and that plans are living documents to be modified and enhanced annually.

Continuation

By the time a strategic enrollment plan is completed, it can be easy to set it on the proverbial shelf. Taskforce members and working groups are tired from the intensity of the process and ready to go back to their seemingly simpler and well-defined roles. A good plan, however, will have identified leaders for every initiative and for the transition from SEP to SEM. For continuation, leadership matters.

As identified in Chapter 3, the fourth phase of the process is implementation. Implementation requires leaders to hold action teams accountable for deadlines. The SEM council needs to have the support of the institutional leadership team to push toward goal achievement. The campus community will be hungry for ongoing communication to better understand why priorities identified in the plan were and continue to be important. In addition, the campus needs regular updates about the progress of the plan to cultivate additional buy-in and remain focused on planned activities.

The continuation of the plan is first the responsibility of the strategic enrollment council. The council needs to motivate and inspire. They need to provide energy and ensure focus. As goals are accomplished, they should be publicly celebrated, and new goals should be identified based on data.

Figure 8-3: Strategic Enrollment Planning Phases

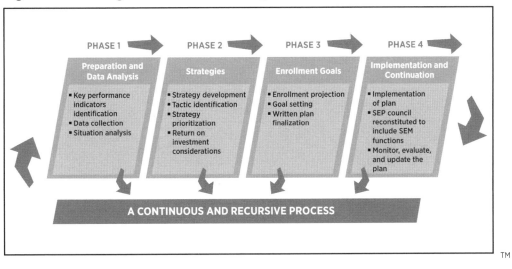

Chapter 3 described four key phases of the SEP process. As the plan continues, the phases of the planning process are repeated. Data is collected. Key performance indicators are reviewed and, perhaps, revised. New performance indicators are added as the environmental scan identifies new challenges/opportunities. Strategies are developed based on the data. The cycle, while continuous, remains data-informed.

Process leaders and the planning participants are critical to the ultimate success of the planning process, implementation, and maintaining momentum. As previously noted: leadership matters.

Dialogue

Although there are many issues for campus leaders to consider in ensuring SEP success, below are some key questions to ask:

- What are the institution's key data metrics?
  - How can you roll those metrics into a user friendly and purposeful dashboard?
  - What will the institution's dashboard look like? Will all units sign on to create their own dashboards that feed into the larger institutional dashboard?
  - How is the institution's dashboard accessible to key stakeholders?
- What are the benchmark goals that the institution wishes to attain?
- How will academic, marketing, recruitment, curricular, co-curricular, and student success programs come together to inform a data-infused strategic enrollment plan?
- How will goal attainment (or goal non-attainment) require a change in assumptions about ongoing enrollment projections in light of changing demographics and other external trends?
- Who will be responsible for keeping tabs on important trends and updating the enrollment projection model every 12 months to ensure informed decision making?
- How will the campus maintain momentum, retain key players in the planning process, and recruit new participants in order to monitor and implement the plan?
- How will the plan's actions and results be communicated to campus constituents, external stakeholders, and governing boards to ensure a sense that the entire campus community is in this together?

CHAPTER 9

Market Positioning

By Ruth Sims

Where are you heading?

As college and university leaders and marketers, we contend with an environment that is out of control. It is, at least, out of *our* control. Economic trends, social changes, rapidly evolving technology, and the prevailing political climate are powerful factors affecting our ability to recruit and retain students, yet we have little or no influence over them.

CHAPTER HIGHLIGHTS

- **Planning identifies gaps between reality and expectations**

- **Effective positioning employs a wide range of electronic and non-electronic venues**

- **Market research clarifies market changes**

This fundamental truth underscores the need for educational institutions to be flexible, nimble, and attentive to the winds of change.

Institutions that turn a blind eye to the environment and meander blithely wherever the road leads are likely to encounter unpleasant surprises. We navigate in an environment where maps are dynamic, and reliable institutional "global positioning systems" are simply unavailable. Chinese philosopher Lao Tzu offered this warning more than 2,000 years ago: "If you do not change direction, you may end up where you are headed."

How does an institution establish its identity in a changing environment? Fortunately, there are core marketing principles to help shape any strategic enrollment plan that remain unchanged from year to year, decade to decade. One example is integrated marketing, which is the unified and synergistic implementation of institutional messages and media—in sharp contrast to sporadic, ad hoc marketing efforts. In addition, central for those involved in an institution's strategic enrollment planning (SEP) initiative is the concept of market positioning: the intentional selection of key features and benefits that define the institution's brand in a competitive context.

Positioning involves determining three things:

1. **Key strengths:** The institution's distinct assets and capabilities in its delivery of the educational experience. These strengths must be documented through qualitative and quantitative research, not based simply on institutional mythology or unsupported aspirations.

2. **Market demand:** An understanding of which institutional strengths are most relevant to and desired by the marketplace, including unique segments within the market, such as traditional students, nontraditional students, and continuing education students. Some of an institution's salient strengths may be different from the factors that internal audiences value. For example, institutional history, longevity, and traditions are rarely of primary interest to prospective students, unless students have had some long-term attachment to the institution, such as following the success of an athletic team. (Note: Few institutions are exceptions. Perhaps only 100 of the 4,500 American degree-granting institutions of higher learning can claim this kind of preferred status.)

3. **Competition:** Examination of competitors' strengths and weaknesses as perceived by the marketplace. Again, these must be documented through quantitative market research. Perceptions of competitors are not a substitute for primary research with target markets.

Figure 9-1 illustrates the process for determining which messages should drive an institution's marketing strategy.

Figure 9-1: Market Positioning in a Competitive Environment

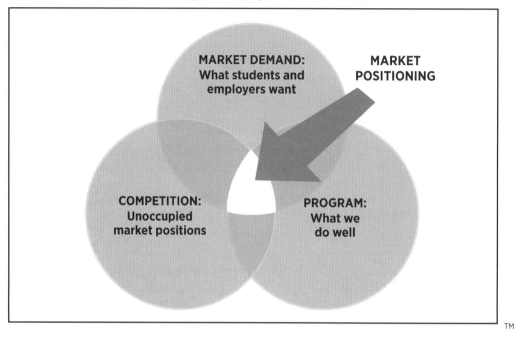

Note that the institution is seeking to differentiate itself *within its primary competitive set*, not among all colleges and universities nationally. There are likely fewer than 50 institutions that have a true national reputation (and another 250 that believe they have a national reputation). It is virtually impossible to find a niche that is unique, given the many similarities that exist among institutions' missions, programs, and target audiences. For that reason, it is far more important for marketing messages to be relevant and true than to be exclusive.

In his book *Selling Higher Education* (2008), Eric Anctil points out that perceptions often drive differentiation more than reality: "Most people do not have the kind of access to colleges and universities that would allow them to make direct comparisons of the numerous characteristics that truly make institutions different from one another." This distinction is difficult for some to accept, but critical to understand as institutions consider their market position and future predicted market share aligned with market demands. Creating a nationally recognized program is difficult and costly. As institutions create strategic enrollment plans, they must carefully consider return on investment for specific goals in order to evaluate where they can realistically fit in the marketplace.

The role of strategic planning in market positioning

Whether or not to attempt to alter an institution's market position is a strategic decision that can be recommended as a strategy or tactic within a strategic enrollment plan.

Ultimately, it is a choice that takes into account the institutional mission, market realities, and the potential return on investment for dollars allocated to shift market position, while keeping in mind the multiple priorities set by the planning subcommittees.

How can an institution change its market position? Strategic planners evaluate and take action when gaps are found between what an institution offers and what the marketplace desires and expects. These actions may be relatively obvious, gap-closing strategies, such as adding new academic programs, or more comprehensive changes, such as improving the quality of classroom teaching institutionwide. Ignoring the gaps is not a viable option; if the key marketing messages that emerge from this process are not sufficiently relevant and substantial, they will not support effective market positioning. In many cases, if not most, closing these gaps and shifting perceptions will be a multiyear process that must be outlined in the strategic plan.

Human communication theory suggests that an individual's identity can be frozen through labeling or stereotyping in the absence of meaningful dialogue: "He is apathetic;" "She isn't good with numbers." The same is true of an institution. It is not uncommon for an outside consultant to hear comments such as, "Twenty years ago, we were a women's college, and we're still remembered that way," or "People think we're basically open admission, but that's no longer true."

For institutions, these frozen images are difficult to alter and can only be shifted through intentional branding strategies that facilitate an ongoing conversation with the marketplace—a conversation that best occurs through market research and interaction, not simply one-way marketing messages. Public relations efforts such as media interviews, story placements, social media initiatives, and strategically planned events can support the thawing of these frozen images, but it will take time to make a noticeable impact on market perceptions of the institution.

Market position strategies and data

As institutions engage in strategic enrollment planning, there are numerous strategies that interconnect with marketing and recruitment efforts. Ultimately, marketing messages and positioning must be intricately linked to how resources at the institution are allocated.

It's an E-world, after all

Today's parents are sprinting to keep up with their children as the creative use of technology is adopted by younger generations. In the same way, educational institutions must have their eyes and ears trained on the new technologies to assess the next hot trend before the current trend fades.

How has this "e-era" changed college marketing? The upward trend of admissions applications as the first point of contact shows that power has shifted from colleges and universities to their prospective students and those who influence them. Students now can learn almost everything they want to know about an institution and make an enrollment decision without any human contact.

Most campuses have begun their foray into the world of e-marketing, some tentatively and some with great enthusiasm. It has not taken higher education long to realize that e-marketing is not free. For most institutions to keep pace, eliminating some print materials or travel recruitment activities will not be enough to fund online marketing. Institutions will need to find new dollars to support competitive e-marketing efforts.

The essential e-marketing tools checklist every campus should employ today includes:

- A formal website governance system that has defined roles and rules for managing the institution's site
- A student-centered website for recruitment that has integrated:
  - A content management system (CMS)
  - User-tested navigation and content
  - A regularly updated search engine optimization (SEO) strategy for key pages
  - Site analytics that are used for ongoing site enhancement
  - A highly visible online inquiry form, campus visit form, and admissions application
  - An online net price calculator
- A website that adapts to each user's device, whether tablet, mobile phone, or desktop
- An e-communications strategy for recruitment
- A goal-oriented social media strategy
- An admitted student website to support yield strategies
- Highly targeted search engine marketing campaigns to generate inquiries for appropriate programs

Effective positioning demands that institutional marketing messages be intentionally and consistently woven through all of these electronic venues.

Build a website driven by student interests

A website is not a mirror into which, Narcissus-like, an institution can gaze lovingly upon its own reflection. Instead, it must be a living résumé submitted to the marketplace in hopes that the institution will be viewed as worthy of engagement.

The central concept of democracy, that all people (and departments) have an equal say, does not work well for college and university websites. An institution yielding to this admittedly powerful cultural bias will find itself with a site that is a patchwork quilt of competing messages. A website must first serve the audiences that are most critical to the institution's future health and vitality. For the vast majority of tuition-dependent institutions, this will be prospective students.

Websites can also serve current students, faculty, staff, and the local community, but the main driver for web resources and functionality needs to focus on the way this tool recruits and engages students who are interested in enrolling at the institution.

The 2015 E-Expectations Report (a joint research effort of Ruffalo Noel Levitz, NRCCUA [the National Research Center for College & University Admissions], OmniUpdate, and CollegeWeekLive) found that the most-valued pages related to academic programs, followed by cost. Colleges and universities must understand that those pages are recruitment pages, not pages designed to serve their currently enrolled (or employed) students/staff.

Research is quite clear on what prospective students want. Despite marketers being enamored with graphic design, researchers Poock and LeFond (2001) reported the following ranking of college website characteristics indicating that website content is indeed king, closely followed by ease and intuitiveness of site navigation, as shown in Table 9-1. These findings have also been verified by more recent studies.

Table 9-1: College-bound Prospects Preferences for College/University Websites

Important/Very Important	Percent	Rank
Content	97%	1
Organization/Architecture	95%	2
Download speed	88%	3
Organization by functional topic (admissions, athletics, etc.)	84%	4
Organization by target audience (applicants, alumni, etc.)	78%	5
Friendliness	73%	6
Distinctiveness	49%	7
Graphics (major emphasis)	49%	7
Graphics (minor emphasis)	40%	8

TM

Source: Poock and LeFond, 2001

The E-expectations research series has tracked students' electronic college search habits since 2005. In terms of content, these studies have shown that traditional students pursue the topics outlined in Table 9-2 first when browsing an institution's website.

Table 9-2: Web Content Priorities for Prospective Students

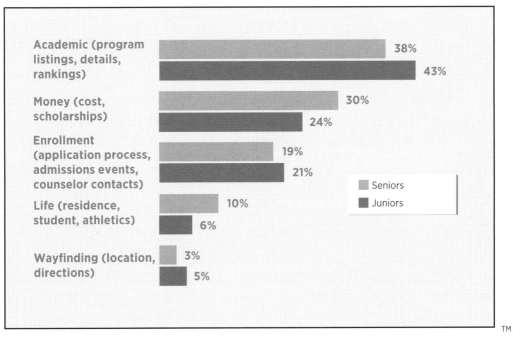

TM

Source: Ruffalo Noel Levitz, 2015 E-Expectations Report

Robust academic program descriptions, complete with faculty profiles, student quotations, and alumni success stories will be significantly more effective than academic catalog-style copy that drones on about the "educational objectives of the business major." Each program description should be written to support the institution's central positioning messages, whether the primary focus is on faculty, practical experience, educational outcomes, or multiple themes.

To mitigate the political forces that often drive website content and design, smart campus managers leverage data from sources such as user-testing (feedback from actual prospective students) and Google Analytics to determine what's working and what's not.

As noted by Durkin (2010), "The ability of individuals to access information in *situ*—i.e., at the time, place, and in the context that is needed—may seem commonplace, but it is evidence of a fundamental shift in the structure of our way of life, our society, and our economy. It is the socioeconomic equivalent of a massive tsunami sweeping across the globe. The surge keeps everything continuously on the move. Information asymmetry asserts that the advantage in any bargaining process (e.g., contracts, purchasing) is always with the party having the most or best information about the deal. In consumer products, the seller has historically held the advantage, while the consumer had to rely on confidence in a brand built by the seller to compensate for lack of information about the actual value. With digital media, the consumer's thumb can just as easily tilt the scale."

The accelerating E-Expectations of students

The ongoing E-Expectations research studies have documented significant changes in students' media habits over the last five years. For example, in the 2009 study, 50 percent of high school seniors reported using Facebook; in 2015, over 70 percent of the surveyed high school seniors used Facebook at least once per week. Over the same time, use of email as an effective communication resource during the recruitment process has remained fairly consistent for prospective students, with research respondents reporting that they not only use email frequently, but are highly likely to open emails from colleges, even those they do not know.

Additional findings from the 2015 E-Expectations study:

- Search engines have become the dominant method for finding college websites.
- Students are much more receptive to receiving text messages from campuses.
- Prospective students are much more drawn to images of a campus than to photos of current students.
- Nearly 80 percent say that a campus website affects their perception of an institution.

Interacting with the market through social media

Social media provides powerful opportunities to connect authentically and transparently with important audiences. By posting real-time content and engaging in direct conversations with prospective students, influencers, and other constituents, colleges and universities can generate an ongoing narrative that demonstrates and reinforces their value proposition.

At the same time, managing social media can be messy. It is time-consuming to maintain and can be difficult to measure in terms of lead-generation and bottom-line impact. As platforms evolve and use shifts, institutions are often challenged to develop a sustainable approach for reaching and interacting with prospective students.

To succeed in this arena, it is imperative that colleges and universities develop a cogent strategy founded on growing engagement and building their brand. An institutional social media plan should answer these questions:

- Which audiences will give us the best return on investment of our time (e.g., traditional students, adult students, parents)?
- What are our goals and how will we measure and evaluate the success of our efforts (e.g., increase in followers, engagement, web traffic, etc.)?
- On which social media platforms will we maintain an active presence?
- How do we intentionally and appropriately integrate key marketing messages into our social media content?
- What are our institutional guidelines and governance processes for social media activities?
- How will we staff the effort in order to cultivate and curate authentic content and maintain an active presence in each outlet?
- How will we coordinate our efforts across the greater college or university enterprise?

Social media management is not a job to be relegated to an untrained work-study student. It is best owned by an enrollment or marketing manager with a clear sense of the goals and objectives of the effort. The social media manager should be engaged in:

1. Providing guidance and insight in the creation or removal of social media assets in concert with the institution's overarching marketing and communications goals.
2. Monitoring social conversations and routing inquiries to appropriate campus offices.
3. Managing enrollment-focused social media channels.
4. Maintaining access to all branded accounts.
5. Coordinating content creators and educating on best practices.

There is value in using student employees to assist with efforts to sustain a successful social media plan. They can be helpful in monitoring assets to alert professional staff to any problematic posts or technical problems. Their own posts regarding their experiences as students can provide valuable insights to prospective students and parents. They can also ensure that professional staff remain attuned to emerging social media trends and new resources. For this reason, some strategic enrollment planning teams include students, often as part of an organized approach for providing a student perspective of institutional strengths and benefits.

For a market on the go: responsive design

Research studies tracking the use of electronic media show that mobile devices are being employed increasingly as a primary way to access the internet, see Figure 9-2. As a result, marketers now need to consider how electronic media—e.g, websites and emails—appear to users on a variety of devices. The solution to this issue is responsive design.

Figure 9-2: Use of Mobile Device to View College Site

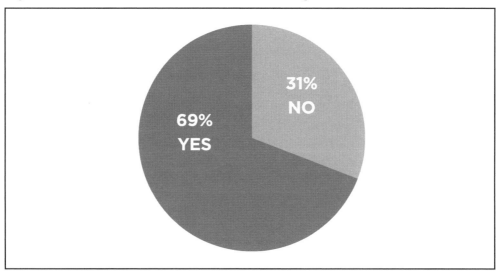

Source: Ruffalo Noel Levitz, 2015 E-Expectations Report

The goal of responsive design is to provide the best possible viewing experience on a wide range of devices, from mobile phones to desktop computers. "Responsive" means that a single email or webpage will fluidly respond to fit any screen or device size. For example, responsive emails will stack elements on a mobile device but display them side-by-side on a computer screen.

Responsive design is no longer optional or a "nice-to-have" feature—it is fundamental to today's electronic media.

Contact-driven branding to raise awareness and motivate response

A common tug-of-war over marketing at colleges and universities is whether to focus on general advertising or direct marketing. Advertising uses mass media such as magazines, billboards, television, and newspapers, and is often considered attractive because it is highly visible to the campus community. General advertising is used to build name recognition and brand image, as well as to reach broad audiences for which target mailing lists do not exist, such as adult students interested in degree completion.

Direct marketing encourages students to respond and take action. As its name implies, it is targeted to the individual through tools such as direct mail, email, and telecounseling. It almost always has a call to action. Direct marketing is a hardworking, productive tool for enrollment managers because it is targeted and measurable. However, it may be invisible to the campus community, leaving enrollment managers open to the criticism that "we aren't doing any marketing."

An evolving concept in strategic enrollment management and marketing is what might be called contact-driven branding, an approach that acknowledges the need for both measurability and the building of awareness. Contact-driven branding is a direct marketing approach with specific messages to specific potential students. Institutions that extensively use student search marketing (purchasing lists of names and then marketing to these prospects) recognize the value of this concept as they observe the many students who do not immediately respond to direct mail or email marketing campaigns, but ultimately enroll because their interest in the institution was activated. In addition to talking with friends and family members about the institution, these students may have gone directly to the institution's website and Facebook page. If the institution's market positioning is well-formed, the messages students receive will be consistent and reinforcing regardless of marketing venue, general or direct. Institutions need to establish measurement systems to track this potential trend.

Online advertising is the new frontier

Advertising online is not for the faint of heart, but online is where both traditional and nontraditional students spend much of their time for both work and play. Paid online advertising can support both general brand awareness for the institution and lead generation for specific academic programs. Typical online advertising initiatives use such venues as:

- Advertising via Google and other search engines.
- Social media-based advertising such as Facebook ads.
- Website retargeting, which captures visitors to your website and presents your message to them as they visit other non-associated websites.

Institutions rarely have the expertise to design, place, and track this kind of advertising with in-house resources, so plan to hire a company knowledgeable about paid interactive marketing when you enter this space.

In instances where using an outsourced vendor partnership to manage your institution's online advertising is an appropriate fit, you will want to ensure that the consultation or agency partner has specific experience with higher education markets and is prepared to be fully transparent about ongoing performance outcomes for your campaigns. A good reference point for beginning this conversation with potential partners is to ask: "How and at what frequency will we learn about the performance of our campaigns and budget spend?" The right partner will be willing and able to share performance metrics for the campaigns on a regular schedule (e.g., monthly), and will be able to discuss performance during a meeting with you by phone or online conference.

You will also be best served by a vendor partner who is willing to invest time to orient you and members of your team to what is happening with the campaigns—and to collaborate with you to refine performance within an open communication relationship where each party is mutually respected for its unique subject matter expertise.

Market research is a dialogue

Since the days of patent medicines, marketing has been viewed as a one-way street. Speak loudly, make enough promises, use the right package colors, and the target will be sold. In college and university marketing, this often has translated into the senior administrator merely wanting a billboard on the nearby highway like that of institution X, or the board members who are certain there must be more students in California or New York who want to attend their small Midwestern school.

In such situations, market research is the great equalizer and clarifier. All institutions, great and small, ultimately must bow to the market's expectations and perceptions. Market research lets the fresh air of the marketplace into the ivory tower.

According to author and educator Kotler (1999), "Companies often fail to recognize that their marketplace changes every few years." The same could be said of institutions of higher education. While higher education may seem slow-moving compared to fields such as business, science, and technology, a host of market factors are in constant flux, ranging from demand for various academic programs to tuition price sensitivity.

Although many colleges and universities are satisfied with the occasional market study, savvy institutions take the pulse of the marketplace regularly. Assessments can be conducted by collecting data elements readily available through national, state, and regional agencies. An ongoing market research plan, linked to performance indicators, ensures the institution is attuned to emerging trends and not taken by surprise with attitude shifts among key constituencies.

The list of possible research areas is extensive; however, the most valuable initiatives will support a strategic enrollment plan by:

1. **Assessing the market:**

   —Image and perception studies: What is the institution's current market position and how does it compare with students' visions of their ideal institution?

   —Academic program demand: How well does the curriculum align with developing market trends? Which programs are likely to encounter the greatest enrollment growth opportunities or declines? What are the preferred modes of program delivery (fully online, hybrid, and/or campus-based), and what course scheduling is preferred (evening, weekend, etc.)?

   —Price sensitivity analysis: What is the optimal tuition level for the institution's market, and how would changes to tuition and financial aid impact enrollment?

2. **Assessing the institution:**

   —Student satisfaction and engagement: What areas are of greatest importance to current students, and what are their satisfaction levels with these items? How engaged are students in the educational experience at the institution?

   —Employee satisfaction: How satisfied, productive, and mission-focused are campus employees as they interact with students?

   —Alumni satisfaction: How do alumni feel about the quality and value of the education they received? What recommendations can they offer for institutional improvements? Will they recommend the institution to others?

3. **Assessing competitors:**

—Competition communications study: What marketing messages and media are competitors using to reach audiences that are also targeted by the institution?

—Market share analysis: What is the institution's share of the market, and where do its competitors rank in terms of market share and quality relative to price?

In the absence of market research, market positioning is reduced to a guessing game that will likely be driven by an incomplete understanding of the environment. In the classic *Harvard Business Review* article, "Backward Market Research," Andreasen emphasizes the need for highly actionable market research rather than research that simply results in "the reduction of the level of ignorance" (1985).

Linking market position with enrollment planning

Most strategic enrollment teams will be focused on some basic long-range enrollment management decisions (e.g., whether to expand market share in secondary/tertiary markets in anticipation of demographic declines in the primary market, whether to reduce or increase sticker price to expand enrollment or reduce the discount rate, and how to develop new programs to be delivered online to the nontraditional undergraduate market). Assuming every research event is driven by the need to answer explicit questions and make specific decisions, Table 9-3 presents a sample strategic enrollment research plan designed to survey multiple enrollment audiences over time.

Table 9-3: Sample Strategic Enrollment Research Plan

Timing	Audience/market segments					
Year 1	Current students	Academic program demand study	High school guidance counselors	Parents of traditional prospects	Transfer students	Community college transfer counselors
Year 2	Prospective students	Competition study	Price sensitivity analysis	Graduate student prospects	Alumni	Employers of alumni
Year 3	Current students and their parents	Withdrawing student survey	Continuing education students	College employee satisfaction	Transfer students	Community college transfer counselors
Year 4	Prospective students	Alumni	High school guidance counselors	Parents of traditional prospects	Employers of alumni	Competition study
Year 5	Current students	Academic program demand study	Withdrawing student survey	Graduate student prospects	College employee satisfaction	Residence hall survey

TM

A Case Study

A public university in a western state had plans to embark on a new branding campaign. As campus leaders evaluated the institution's strengths, they concluded that their racial and ethnic diversity, which extended to students, faculty, staff, and administrators, was their primary market positioning asset.

Just before launching the campaign, however, they sought market research to confirm their direction. The research showed that, of 25 college choice factors, diversity was ranked 24th in importance by their prospective students. Further qualitative investigation revealed that, because the institution's students came from homes, schools, communities, and workplaces that were highly diverse, diversity was a fundamental expectation, not a distinction. As a student buying motive, diversity would have been a barrier if absent, but its presence was not viewed as exceptional.

Although this was a large campus with an undergraduate enrollment of more than 10,000, the research suggested that students were seeking a high degree of faculty engagement in and outside the classroom as their primary institutional characteristic.

Today's admissions counselor isn't disposable

A single admissions counselor at a small, private college or university could easily be held responsible for enrolling 50 to 200 students for a fall semester. If the institution averages $15,000 in net revenue per student, that recruiter is accountable for generating roughly $750,000 to $3,000,000 annually in institutional income. In the business world, that kind of salesperson would be highly valued and the target of vigorous employee retention efforts. In higher education, that recruiter is often at the bottom of the ladder in terms of compensation and prestige. A revolving door for the admissions counselor position is generally accepted at many institutions.

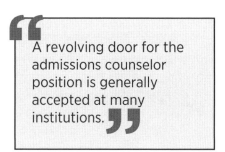

A revolving door for the admissions counselor position is generally accepted at many institutions.

Where does this attitude come from? It may be a vestige of earlier eras when many campuses did not need to market themselves and could simply process applications, and frankly, at times it arises from the academy's assumption that the institution will just sell itself based on the superiority of its academic programs.

An admissions counselor holds significant responsibility in his or her hands. According to NACAC, the mean student-to-college counselor ratio is 1 to 348 and the mean number of applications per admission officer is 620 (2013).

Institutions that recognize the value of well-trained, professional admissions counselors are beginning to invest in developing the position into one that requires:

1. A broader focus on marketing, as counselors represent the brand image of the institution.

2. The ability to interact effectively with diverse populations from a variety of cultures and ethnicities.

3. Strengths in relationship-building and management, with a focus on determining fit between the institution and the student rather than simply on selling.

4. A firsthand knowledge of the use of technology in recruitment, from social media sites to text messaging.

5. An understanding of strategic marketing communications and the role of advertising, direct marketing, one-on-one interactions, and other tools.

6. Expertise in a variety of college financing solutions.

7. The ability to broadly and specifically articulate the institution's market positioning in a compelling way.

W. Kent Barnds—vice president for enrollment, communication, and planning at Augustana College in Illinois and a 20-year admissions veteran—observed, "The senior enrollment management role at institutions is becoming increasingly important. More and more enrollment officers are serving at the cabinet level, are engaging with boards of trustees, and are involved with institutional strategic planning. We've got to find a way to groom the next generation for this kind of role, and it starts with investing in our own counselors" (personal communication).

Viewing admissions counselors as valued employees to be developed, rather than disposable assets to be recycled, requires an institution to:

1. Conduct succession planning for key positions and promote from within whenever possible.

2. Cross-train employees on multiple functions (e.g., financial aid), enabling counselors to build a robust skill set.

3. Offer a clear career path within the enrollment management function.

4. Improve compensation in relation to other institutional positions, offering internal recognition and financial rewards matching the importance of the role.

The 2013 National Association for College Admissions Counseling (NACAC) *State of College Admission Report* indicates a median salary for college admissions counselors at all levels of experience of $35,800. According to the College and University Professional Association for Human Resources, the entry-level annual giving officer earns an average of approximately $43,000, as does the entry-level alumni relations officer—a 20 percent difference in pay (2015).

Conclusion: Dull or differentiated?

Good market positioning is not pixie dust sprinkled over an institution in an attempt to make it more attractive to the marketplace or a coat of paint that disguises defects and deficiencies. It requires an investment in research, planning, and marketing strategies that both strengthen the institution by placing it in the intense spotlight of market expectations and allow it to move forward by highlighting its relevant strengths. For strategic enrollment planners, well-executed market positioning can help catapult an institution out of dull sameness into a place of distinctiveness that truly matters.

Dialogue

Use this discussion guide in your marketing and enrollment management teams to facilitate changes in attitudes and priorities:

- What key marketing messages are you using today with prospective students? Do these messages fit the criteria of being at the intersection of institutional strengths, market demand, and competitive opportunity?

- Is there a gap between the institution's current market position and its ideal position? How can strategic planning help to close that gap?

- What market research do you need to ensure that the strategic planning team has a comprehensive, data-informed understanding of the institution, the market, and the competitive context?

- How are you ensuring that your institution's website is driven by audience needs, not simply by institutional interests? Does the relative emphasis by audience on your institution's homepage match the importance of those audiences to your institution's future?

- Is your campus making a sufficient financial investment in e-marketing strategies, or are you acting as if tools, such as social networking, are free?

- How will you evaluate your current marketing practices that use social and/or electronic media to generate interest and help support the institutional brand?

- Is your institution intentional about providing a career path for admissions personnel? Are junior and mid-level admissions staff compensated at a level commensurate with institutional advancement staff and other comparable functions?

CHAPTER 10

Financial Aid, Pricing, and Positioning

By Wes Butterfield and Scott Bodfish

Have we reached the tipping point in college affordability? As we look across the college landscape, we see several major issues. Rising college costs, declining institutional yield rates, increased family borrowing, shifting demographics, increasing discount rates, and decreasing purchasing power of federal aid are just some of the reasons campuses need to optimize their institutional financial aid and consider pricing strategies (see Figure 10-1).

CHAPTER HIGHLIGHTS

- **Cost is a concern for both colleges and families**

- **Many campuses deal with enrollment challenges by increasing financial aid budgets**

- **Assistance with college financing is imperative, particularly for first-generation families**

The rising cost of college

The rising cost of college has been at the forefront of conversation around college campuses for a number of years. According to the College Board, *Trends in College Pricing*, from 1985-86 to 2015-16, the average published tuition, fees, room, and board at private nonprofit four-year institutions rose by 139 percent, from $13,551 (in 2015 dollars) to $32,405. The average published price at public two-year colleges rose by 142 percent, from $1,419 (in 2015 dollars) to $3,435, while the increase for in-state students at public four-year institutions was 222 percent, from $2,918 to $9,410 (College Board, 2015). Cost increases have slowed since the Great Recession of 2008, but cost remains an area of concern for both colleges and families.

One way campuses are addressing the rising cost of attendance is to expand the base of students they are trying to influence. However, a frequent consequence of trying to influence a larger number of students is a decline in yield rate: the percentage of students who enroll at an institution compared to the number of students who have been offered admission. Since 2005, both public and private four-year institutions have seen declines in yield rates. In 2005, public institutions experienced a 43 percent yield rate with steady declines down to 36 percent in 2014. Private institutions have seen yield slide from 35 percent in 2005 to 26 percent in 2014 (Ruffalo Noel Levitz, 2014). This decline is due, in part, to institutions increasing the number of students in their enrollment pools who are less interested in them specifically.

The slide in yield also stems from shifting demographics (Chapter 1). Data from the Western Interstate Commission for Higher Education suggest we are coming out of a demographic low point, but the variation in high school graduation numbers by state is more problematic, depending upon the recruiting base. For example, if a campus is located in the Northeast or parts of the Midwest, high school graduates are at historic lows.

To respond to changing demographics and increased competition, colleges and universities are increasing their attention to price and financial aid.

Figure 10-1: Have We Reached a Tipping Point in College Affordability?

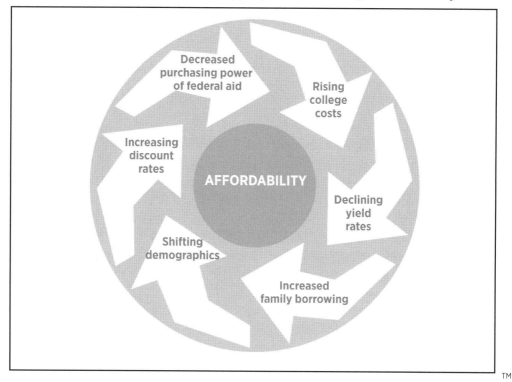

™

In this chapter, we will discuss how to address these issues illustrated in Figure 10-1, with a focus on the pricing strategies and financial aid structures that can help colleges manage affordability.

Pricing and positioning

The "sticker price" refers to the published amounts for tuition, fees, room, and board that colleges and universities charge students to take classes (tuition), use various services (fees), live in residence halls (room), and eat in dining facilities (board). Most of the focus of pricing strategy is in setting tuition, since this represents the largest source of enrollment-related revenue. Fees historically have been tied to specific services, such as technology fees and lab fees and are typically presumed by consumers to reflect the actual costs of services provided. At public universities, fees are often a significant source of revenue, especially when tuition rates are set by state agencies. Room and board costs are relevant to those institutions with a residential population and are in part a function of prices that institutions are charged by vendors (especially for dining services).

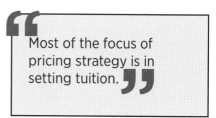

Most of the focus of pricing strategy is in setting tuition.

However, the majority of college students do not pay the sticker price. Most students receive some form of gift aid that, from an economic perspective, acts as a discount off the sticker price. While gift aid from non-institutional sources effectively discounts the price students pay, the general practice is to regard gift aid from institutional sources as "discount."

Tuition discounting

Tuition discounting describes the practice of offering institutional gifts to help defray the cost of attendance. While the National Association of Colleges and University Business Officers (NACUBO) provides discount rate definitions that use both funded and unfunded awards, the discount rate is commonly calculated based on the average of all unfunded institutional gift aid awarded to students divided by the sticker price (usually tuition and fees for a year of full-time enrollment). Two versions of the discount rate are defined in Figure 10-2 below. The discount rate is often used as a key indicator of institutional financial viability. A high discount rate is typically taken as a sign that an institution is less effective in competing for students than other institutions with lower discount rates.

Figure 10-2: Formulas for Tuition Discount Rate

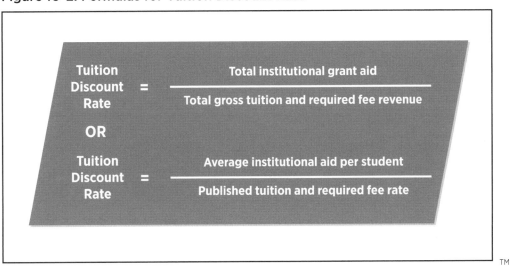

Tuition discounting has historically been used most often by four-year private, not-for-profit institutions. Since their sticker price is generally much higher than the sticker prices that four-year public institutions charge to in-state residents, in large part due to state subsidies, private institutions that have substantial competitive overlap with four-year publics have used institutional gift aid (both need-based and non-need-based) in an effort to remove price as a barrier to enrollment.

However, as government subsidies of public colleges and universities have stagnated and/or declined, many four-year public universities have begun to use institutional gift aid to discount tuition for selected student segments, such as non-resident students. For-profit institutions are also introducing discounting strategies as the enrollment growth rate in this sector has stagnated and competition has increased.

Pricing practices

A framework for determining an institution's price position relative to competitors is to map the position on two axes: sticker price and discount rate. This creates four quadrants, as shown in Figure 10-3. Three of these represent different types of pricing strategies:

* **High sticker price/high discount:** This pricing strategy is effective in markets where dominant competitors are competing on scholarship.

\# **High sticker price/low discount:** This pricing strategy is typical of selective institutions that have a strong brand appeal and can command premium prices.

+ **Low sticker price/low discount:** This pricing strategy is for institutions where there is very little differentiation in product offerings or distinctive brand attributes and lowest price is generally the deciding factor.

X **Low sticker price/high discount:** While this is a potential position in the matrix, it is not viable as a pricing strategy.

Figure 10-3: Pricing Strategies

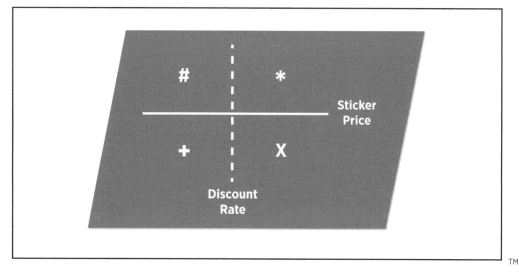

Campuses set prices (tuition, fees, and room and board charges) in one of three ways:

- Competition-driven: Prices are set using a benchmark set of competitors (for example, keeping a school's tuition in the middle of a set of competitors).

- Market-driven: Prices are set using information about the price behavior of prospective students (for example, after research on price response among the schools' inquiries, it is determined that tuition should not be increased by more than 3 percent).

- Budget-driven: Prices are set so that the total revenue generated from the expected student enrollment meets a target amount that enables the institution to balance income and expenses.

In reality, most campuses attempt to incorporate all of these—a pro forma budget is developed and the tuition rate required by the pro forma budget is compared to expectations of competitor price increases and some sense of market sensitivity, usually communicated through admissions and financial aid representatives.

Each method presents certain challenges. The competition-driven method assumes that the benchmark set represents the actual competition for students. It also assumes that the prices charged by competitors reflect the pricing that the market is willing to bear. The budget-driven method by itself does not incorporate any information about how prospective students will respond to a price increase, since it does not incorporate any information that reflects market behavior. It may risk overpricing as well as underpricing.

The market-driven method depends on the validity of the research. We would consider polling admissions and financial aid staff as a type of market research; however, while these individuals are closest to the actual behaviors of prospective students, they may not accurately represent actual price sensitivity. Often, they tend to assume greater sensitivity to price increases than actually exists.

Price sensitivity

It is increasingly common for institutions to engage in price sensitivity research. This type of research can influence both pricing and financial aid strategies. Systematic methods of measuring price sensitivity ("elasticity of demand") incorporate survey research with a representative sample of the "market," usually prospective students. When researching price sensitivity in order to set a price for traditional-age undergraduates, it is desirable to survey both students and parents, as the decision to enroll at a specific institution is usually made jointly and because parents typically pay more attention to price than students—both sticker price and net price. The validity of the research results are a function not only of sample size, but also the design of the survey project.

For example, asking a very direct question like, "How much would you be willing to pay in tuition to enroll at institution X?" would seem to capture how individuals would respond to an increased price at the institution. However, this type of question in a survey environment usually results in responses that lowball the actual willingness to pay. Respondents tend to assume that it is to their advantage to provide the lowest response to the question in the belief that this will limit price increases.

The preferred method is to provide a variety of pricing scenarios that introduce changes in price and ask respondents to rate their level of interest in each scenario. This method allows the researcher to compare the change in level of interest with the change in price to infer price sensitivity. This type of design provides a result that tells the institution that increasing tuition beyond a certain percentage from its current level would reduce demand by a corresponding amount.

Another important consideration when fielding research to measure price sensitivity is whether the questions should be framed in terms of sticker price or net price. Since most students do not pay the sticker price, it would seem that the best approach would be to use questions that refer to net price. However, there is evidence that in the early stages of the formation of a set of schools to consider (usually prior to application), some people rule out certain institutions as too expensive. Since there is generally little specific information about the amount of financial aid students would realistically be awarded from institutions until after they have applied to a school (though more information is available with the advent of net price calculators), the assumption is that the determination not to consider certain schools because of price is a function of the sticker price and not the net price.

There is also evidence that financial aid, usually in the form of a scholarship award, is influential in the choice of a school and that the influence of the scholarship is independent of the discount effect of the scholarship. In other words, large scholarship offers can be influential regardless of the price, sticker or net. So while it is possible to design questions that test how people respond to changes in net price, designs that allow the independent measurement of changes in sticker price, in financial aid award, and in net price provide better information for developing a pricing strategy using market research.

Conjoint designs are used in research applications where the researcher is interested in measuring the influence of changes in the level of different attributes. For example, a conjoint design can be used to tell whether improvements in fuel economy are more influential than rebates when purchasing an automobile and what combination of gasoline MPG and rebate are optimal. With a conjoint price sensitivity research design, a survey can be developed to measure the influence of sticker price as well as financial aid.

Campus examples of pricing strategies based on price sensitivity research

1. In the face of constraints on resident tuition increases, a public university investigated the feasibility of greater increases in non-resident tuition as a way of generating new revenue. Historically the institution had kept non-resident tuition rates low in the belief that few families would be willing to pay the higher costs when in-state publics were so much more affordable. Pricing research showed that there was much greater willingness to pay among out-of-state families than had been expected, showing that they were underpriced in their out-of-state market.

2. A private university had been the lowest-priced among a key group of private competitors. After several years of aggressive tuition increases, there was still little change in its relative position among these competitors, and university officials were concerned that continuing to increase tuition at a rate greater than their competitors would result in creating a barrier to enrollment for students, especially key demographic segments that were believed to be especially price sensitive. By periodically conducting research on price sensitivity, the university monitors the elasticity of demand at future levels of increase to get an early indication of when they have reached a tuition level that triggers excessive price sensitivity.

Resetting tuition

Several private institutions have "reset" their tuition level, cutting tuition significantly and adjusting their discounting levels accordingly. Several have been successful (as measured by increases in enrollment), while others have reduced tuition with little change in enrollment. While it would seem intuitive that reducing price would always result in more enrollment, the fact that some institutions have reset tuition without generating more enrollment suggests that the success of a price reduction strategy depends on more than just announcing a price cut.

One factor that accompanies most successful price reductions is an effective marketing plan that makes use of advertising to publicize the new price position, especially to groups that may have been ruling out the institution because of assumptions about high price (prospects who never inquired and inquiries who never applied).

Another factor that determines the success of a price reduction is the extent of price sensitivity in the school's market. If the current sticker price of the institution is at a level that most families would expect to pay for that type of institution, then price probably isn't a barrier to enrollment. Reducing price would not result in generating increased interest in the institution.

Differential pricing

Where there are differences in demand based on the program of study, it may make sense to charge different prices, a practice known as differential pricing. This can take the form of either higher tuition or additional fees for programs with stronger demand. Differential tuition can be problematic when students in different programs are enrolled in the same courses, and so program-specific rates are the more typical means for implementing a differential pricing strategy.

Differential pricing is found more frequently among graduate programs than it is among undergraduate programs. While unvarying undergraduate tuition and fees are generally associated with a broader college experience (general education courses, student life programming, extracurricular and co-curricular activities, etc.), differential pricing is used when students are largely paying for instruction in their specific program of study, e.g., non-traditional undergraduate programs and graduate programs.

Differential pricing by program is usually implemented when some programs are more expensive to deliver than others or when the employment outcomes (starting salaries, employment rates) are more robust than others. This presumes that the institution is able to assign costs to programs that accurately reflect their direct expenses. But another rationale is to charge a premium price for programs where the demand for the program is inelastic relative to other programs, where there is less interest, or where there is more competition.

Differential discounting by program is a mechanism for responding to differences in the elasticity of demand across programs, especially for full-time undergraduate populations where differential pricing of tuition is problematic.

Tuition guarantees, freezes, and rebates

Several colleges and universities have implemented a "tuition guarantee"—a pricing strategy designed to increase enrollment by guaranteeing that a student's tuition will not increase over a specified period of time, usually the length of time required to complete the program. This strategy may also be effective in reducing attrition, especially among students with high levels of need where the ability to pay may not increase in line with the rate of tuition increases.

A disadvantage of a guaranteed tuition plan is that it tends to force institutions to implement even greater tuition increases for each new cohort since expenses associated with a cohort generally do not remain fixed over the years students are enrolled at the guaranteed rate. An increase in student interest that a tuition guarantee may generate when first announced might not continue in subsequent years, especially if it tends to drive tuition significantly above where competitors are priced.

> " Tuition freezes are more likely to result in increased enrollment of returning students than in increases in new student enrollment. "

A more common pricing strategy in response to market concerns about sticker price is a tuition freeze, where the institution keeps tuition for all students at the same level as the prior year. Since most colleges and universities increase tuition each year, a freeze can be a competitive advantage. However, it is worth bearing in mind that when new students are making enrollment decisions, they rarely compare the price that they will be charged with the price the institution charged in the past. Tuition freezes are more likely to result in increased enrollment of returning students than in increases in new student enrollment, especially among returning students who are less able to afford increased prices.

Another pricing strategy designed to increase enrollment is to offer some form of rebate if students take longer than the standard length of time to complete their education, most commonly four years for a bachelor's degree. This strategy can be effective for students who are concerned that it may take them longer than four years to earn their degree. Since market perceptions generally are that students attending public universities take longer than four years to graduate, rebates can be an effective strategy for a public university if price is a barrier in the university's market. Some private colleges and universities adopt this strategy to reinforce their commitment to "on-time" degree completion.

Per-credit or zone

At four-year institutions, the normal model for full-time undergraduate tuition is a flat tuition amount per semester or per year for any number of courses within a range that represents full-time attendance, such as 12 to 18 credit hours per semester. Two-year institutions typically charge per credit hour regardless of the number of courses taken. Nontraditional undergraduate programs and many graduate programs also charge tuition per credit hour or per course.

Charging tuition per credit hour provides students with a means of managing the affordability of college to meet their individual circumstances. Students can take a smaller course load and work, or keep tuition payments each term lower than if tuition were charged at a flat rate based on a larger course load. It also is well-suited to students who don't fit the traditional, residential college model, such as nontraditional students, commuter students, and "swirling" students (Chapter 12).

One commonly heard concern with per-credit-hour tuition plans is that they may encourage students to take longer to complete their education, as there is an implicit economic incentive to take fewer credits per semester (typically the average rate at which a student needs to take classes in order to complete their degree in four years). However, a recent study of pricing plans Ruffalo Noel Levitz conducted for a set of large, public institutions found no evidence that per-credit-hour models led to lower retention or graduation rates. In the study, half of the universities had per-credit-hour pricing and half charged a flat tuition rate for students taking a full-time range of credit hours. Data were analyzed to see whether or not schools that had per-credit-hour pricing had lower retention or graduation rates. After controlling for average test scores of incoming freshmen, percent of students on Pell (as a measure of need), and admissions acceptance rates (as a measure of selectivity), there was no statistically significant difference in either retention rates or graduation rates between the two groups of schools.

Financial aid

Many campuses deal with enrollment challenges by funneling additional funding into financial aid budgets, which drives up institutional discount rates. Multiple factors are at play in the rise of discount rates. Demographic factors (Chapter 1) are one force. Student subsidies from both federal and state sources are flat or, in some cases, being reduced. The economic downturn of 2008 had multiple influences, from the loss in home value, to an increasing reluctance to borrow and the loss of alternative loan options.

The decreasing purchasing power of federal aid and state appropriations is affecting students' ability to attend a college or university. Federal grants reached an all-time high in fall 2010-11, accounting for 44 percent of all grant types for students across the country. This percentage slowly declined to 37 percent in 2014-15. Institutional aid from campuses has filled the gap, growing from 35 percent to 41 percent during this same period. Meanwhile, state grants have remained flat nationally (College Board, 2015).

During this same timeframe, student and parent loans have declined, from $120.8 billion in 2010-11 to $106.1 billion in 2014-15 (College Board, 2015). Colleges and universities will need to continue to show families they are worth the cost if families are to continue to invest in higher education.

How are campuses responding to the above issues? They are restructuring their financial aid to maximize its impact.

Begin with an analytical framework

A sound financial aid awarding structure begins with an analytical framework guided by data. Most campuses struggle with the trade-off in three broad areas—enrollment headcount, academic quality or credentials, and finances (cost, net revenue, discount rate, etc.). In most cases, campuses may want to increase all three areas, but generally speaking, that is a virtually impossible goal to achieve. Creating a rank order for headcount, quality, and finances is a strong starting position for developing an analytical framework.

From there a campus needs to understand the principles for moving a student population. By analyzing your campus data, you will be able to make decisions based on facts, not conjecture. In an ideal state, families would understand their financial need through tools like the Free Application for Federal Student Aid (FAFSA) and have the willingness and ability to pay the amount the analysis indicates the household can pay. On the other end of the spectrum, campuses would understand a family's need and have the willingness and ability to fill the gap between the cost of attending the institution and the family's need. Unfortunately, most campuses have a limited pool of institutional dollars to provide to families.

Figure 10-4: Base Analytical Framework

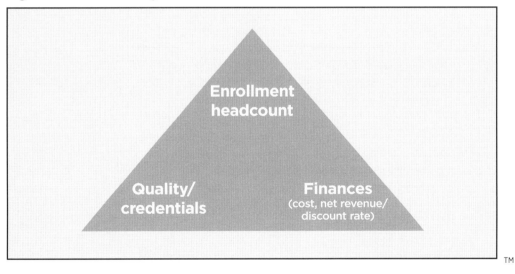

A strong analytic framework prioritizes three broad ingredients: enrollment, quality and finances as shown in Figure 10-4. There are many campuses exploring what is the "right size" for their institution. Bigger is not always better but understanding what is the best size for an institution to best fulfill its purpose is imperative. The academic credential is a forward-facing metric unfortunately used at times to determine institutional quality. Many campuses are looking to move their campus to "the next level." And the finances piece can be daunting. Keeping track of overall revenue, discount rates and net tuition revenue are the fuels for many campus engines.

The second key variable, willingness to pay, is more challenging to measure. In most cases, a student's willingness to pay can be measured by evaluating an institution's yield rate. However, a student's or family's willingness to pay varies and is influenced by a number of factors. Willingness to pay will vary from person to person in education, as in any other major purchase.

For example, consider two individuals with daily commutes to work who, because of where they live, cannot use public transportation. They each need a car to get back and forth to work and both have the ability to spend up to $30,000 on a vehicle. The type of car each person chooses will vary based on individual preferences. The first driver may believe that any reliable car with four wheels will be sufficient to go back and forth, and in this case the person spends only $15,000. The second driver desires a few more comforts in the car he or she chooses to drive and spends close to the financial limit of $30,000. Neither person is wrong in their reasoning. The type of car each person chooses will be based on more than simply what each can afford. The car model and options will vary based on the relative importance of a number of variables. This thought process is very similar to the willingness to pay for higher education. While some families aren't willing to extend very far for higher education, others are willing to overextend to help their students reach for a more selective campus experience.

Academic ability can also influence willingness to pay. Top academic students are not only admitted to multiple institutions, they are more likely to be offered large academic scholarships, which may actually reduce their willingness to pay. Geography can also play a role, as can having a parent or other significant relative who is an alumna of an institution. Some students are willing to pay more to be near their significant other, or to have an opportunity to continue to play their favorite sport.

Just as students and families have to make choices about the characteristics of the ideal college experience, institutions also have to make choices about what type of students are best to continue their visions, missions, and values. Campuses must consider the trade-offs between improving quality and shaping their classes with students who have the desired characteristics the campus wants, while striving to maximize net revenue.

In an optimal analytical framework, a campus should experience its desired level of enrollment, and the enrolled class should generate the ideal amounts of net revenue. The optimal structure should also be mindful of institutional discount rates and allow a campus to enroll specific market segments.

Market segmentation

As part of an optimal financial aid framework, a campus must consider which market segments it wants to influence with financial aid, understanding that different segments may require different levels of financial aid to enroll students.

Using your campus data for your admitted student population, a rational approach to market segmentation begins with identifying *like* populations. *Like* student populations are students

> " As part of an optimal financial aid framework, a campus must consider which market segments it wants to influence with financial aid. "

who react similarly to specific amounts of financial aid. Admitted students are the best group of students to analyze. In most cases, if students are not admitted, you are not going to focus your financial aid efforts on them. Traditional populations that may react similarly to aid include geography (in-state, out-of-state), student type (commuter, residential, athlete, direct from high school, adult), or majors and programs. This reaction or behavior is measured by yield rate. Every campus is unique, so these populations will vary.

After clusters of like students have been identified, the campus determines how it wants to intervene financially with each group. To illustrate, imagine that a campus wants to award full-tuition scholarships for a portion of its enrolling student population. The first step is to determine the academic boundaries for the potential student population. How many scholarships does the campus want to award? What type of yield rate did students of this caliber have in the past? What type of non-financial activities are in place, and how can these activities be modified to maximize yield?

One final note about segmented populations: remember that all segmented populations should equal the sum of their parts. If a campus has identified an in-state, out-of-state, athletic, and high-scholar population, for example, the sum of those four groups should be your entire admit pool. For the sake of analytical review, students should only show up in a single, segmented population. So in this example, a high-scholar athlete who lives close to campus should be placed into the population of greatest yield influence.

Developing a scholarship program

What is the purpose of the campus scholarship program? Harvard began using merit scholarships in the 1930s to attract top-ranking scholars from around the country, and this practice has become commonplace on campuses nationwide (Karabel, 2005). Today, campuses are still using scholarships the same way. They are used to attract a certain type of student and hold their interest throughout the recruitment process. Institutions without strong name recognition must showcase a robust scholarship program to grab a student's initial interest. These campuses must then spend substantial time communicating about mission, vision, and values to help the student understand their experience difference.

The second purpose of the scholarship program is to influence specific populations of students—a purpose which is similar to market segmentation. If a campus wants to develop a strong choral music program, for example, it may invest in scholarships targeted at this specific population. Remember, the same questions must be answered for specific population awards: What is the purpose of the award? How many students will enroll? What is the cost? There must be an understanding of how these students will positively affect enrollment. Ultimately, the institutional scholarship program should support the admissions objectives. One of the great struggles on many campuses is to help other offices understand that the best scholarship programs are those where the scholarships are used to positively affect enrollment behavior. If scholarship dollars are used for any other purpose (and there may be other purposes for some scholarships), they aren't being used to positively affect enrollment.

After identifying the students to influence with the scholarship program, campuses promote their scholarships and continue to award scholarships until their enrollment objectives are met. Scholarship programs that best stimulate positive enrollment behavior are easy to understand and allow the student population to self-qualify to determine where they may fall in the awarding matrix. Tools like a net price calculator (NPC), which all campuses should now have easily accessible on the institutional website, can be wonderful recruiting aids if the parameters allow a student to self-qualify. Ruffalo Noel Levitz has been aggregating net price calculator information since the 2008 federal NPC mandate, and the data indicate that the primary goal of NPC users is to understand scholarship opportunities. Of the more than 5.68 million users tracked, over 70 percent of the users moved through the initial scholarship portion of the Ruffalo Noel Levitz net price calculator. The number of students who completed the entire calculator was about 33 percent of those who started the process (see Figure 10-5).

Figure 10-5: Ruffalo Noel Levitz Net Price Calculator Results Through November 2015

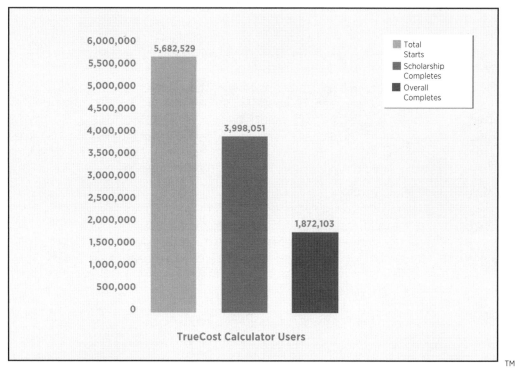

TM

So what is the takeaway regarding your NPC? You should place your campus calculator in a highly visible area on your campus website, and make sure to accent the scholarships you offer. Your NPC can provide an entryway for prospective students and their families who are experiencing initial sticker shock.

A number of campuses may not offer a robust institutional scholarship program. In these cases, the goal is still to try to lower anxiety by helping families understand college affordability on your campus. Strong communications about assistance with college financing are imperative, particularly for first-generation families.

Measuring student response to your net price offer

Scholarship offers are on the streets—now what? On an annual basis, each institution should measure the results of the institutional scholarship program. By reviewing the total institutional gift aid awarded to students, a campus can understand receptivity to its award offers. Table 10-1 helps explain this concept. This example analyzes the amount of total gift offered to students at a small campus. Why gift aid? Remember, most families respond positively to gift aid, so by analyzing the sources of gift aid, we can look at how the amount of aid provided to students affects decision-making. We see very different reactions based on yield or enrollment rates depending on the amount of aid provided. In the example in Table 10-1, overall scholarship yield was 43 percent. When the campus met less than 45 percent of a family's need, the enrollment rate dropped to 24 percent (need is based on the results of the family's Expected Family Contribution (EFC) minus the indirect cost of the institution). On the other end of this example, when the campus met more than 62 percent of the student's need with gift aid, the enrollment rate jumped to almost 63 percent.

Table 10-1: Example of Price Sensitivity Based on Percentage of Need Met With Gift Aid at Ruffalo Noel Levitz University

Need Met with Gift Aid	Enrollment Rate	Number of Cases
<45% (<$10,000)	24%	78
45%-62% ($10,000-$15,000)	48%	73
>62% (>$15,000)	63%	51
Total	43%	202

TM

Where is the right point to land? The answer is based on institutional goals. Note the number of students enrolling at each gift aid break. Although we are only enrolling students at a 24 percent rate on the lower end, 78 students accepted this award. This campus may not be able to afford to increase this tier of students much more than its current level. The 78 cases (or students) is a large number compared to the overall number of cases reviewed. The campus may determine the expenditures spent on this group of students are sufficient for its overall goals.

Another way to analyze gift aid effectiveness is to review merit offers. The previous example may be a useful tool for campuses not offering a merit scholarship program. In Table 10-2, we see the effectiveness of merit scholarships based on students who do not qualify for aid (low-need or no-need students). By reviewing low-need or no-need students, we are able to measure price sensitivity based on students who don't qualify for anything besides scholarships.

Table 10-2: Example of Price Sensitivity Based on Merit-Aid-Only

Merit Offer	Enrollment Rate	Number of Cases
<$2,999	6%	30
$3,000-$4,999	42%	53
$5,000-$6,999	60%	30
>$7,000	75%	12
Total	39%	125

TM

Students who received less than $3,000 in the merit scholarship program only enrolled at a yield rate of 6 percent. The overall average enrollment rate was 39 percent. In this case, the campus may need to increase its merit level threshold to see more lift from this group of students—based on the campus needs. Also, this campus may be awarding the smallest award to the lowest academic performers, and it may not be able to support more than the 30 cases enrolling. But is the movement of limited financial aid resources the only option for a campus? The next section has other non-financial factors to consider.

Control for non-financial variables

Student decision making isn't always about the best financial aid package, so campuses have to be mindful of other factors. For example, one of the strongest non-financial variables that can affect enrollment rate is the campus visit experience. Most institutions will see a lift from students who visit their campus.

When you meet students and their families face-to-face, you have the best opportunity to change or influence decisions. When you have prospective students on your campus for an individual visit or small group, you should see lift. If not, you can review the things you can control. What are the key takeaways from your campus visit experience that every student should be aware of? What differentiates your campus from the other schools that might be on their visit list? It is helpful to develop a list of key messages and themes to be used by the admissions and financial aid teams, and perhaps other outward-facing offices, such as development and alumni affairs.

Once the messages are in place, view your campus through the eyes of a prospective student and his or her family. Review the route your prospective families take to get to your campus. Where are you having them park? Are they walking through the main entrance of your campus? When was the last time you took the *money walk*? This is the walk that you should take annually to assess the campus. What are your families seeing? Where are the cracks in the foundation, the dumpsters, and the deferred maintenance? At times, students base their decisions on the little things. You can't control everything, but there are many aspects of the visit experience you can influence.

Develop a strategic financial aid plan

Once you have gathered campus data to develop your analytical framework, you will need to review the data to develop a strategic financial aid plan. Your yield rates in various combinations of academic criteria and financial need can help you better understand the relationship between ability and willingness to pay at your institution. On one axis, you will create academic ability boundaries for your financial aid plan. The academic boundaries are based on your individual campus. Many campuses use high school grade point average, standardized exams, class rank, or other factors to group students with similar academic characteristics. Reviewing changes in yield rates based on your academic boundaries will allow you to segment your population.

> " Your yield rates in various combinations of academic criteria and financial need can help you better understand the relationship between ability and willingness to pay. "

On your other axis, you will measure yield rates by ability to pay, as measured by expected family contribution or need. Many campuses use the FAFSA or Student Profile. As mentioned, the goal is to determine the financial strength of the household and its ability to assist with financing their student's education.

With students identified by academic boundaries and financial need, and after a thorough review of yield patterns from like students, the campus can now begin awarding financial aid packages. There are a number of factors to consider during development of the financial aid plan. Direct cost, admitted and enrolled students, state and federal subsidies (and potential changes in these areas), scholarship levels, the segmented populations the campus has identified, and the overall aid package all need to be reviewed and boundaries need to be set for each component.

Table 10-3 is one example of how the financial aid framework might look based on ability to pay and willingness to pay.

On the x-axis of the table are the academic boundaries, and on the y-axis is ability to pay. Within this framework, *like* students are captured in each of the awarding cells. The goal of a framework like this is to create a financial aid awarding structure for students within the cells that would contain similar aid components—scholarships, grants, work, and loans. The E and NE in the example are the enrolled and non-enrolled students falling into each cell. Remember that this is simply an example, as boundaries and subpopulations are specific to each institution.

If we are successful in developing a strong analytical framework, our financial aid structure should accomplish four objectives. The first and perhaps most important objective is to make the institution affordable to those who are willing to pay its cost without spending more than necessary to enroll and retain each student. In 2015, students enrolled at their first-choice institutions 55 percent of the time (Eagan et al., 2015), and developing a sound financial aid structure allows us to maximize this group of students. The second objective is that the plan will contribute directly to new and returning student enrollment goals. The third objective is that the plan will optimize the distribution of aid to serve more students. The plan allows the institution to move away from a first-come, first-served mentality. Finally, the plan maximizes net tuition revenue so the institution can maintain and improve the quality of its programs and services.

Table 10-3: One Example of a Strategic Financial Aid Matrix

	Willingness to Pay									
	Ability Level I		Ability Level II		Ability Level III		Ability Level IV		Ability Level V	
Ability to Pay	E	NE	E	NE	E	NE	E	NE	E	NE
Very High Need	Cell 1		Cell 2		Cell 3		Cell 4		Cell 5	
Need Level 5	Cell 6		Cell 7		Cell 8		Cell 9		Cell 10	
Need Level 4	Cell 11		Cell 12		Cell 13		Cell 14		Cell 15	
Need Level 3	Cell 16		Cell 17		Cell 18		Cell 19		Cell 20	
Need Level 2	Cell 21		Cell 22		Cell 23		Cell 24		Cell 25	
Low Need	Cell 26		Cell 27		Cell 28		Cell 29		Cell 30	
Merit Aid Only	Cell 31		Cell 32		Cell 33		Cell 34		Cell 35	
Full Pay	Cell 36		Cell 37		Cell 38		Cell 39		Cell 40	
Premier	Cell 41		Cell 42		Cell 43		Cell 44		Cell 45	
Special Talent	Cell 46		Cell 47		Cell 48		Cell 49		Cell 50	
Employee Benefit	Cell 51		Cell 52		Cell 53		Cell 54		Cell 55	

™

Manage results through routine management reports

Once the framework has been developed and deployed, it is imperative to measure the success of the financial aid plan. A sound reporting structure will ensure that the enrolling student class doesn't sneak up on you. You should have a series of reports monitoring awards from the beginning of your recruiting cycle through the point when students enroll at your institution. Once financial aid awards have been sent, you need to develop reports to help understand how many awards have been sent out and who has received the awards. By understanding the number of awards offered, you are able to understand your potential exposure in real-time, which is invaluable.

Another way to monitor your awarding structure is to observe and report how students respond to their financial aid awards. There are several key, measurable items to capture with a well-developed qualification scale. The main goal is to understand the award reaction based on a student's impression of the award. Where the institution ranks within the student's list of institutions is also important to understand. Remember, a student is more likely to enroll at his or her first-choice school.

What is the student's reaction to the financial aid award? Did the award meet the student's needs, exceed, or miss expectations? By understanding the reaction to the award, you are able to determine if the financial aid strategy is working and can evaluate the next steps in a student's decision-making process. This gives the institution an opportunity to further influence the student's college selection.

Table 10-4 is a sample qualification scale. On this scale, you see a number-based system measuring the student's interest in the institution. The financial aid award reaction code measures how the student feels about the financial aid package.

Table 10-4: Qualifying and Financial Aid Award Reaction Scales

Accepted Student Qualifying Scale:	
Code	**Description (Student reaction to institution)**
1	Ruffalo Noel Levitz University (RNLU) is top choice, will deposit
2	RNLU is top choice, will deposit pending receipt of adequate aid award
3	RNLU is among top 2-3 choices, may deposit
4	RNLU is not among top 2-3 choices, unlikely to deposit
Financial Aid Award Reaction Scale:	
Code	**Description (Student reaction to financial aid)**
A	Award exceeds expectations
B	Award is sufficient to enroll
C	Neutral or non-committal
D	Award is not sufficient to enroll
E	Appeal, student has requested a review of his/her aid

TM

Over time, the two-code system may be extremely predictive of enrollment. What is the yield of students coded a 1C? How does this differ from a 2A? What is the strategy for students who are coded an E and need a financial aid package review? The codes allow the institution to react and determine how it will intervene with students throughout the cycle.

For example, if your institution works with a high percentage of first-generation college students, you may want to consider adding a cost worksheet with the financial aid package, outlining all of the costs a family will potentially incur during the first year.

Implementation of supporting strategies and tools

The final step in your financial aid framework is to create a structure that you can evaluate on an annual basis. You should be prepared to modify and tweak your structure. Which cells performed well? Which subpopulation reacted well to the award structure? What did you miss, and what are you prepared to do about any holes in your structure?

Develop your financial aid structure with both new student enrollment and degree completion in mind. Look to create a clean, straightforward structure, free from financial aid barriers. In addition, the campus should develop financial aid options with institution-specific student populations in mind. Are you offering payment options (10-month, 12-month, etc.)? Does your financial aid award and billing information share some of the same characteristics and convey a clear, streamlined message?

If you feel your structure is sound but doesn't seem to be enrolling the optimal pool of students, you may need to step back to determine if you are priced appropriately. What are your options when you find that you have reached the maximum amount of financial aid that you can provide to students? When you feel that you are discounting the cost of your student population more than other campuses in your marketplace and aren't generating enough net tuition per student, where do you turn? Financial aid is not a silver bullet; it is simply a structure for managing and awarding your limited funds.

Dialogue

Pricing and financial aid strategies are key considerations for any strategic enrollment planning project. As with any dimension of enrollment planning, discussions and decisions should include broad representation from key institutional departments: finance, financial aid, admissions and recruitment, marketing, and even retention. Key questions include:

- Do you know how your price is perceived within your primary market?

- Do you regularly have conversations about the difference between managing the discount rate as a distinct effort from managing net revenue?

- Do you understand how your price and your financial aid offers compare to both your peer and competitor institutions? Have you used other schools' net price calculators to understand their financial aid and pricing structures? Have you explored their websites to see how they are marketing themselves?

- Is your own net price calculator in a highly visible place on your website?

- Have you been intentional about your marketing messages regarding price and aid, and are those messages helping you to position yourself against your peers and competitors? Are you sufficiently differentiating yourself in relation to price, value, and outcomes?

- Are you sending early offers of merit aid to all accepted students and sending all financial aid awards as early as possible?

- Do you regularly conduct follow-up phone calls after aid awards are sent to gauge student and family reaction?

- Can you be nimble in adjusting awards during the decision cycle if early indicators warrant?

- Are student success and retention efforts sufficiently integrated with financial aid planning? At some institutions, net revenue per student increases as students are retained because prices go up while financial aid awards remain stable. Are you helping students to plan for annual cost increases? Are you using financial aid to create retention incentives?

- Do you have ample financing options available? If you have technical programs with high tool costs, can students finance those purchases, rent, or even borrow tools until they are sure they are in the right program?

CHAPTER 11

Recruitment Strategies

By Sarah Coen

"The nicest thing about not planning is that failure comes as a complete surprise and is not preceded by a period of worry and depression."—Sir John Harvey-Jones

Student recruitment is a crucial component of a strategic enrollment plan (SEP). To reach a desired state, a campus must recruit the students who fit that planned state. This desired group may include traditional undergraduate, graduate, and nontraditional students. This chapter will mainly describe traditional undergraduate practices, though most, if not all, of these practices can apply to other populations. We will address specific practices related to adult, online, and graduate students in Chapter 13. An annual plan plays a pivotal role in the SEP process and, at most campuses, is separated by traditional, transfer, graduate, and nontraditional plans. It must not only be data-informed, but also in alignment with the overall goals contained in the SEP.

> **CHAPTER HIGHLIGHTS**
>
> - **The annual recruitment plan should support SEP goals**
>
> - **Building relationships is key**
>
> - **Subpopulations require differing approaches**

The quote above by Sir John Harvey-Jones sums up how many campuses feel about developing an annual recruitment plan. Often, recruitment plans are little more than a laundry list of recruitment activities or a calendar of admissions events—neither of which represent a plan. A well-conceived recruitment plan is an organized thought process and communication tool that describes what the institution wants to achieve and how it will accomplish it. In short, it is the roadmap to reaching new student recruitment goals.

A primary difference between an SEP and an annual marketing and recruitment plan is that the marketing/recruitment plan is typically developed within the office of admissions—where accountability lies—while the SEP is developed with the involvement of a wide range of offices including faculty, staff, and administration throughout the campus. For example, if the SEP calls for an increase in academic profile, then the annual recruitment plan should include supporting strategies, such as purchasing high-ability student names for search and aggressively recruiting them to campus. The admissions team now needs to take this action item and determine which purchased names can best shape the desired profile. The strategic enrollment plan drives the priorities of the admissions office and requires the leaders within admissions to determine the steps needed to reach the strategic priority.

Consider Table 11-1 from the *Marketing and Student Recruitment Practices at Four-Year and Two-Year Institutions* (Ruffalo Noel Levitz, 2016), which shows the percent of institutions that have an annual recruitment plan and the percent that consider theirs to be of excellent quality.

Table 11-1: Prevalence of Recruitment Planning by Institution Type

My institution has a written annual recruitment plan		
	Percent of respondents in agreement	
Type of institution	**Yes**	**Yes, and it's of excellent quality**
Four-year private	85.1%	15.5%
Four-year public	81.6%	22.5%
Two-year public	86.7%	NA

TM

Source: Ruffalo Noel Levitz, 2016 Marketing and Student Recruitment Practices Benchmark Report

Even though the majority of respondents reported having plans in place, a significant number failed to rate their plan as excellent. The recruitment of new students has become fiercely competitive and requires masterful planning and execution. Planning alone does not ensure results, but it does provide disciplined appraisal, goal setting, and strategizing that can minimize failure. Developing an annual recruitment plan that includes defining the current state, setting goals, identifying strategies, and writing the action plans can vastly improve the chances that new student recruitment and net tuition revenue goals will be met.

Defining the current state of recruitment

The initial step in recruitment planning is to document the current state of enrollment through the use of historical data, market research, and an articulation of the internal and external environments in which the enrollment effort must be carried out. This step usually involves the following tasks aligned with the SEP process:

1. Review the institutional mission statement that describes the basic reason for the existence of the organization.

2. Confirm the primary target markets and enrollment growth strategies your campus is pursuing and has outlined in the SEP.

3. Review the SEP and mission statement, making sure they are consistent with each other.

4. Assess current strengths, weaknesses, opportunities, and threats, or driving forces (combination of strengths and opportunities) and restraining forces (combination of weaknesses and threats). These driving and restraining forces should be included in the situation analysis and represent many of the forces that must be overcome—and exploited—in order to achieve enrollment goals.

Supporting data for recruitment planning

Chapter 5 discusses the importance of data-informed rather than data-driven planning. This holds true for the annual recruitment plan as well as the SEP. Unfortunately, what tends to drive most recruitment goals is the number of students needed to support the operating budget. A much better approach is to compile and review historical recruitment and admissions data, both overall and by specific program. Basic funnel and stream metrics (prospects, inquiries, applications, acceptances, deposits, and matriculants) should be included in the situation analysis, as well as any research pertinent to the planning process (e.g., source code analysis, territorial analysis, conversion and yield analysis, campus visit analysis, SAT analysis, and competition and market share analysis).

In addition to historical funnel and stream data, it is important to consider other data and research that can help drive the recruitment plan. The list of data below could be collected as campuses begin to write their SEP, as noted in Chapters 4 and 9.

1. Review appropriate demographic trends and environmental data, such as:
   - In-state high school population and other important markets;
   - Graduation rates and projections;
   - Migration patterns (percent expected to stay in state or leave state for college);
   - Preferred majors by high school graduates;
   - SAT/ACT test score analysis;
   - Education attainment patterns of adults in the primary market; and
   - Job/Industry trends in the primary market.

2. Evaluate any information from recent competition studies to include:
   - Five-year enrollment patterns;
   - Tuition and institutional aid of primary competition;
   - Key recruitment themes and messages (as seen on competitors' websites and in literature); and
   - Market share of your institution compared with primary competition.

3. Review results of recent market survey research, to include:
   - Lost inquiry study;
   - High school counselor survey; and
   - Admitted student questionnaire survey (for enrolled and non-enrolled students).

4. Use data to confirm target markets.

5. If necessary, conduct a program-by-program (major fields of study or concentrations) analysis and establish desired enrollment state and marketing/recruiting needs.

6. Develop a list of recruitment planning assumptions (e.g., staffing, budget, and competition).

Annual goal setting

While SEP calls for three-, five-, or seven-year enrollment goals, recruitment plans call for annual recruitment goals. Recruitment goals must be quantified and understandable to all who are accountable for achieving those goals. These goals must also be shared with all members of the enrollment team and the broader campus community.

As stated in Chapter 7, campuses must determine whether they want to increase, maintain, or shrink enrollment. The examples shared in that chapter are worth repeating here, as they should also guide the annual recruitment planning process:

- **Increase** enrollment, because a campus is focused on growing net tuition revenue, has capacity to grow, and has academic programs with growing demand.

- **Maintain** enrollment, because an institution has little or no capacity to grow but may have other enrollment goals, such as improving academic quality, shaping the enrollment in specific academic programs, improving the geographic and/or socioeconomic diversity of the student body, etc.

- **Shrink** enrollment, either by design (perhaps due to focusing on higher student academic quality and/or a narrowed set of academic offerings) or by necessity (e.g., the catchment area is regional and there are declining high school graduates, there is declining employer support for students pursuing master's programs, there is increasing competition from a lower-cost provider, or there is declining demand for the academic programs that have been offered historically).

The following points are also important to the goal-setting process:

- Goals are an expression of the outcomes of the recruitment plan.
- Goals are derived directly from the enrollment planning process.
- Goals are most often, but not always, expressed quantitatively and relate to desired enrollment outcomes. If a goal is not measurable, it should at least be recognizable and qualitative in character.
- Generally, recruitment plans contain no more than three to five major goals.
- Goals are stated as simply and concisely as possible.
- Effective recruitment plans begin with a clear understanding of the goals that must be achieved in order to succeed.
- Goals are always supported by one or more strategies.
- Goals are mutually agreed upon by all whose efforts will achieve them.

Table 11-2 provides a framework for setting funnel and stream goals. This framework should be used for setting both the overall new student enrollment goal, as well as other subpopulation goals (transfer, honors, graduate, out-of-state, etc.).

Table 11-2: Admissions Funnel Framework: Quantitative Enrollment Goals

Enrollment goals for each funnel stage						
Stage	Year one final	Year two final	Year three final	Year four final	Four- to five-year average	Next year's goal
Prospects						
Progression percent						
Inquiries						
Conversion percent						
Applicants						
Completed applications						
Accept percent						
Accepts						
Yield percent						
Confirms						
Capture percent						
Enrolled						

TM

Table 11-3 provides some examples of the goals that might drive a recruitment plan.

Table 11-3: Examples of Typical Recruitment Planning Goals

Recruitment goals

Overall goal: Enroll a total of 2,200 new students for fall 2016, consisting of 1,500 new freshmen and 700 new transfer students. This is compared to 1,862 new students in fall 2015 (1,190 FTIC/672 transfer).

Goal one: Enroll an entering class with an average high school grade point average of 3.2 or better (vs. 3.15) and an average ACT score (or equivalent) of 23 or better (vs. 22.5).

Goal two: Achieve 10 percent domestic minority representation in the entering class (150 students vs. 125).

Goal three: Achieve 6 percent out-of-state representation in the first-year class, vs. 3 to 5 percent in recent years.

Goal four: Increase new student enrollment in the College of Arts and Sciences by 125 students, from 750 to 875.

TM

Additional note about the evolution of funnel theory and management

For decades, enrollment managers have shaped their recruitment strategies around a stage-based enrollment funnel (Figure 11-1), moving students linearly from prospect to inquiry to applicant to decision to deposit to enrollee. There was a direct correlation between the top of the funnel and the bottom; to increase the number of enrolled students at the end, campuses were encouraged to increase the number of prospective students at the top. This model worked well when campuses had more direct control over the information-gathering process for prospective college students.

Figure 11-1: Enrollment Model: Traditional vs. Current Student Behavior

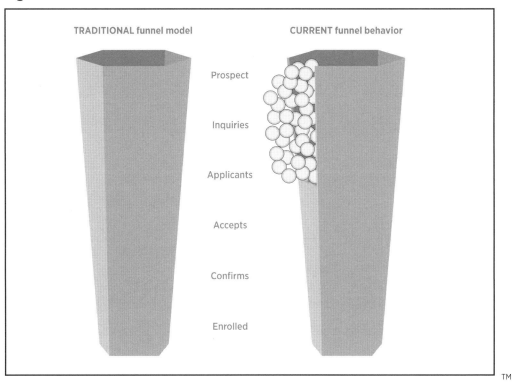

However, that orderly flow has been severely disrupted during the last decade. Due to shifting demographics, technological changes, major shifts in the mindset of prospective students, and the role of parents in the enrollment process, the traditional funnel management approach is no longer adequate in and of itself for both predicting student behavior and giving enrollment managers a reliable model for their recruitment strategies.

In today's college search environment, the traditional funnel has evolved, with a model emerging that Ruffalo Noel Levitz calls the student engagement stream, a concept that gears campuses to consider the most effective ways to engage and re-engage students across the entire student lifecycle.

Figure 11-2: Stages of the Student Lifecycle: Engagement Stream

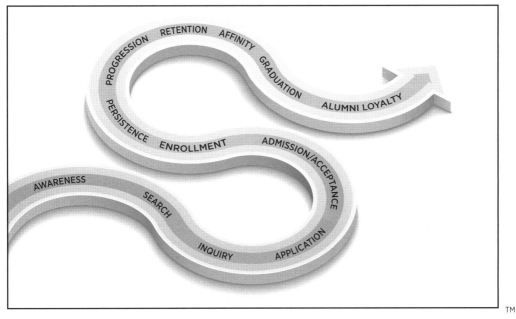

TM

Tables 11-4 and 11-5, from the Ruffalo Noel Levitz *2014 Admissions Funnel Benchmarks Report*, illustrate the average conversion and yield rates for both four-year public and private institutions from 2008 to 2014. And while the funnel concept has evolved into the stream, it is still important to measure such rates to determine the students' level of engagement with the institution.

Table 11-4: Four-Year Private Institutions—FTIC Student Funnel Rates

Median Funnel Rates	2014	2013	2012	2011	2010	2009	2008
Conversion rate from inquiry to application (all inquiries)	15%	15%	16%	17%	15%	15%	13%
Conversion rate from inquiry to application (not counting inquiries who made their first contact by submitting an application)	9%	9%	10%	11%	10%	10%	NA
Admit rate from application to admit (all applications)	65%	64%	64%	64%	66%	65%	71%
Admit rate from application to admit (completed applications only)	89%	89%	86%	86%	86%	86%	87%
Yield rate from admission to enrollment	26%	27%	29%	31%	29%	29%	31%
Capture rate from deposited to enrollment	91% (Melt: 10%)	90% (Melt: 11%)	91% (Melt: 9%)	91% (Melt: 9%)	88% (Melt: 12%)	88% (Melt: 12%)	90% (Melt: 10%)

TM

Source: Ruffalo Noel Levitz, 2014 Admissions Funnel Benchmarks Report

Table 11-5: Four-Year Public Institutions—FTIC Student Funnel Rates

Median Funnel Rates	2014	2013	2012	2011	2010	2009	2008
Conversion rate from inquiry to application (all inquiries)	30%	34%	33%	33%	35%	34%	33%
Conversion rate from inquiry to application (not counting inquiries who made their first contact by submitting an application)	17%	19%	22%	24%	23%	21%	NA
Admit rate from application to admit (all applications)	70%	67%	66%	69%	66%	65%	66%
Admit rate from application to admit (completed applications only)	89%	88%	85%	81%	82%	85%	71%
Yield rate from admission to enrollment	36%	37%	38%	40%	41%	43%	38%
Capture rate from deposited/confirmed to enrollment	94% (Melt: 7%)	95% (Melt: 6%)	95% (Melt: 5%)	95% (Melt: 5%)	93% (Melt: 7%)	91% (Melt: 9%)	92% (Melt: 8%)

TM

Source: Ruffalo Noel Levitz, 2014 Admissions Funnel Benchmarks Report

When an institution's conversion and yield rates fall below the national average, it typically indicates that new or improved strategies need to be considered in order to engage students at that particular point in the stream. For example, if a private institution has been converting admits to enrollees at a rate of 20 percent, instead of the national average of 26 to 27 percent, the campus might consider enhancing its post-admit communication plan to include messages of value and outcomes. This may also indicate an opportunity to improve the effectiveness of the institution's financial aid strategy.

As a campus seeks to sync its recruitment and SEP, the understanding and management of these important rates and use of these metrics (and how they are changing) is critical to align action with goal setting and a basic underlying foundation of strong new student recruitment. Campuses must focus throughout the stream/funnel, but need to remain keenly aware of the bottom lines—the number of students enrolled and graduated. As the enrollment team works to engage students at each phase of the student lifecycle, the goal should be to use data, including conversion and yield metrics, to meet stated enrollment goals. Ideally, the team will build an entering class that will not only enroll, but retain, graduate, and give back to the institution.

Recruitment strategies

The next step is identifying the strategies needed to reach annual goals. Strategies should include a connection to the institution's mission and values, which link academic, co-curricular, and enrollment planning and align them with fiscal planning. Effective recruitment plans include a variety of strategies that will vary by institution type and by student population, but some are central to any plan. While the following list of strategies is not exhaustive, it does represent the essential elements of new student recruitment.

Building the prospect and inquiry pools

Even with the changing dynamics, prospect and inquiry pool development is important to any sound recruitment program. A successful admissions operation will intentionally and consistently manage the development of a prospective student pool and inquiry pool to reach the desired goals for new student enrollment. Although the shape, size, and characteristics of these pools are changing (mainly as more students are waiting to make the initial contact with the institution at the applicant stage), it is still essential to understand how pools are built, which sources are more predictive of enrollment, and what opportunities for improvement exist to strengthen communication at each stage. The critical element in the development of these pools is that they are of the right quantity and quality to reach enrollment goals. Simply filling the top of the funnel does not mean that enrollment goals will be met.

Inquiries can be categorized into four distinct types, each converting and yielding at different rates. Campuses should attempt to develop an appropriate mix of inquiries that will achieve the targeted percentage goal from inquiry to applicant to enrolled.

1. **Student-initiated:** These inquiries often convert and yield at the highest rates, since they come directly from students as they express an interest in the institution. These include standardized test scores, applications as first source, emails, phone calls, and campus visits, among others. It is wise for campuses to heavily focus on strategies to get more student-initiated contacts into the inquiry pool.

2. **Travel-initiated:** These are cultivated during counselor travel, including high school visits, college fair programs, community college meetings, employer visits, off-campus receptions, and other events. They are a direct result of the territory management model discussed later in this chapter.

3. **Solicited:** These are prospective student names that are purchased from a variety of sources (e.g., ACT, College Board, NRCCUA, and CollegeFish.org). Once the prospective student expresses interest, either as a result of a direct mail or email campaign or at any time during the recruitment cycle, he/she should be entered into the inquiry pool. This may also include a subset of search names that are directly loaded into the inquiry pool using a predictive model score or some other qualification technique.

4. **Referral:** These are names provided to the admissions office by alumni, faculty, intercollegiate athletics, churches, and others. Creating a plan for generating or asking for these referrals is an important step in building the inquiry pool.

Table 11-6: Example of Initial Inquiry Source Code Report

Source	High school visit	ACT test submitted	NRCCUA search name	College fair	Web inquiry	Application as first source
Inquiries						
Current year						
Last year						
Difference						
Applications						
Current year						
Last year						
Difference						
Accepts						
Current year						
Last year						
Difference						
Confirmed/Enrolled						
Current year						
Last year						
Difference						

TM

It is equally important to understand how various inquiry sources impact student engagement and, ultimately, enrollment. Enrollment officers will want to create a basic inquiry-by-source report (see Table 11-6) that tracks the volume of inquiries by source.

Qualifying the pool

Qualification is a systematic process designed to determine the level of student interest in an institution's prospect, inquiry, applicant, and confirmed student pools. Students can be qualified through operations and market research, reply mechanisms (including the initial prospect card), by telephone, or through other personal contact. Qualification has two goals:

1. Identify and target students who are genuinely interested in the institution.
2. Remove students with little or no interest in attendance.

An effective qualification system allows the enrollment management team to focus scarce resources on those students with the greatest *propensity* to enroll. See Figure 11-3.

With *grading*, an institution rates the desirability of prospective students at the prospect, inquiry, applicant, and decision stages. This is generally accomplished by examining student characteristics, such as academic profile or racial/ethnic category (objective assessment), and through personal contact (subjective assessment). An effective grading system allows an institution to focus resources on those students it has the greatest *interest* in enrolling.

There are a number of advanced methods, such as statistical modeling or predictive modeling that can identify the best prospects for a campus and make the qualification process much more precise. The data-informed nature of these methods also makes them well suited for the SEP process, in addition to recruitment planning.

Figure 11-3: Influence Continuum

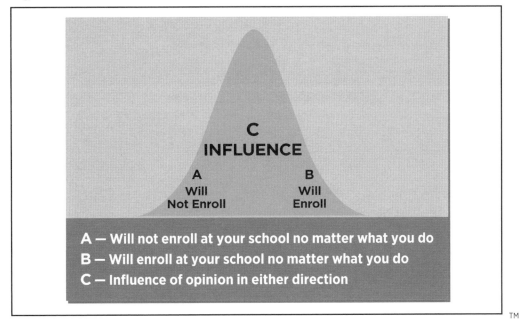

C
INFLUENCE

A
**Will
Not Enroll**

B
**Will
Enroll**

A — Will not enroll at your school no matter what you do
B — Will enroll at your school no matter what you do
C — Influence of opinion in either direction

TM

Student search

Student search plans should build awareness of an institution in primary, secondary, tertiary, and national markets, when appropriate. However, today's student search process needs to be approached differently than in previous years, giving less attention to response rates and focusing more on actual enrollment rates. With the increase in stealth shoppers (those whose first formal contact with the institution is as applicants), student search has shifted from a response mechanism to a critical process for building institutional awareness. Institutions are finding that, by getting their brand into the marketplace much earlier, their applicant pools are increasing even if their inquiry pools are not growing as quickly.

Beyond the name purchase itself, institutions are placing increased efforts on direct marketing campaigns for search names. It is not uncommon for today's search campaigns to include multiple messages, in both written and electronic form. The old way of sending a search piece and waiting for a response no longer works. Consider the data in Figure 11-4.

Figure 11-4: Written Communications a Prospective Student Received by Stage

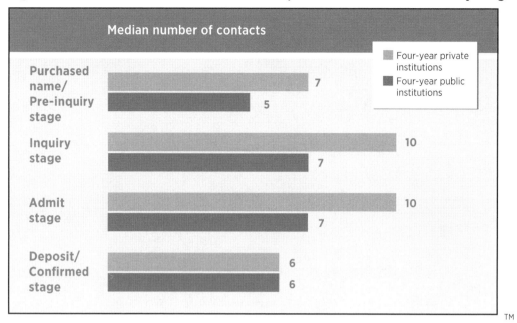

Source: Ruffalo Noel Levitz, 2016 Marketing and Student Recruitment Practices Benchmark Report

Consider these two strategies when implementing a successful search campaign:

1. **Treat student search as a continuous process throughout the academic year.**
   Today's students explore colleges when *they* are ready, not when the institution is. Campuses must be constantly ready to communicate with them throughout the year. In addition, the communication timeline for college-bound high school students has expanded in both directions. More sophomores take the PSAT than juniors (College Board, 2014), which has pushed the recruitment communication cycle earlier. At the other end, consolidated data from Ruffalo Noel Levitz clients shows nearly 30 percent of students who ultimately enrolled entered their inquiry pool as rising seniors the summer before their final year or during the fall of senior year. This also illustrates an advantage of an engagement stream approach compared to a stage-based funnel. A junior who has inquired and applied is likely to exhibit different behavior and decision making than a student who applies in the fall of senior year. Yet the funnel model would treat both of those students as if they were in the same stage. A continuous stream model would instead place those students where they reside in the *enrollment decision* process, with the senior likely to be further along and quicker to make a decision.

   Prospective students are a reflection of consumers today—more students are waiting to make contact with campuses because they can learn so much about an institution independently, without the campus knowing. However, students still lack an ability to accurately assess fit, which can affect yield, melt, and attrition. Campuses therefore have to be quick to engage students, help them assess *fit*, and build a relationship that leads to enrollment for students who are a good fit.

In addition, campuses have to engage students across multiple channels—via mail, email, web, social media, phone, and in person—to reinforce the institutional brand and give students incentive to keep progressing toward enrollment. This should be done at every point in the process, from the sophomore PSAT prospect to the late-term senior. While the range and timing of communications may seem daunting, they also give campuses a wide net to cast for students.

2. **Analyze and filter communication strategies to prospects by level of yield.**
   For many campuses, past list-purchase practices determine the number of students searched, without regard for what percentage of the enrolled student population came from the search pool. This can lead to an incomplete canvassing of an institution's primary and secondary markets. For instance, a combined prospect list might contain only 40 percent of an institution's enrolled class, leaving the other 60 percent to chance.

   A strategic student search campaign requires knowledge of how many of an institution's enrolled students came from its prospect pool, regardless of how those students eventually became applicants—and regardless of whether the prospect responded directly to the solicitation/search. This last point is key, because in the era of stealth shopping among prospective students, many will independently research a campus by visiting its website, Facebook page, YouTube channel, or other channels. They may actually be engaged with a campus, even though they are not making contact as a traditional inquiry.

   Once a campus understands the behavior of how students in its pool are moving toward enrollment, the institution can develop strategies to filter communications across different channels and with different audiences. For example, a campus could:

   - Extend marketing communications traditionally reserved for inquiries to prospects (or subsets of the prospect base).
   - Allocate communications by predetermined level of interest and yield within prospect pools—reaching all prospects with some communication, but saving more intensive and expensive communications with groups more likely to enroll.
   - Build an engaging web and online presence that connects with the stealth shopper but also appeals to students in the marketing communications flow who want to continue to research a campus without direct contact.

Marketing and communication

Strong prospective student communication plans begin with an understanding of the institutional image and brand. Branding is generally an institutionwide initiative that involves university relations and enrollment management (at the very least), and should also be part of institutional strategic planning initiatives or discussions. As outlined in Chapter 9, branding is what an institution is known for or wants to be known for—what makes it unique and distinctive. For branding to be effective in new student recruitment, an institution must continually assess how to deliver on the promise of its brand. If a brand communicates "student success is our business," then graduation rates must be well above average, retention initiatives must permeate institutional planning priorities, and alumni successes must be well-tracked and documented.

Messaging involves the expression of key strengths that speak to the institution brand and may include some targeted messages for selected audiences. Messaging helps to translate why the brand has value for the audience. Unfortunately, many colleges miss the mark when it comes to selling value. The focus of the key messages tends to be more about the atmosphere of campus (student life, religious affiliation, facilities) than on the actual product—the academic experience and related outcomes. While co-curricular offerings are important and do drive some students' decision making (e.g., playing a sport and/or receiving a scholarship to play a sport), the majority of students enroll and graduate because of the quality and outcome of the academic program.

Once the key messages have been identified, the challenging task of communicating them to prospective students and their families begins. Building effective communication plans for today's prospective students can be daunting, to say the least. While it is clear that students use many forms of technology, including web, email, social media, phone, and texting to communicate, research also suggests that they still rely on traditional communication. In the 2015 Ruffalo Noel Levitz report, *High School Students' and Parents' Perceptions of and Preferences for Communication With Colleges*, 37 percent of students reported that they preferred direct mail for their first contact with a campus.

One common misperception is that marketing ends when a student is admitted. This is a mistake, especially as more students apply to multiple institutions than before the advent of online applications, pre-populated applications, and the Common Application. Effective communication plans should be integrated with the recruitment process, begin at the search stage, and continue until the student is enrolled. Even after students have made a deposit, it is wise to keep communicating with them and create compelling reasons for them to see their enrollment all the way through.

As with student search, marketing and communication metrics are changing. Given the importance of marketing to recruitment, as well as the importance of recruitment to SEP, campuses should consider tracking metrics such as:

- Institutional awareness in primary and secondary markets (how many students in those markets have heard of the campus prior to any contact?).
- Awareness of primary strengths and academic offerings (for what is the institution known?).
- Awareness of the primary strengths and academic offerings of main competitors.
- Impressions of the value of a degree from the institution (such as job opportunities, post-baccalaureate study, and alumni success).

Some of these metrics, such as institutional awareness, may be quantifiable. Others are more qualitative (such as most-recognized academic offerings), but can be tracked year-to-year to discern whether the campus is reaching its desired state in its target markets. Depending on the research capabilities of the institution, a campus may want to engage outside, specialized market research services to periodically examine some areas (at the beginning of the SEP process, then again every two to three years while moving toward the desired state).

Territory management

Territory management assigns the recruitment and enrollment of students from a specific geographic area to one or more admissions representatives. Objectives include:

- Establishing application and enrollment goals by territory. These goals should be aligned with any new market development goals that are outlined in the SEP.
- Empowering admissions staff to develop territorial recruitment strategies.
- Providing recruitment staff with budget responsibilities within their territories.
- Making certain that the same staff member works with a student from point-of-inquiry through enrollment.
- Assigning responsibility for transfer and adult students to a dedicated transfer/adult counselor(s).

Relationship building is probably the single most important duty of the territory manager. The territory manager should build relationships with secondary school counselors, community college advising staff, and prospective students and their families during school visits, college fairs, and receptions. Face-to-face relationships may be time consuming, but they provide great value when it comes to enrollment. By developing personal relationships, the territory manager has the greatest ability to motivate students to take the next steps toward enrollment.

Tracking the conversion and yield metrics for each counselor/territory is an important part of the territory management model. Table 11-7 provides a framework for territory metrics.

Table 11-7: Example of Framework for Territory Analysis Report

Territory/ Counselor	Territory 1	Territory 2	Territory 3	Territory 4	Territory 5
Inquiries					
Current year					
Last year					
Difference					
Applications					
Current year					
Last year					
Difference					
Accepts					
Current year					
Last year					
Difference					
Confirmed/Enrolled					
Current year					
Last year					
Difference					

TM

Campus visit programming

When a prospective student begins to envision him/herself as a member of the campus community, the likelihood of the student applying and enrolling goes up dramatically. Therefore, virtually every strategy contained within a recruitment plan is designed to attract a prospective student and his/her family to visit the campus, and these campus visit strategies are arguably the most important ones implemented during the admissions cycle.

There are many types of campus visit opportunities, including both individual and group options. Often, the mission and size of the institution will determine which are best for the students they serve.

1. **Individual visits:** Prospective students and their families should be encouraged to visit campus individually. This visit could include meeting with admissions staff, taking a campus tour, sitting in on a class or meeting with a faculty member, meeting with financial aid staff, and spending the night in the residence hall (some of these visit elements will depend on the type/size of the institution).

2. **Group visits:** These events are also very important in the recruitment process and need to be targeted to the appropriate audiences, depending on the time in the recruitment cycle. Group visit opportunities include open houses for inquiries and applicants in the spring and fall, an admitted student day as a way to increase yield, and a college-planning workshop event targeting high school juniors and sophomores.

3. **Transfer visit days:** For most transfer students, the typical open house events will not be appropriate. It is much more effective to host an event that focuses on common transfer student concerns (transfer of credit, paying for college, availability of classes, introduction to other transfer students, etc.).

A note about financial aid

While we cover approaches to financial aid and pricing in Chapter 10, a few comments about the relationship of financial aid to recruitment and admissions are in order. It is essential to have a strong working relationship between admissions and financial aid. Any breakdown in communication between the admissions office, financial aid office, and the prospective student and parent(s) or family members will generally undermine new student enrollment goals. This is true even if a campus has a competitive scholarship and financial aid program in place. The two offices should jointly create a communication plan for students and parents that explains the details of the financial aid process *and* communicates the value of earning a degree from the institution. This plan might include the following:

- Post your net price calculator on the website in a highly visible area so that students and parents can easily find it. Ideally, this calculator will include estimates for merit aid awards as well as federal aid so that it delivers the most competitive net price estimate possible.

- Send early offers of merit aid to all accepted students. Consider including this right on the acceptance letter or in a follow-up letter to arrive within a week of original acceptance.

- Mail financial aid award letters as early as possible. Include payment plan options in the letter.

- Ramp up financial aid follow-up calling efforts. Train and/or retrain staff on this strategy. As an institution, make sure it is clear to the frontline staff what the policy is when families negotiate and to determine if more aid will be offered to families who need or ask for it.

- Develop creative financing options for students. Are there additional types of payment plans to offer (10-month, 12-month, etc.)? Make sure admissions and financial aid staff know how to respond when a family asks for additional assistance.

- Create a cost worksheet and enclose it with the financial aid award. This worksheet will list all of the costs a family may incur during the first year.

- Ensure the bill is accompanied by some type of personalized letter to parents. The letter should include:
  - A personalized message;
  - Statement of value/outcomes;
  - Contact information for questions; and
  - Payment plan options.

- Include more in-person appointments with financial aid staff in pre-summer orientation programs. One general financial aid session will likely not be sufficient for most families.

Data and reporting

The importance of data has been discussed throughout this book as it relates to defining the current state and goal setting. It is also important to develop data and reporting structures as part of the recruitment strategy to move the campus to the desired state. Campuses should create a basic package of weekly and monthly reports to monitor the progress of the marketing/recruitment program and evaluate the effectiveness of key marketing and recruitment strategies. This monitoring will also provide data for recruitment-related key performance indicators. Table 11-8 shows an example of a report that can track progress for various strategies outlined in the recruitment plan and, ultimately, the SEP.

Table 11-8: Example of Framework for Recruitment Strategy Report

Report title	Variable	Variable	Variable	Variable	Variable	Variable
Inquiries						
Current year						
Last year						
Difference						
Applications						
Current year						
Last year						
Difference						
Accepts						
Current year						
Last year						
Difference						
Confirmed/Enrolled						
Current year						
Last year						
Difference						

TM

Because of the importance of data in the marketing and recruitment operation, an increasing number of institutions have created a data analyst position within enrollment services to manage the admissions database, produce reports, and support implementation of all communication streams (direct mail, electronic, and telephone).

Putting strategies into action—Developing action plans

As described in Chapter 6, but important to reiterate here, the final step of the planning process is to devise action plans for each of the key strategies. Each strategy must be supported by one or more specific activities necessary to successfully accomplish the strategy/objective. The activities, taken in total, comprise the action plan. This will be the most detailed and time-consuming part of the planning process. The action plans represent the guts of the plan.

Good action plans always include the following components:

1. **What will be done?**
   Specifically describe a quantifiable and measurable activity.

2. **When will it be done?**
   Provide timetables that clearly show key dates and deadlines.

3. **Who will be responsible?**
   Designate clear assignments of responsibility for performing important tasks.

4. **How much will it cost?**
   Provide budget information showing whether the strategy will save money, increase overall costs, or be budget neutral.

5. **How will accomplishments be tracked?**
   Establish and list the methods of evaluation or control that will be used to monitor progress and measure success or failure of the actions.

The following reminders help to develop effective activity/action plans, which can be tracked using an action plan report similar to the strategy report shown in Table 11-8.

- One or more action plans may be needed to implement a key strategy (e.g., a separate action plan for each individual student search implemented by the institution and action plans for different types of campus visit events).

- A description of the activity should be provided.

- The timetable should include a date by which each task should be completed. If appropriate, it is also permissible to designate an activity as "ongoing."

- Note responsibility for the implementation of the activity/action plan. This may be an individual, a committee, or a functional area.

- Include in the budget section *any anticipated new or reduced direct expenses not currently budgeted* that will be incurred in implementing the activity.

- Evaluation and control may be as simple as indicating that the activity has been fully or partially accomplished, or may link back to conversion and yield rates.

- The activity/action plan should be complete enough to provide direction to those responsible for its implementation.

Focusing on subpopulations

As we further advance recruitment practices, development of specific subpopulation strategies is increasingly critical. Given current high school graduation projections, enrolling subpopulations may, in fact, help campuses achieve or exceed enrollment goals. Three of these subpopulations—adult, online, and graduate students—we treat comprehensively in Chapter 13.

Like any other element related to SEP, institutions should take a data-informed approach to determine which subpopulations to pursue, how the enrollment of those populations will strengthen the SEP process and move the institution closer to its desired state, and how to track key metrics related to their enrollment. The campus should avoid targeting specific subpopulations based on existing assumptions about those students, or a general notion that the campus needs a subpopulation, without researching the cost and benefits of recruiting students with those characteristics.

In addition, institutions should develop specific communications tailored to those subpopulations. The campus website should have pages dedicated to those student populations, and targeted communication flows should address their concerns and interests. As presented earlier in this chapter, many of the general recruitment strategies for traditional students are also well-suited for recruiting subpopulations.

Transfer students

Transfer students approach receiving campuses with a frame of reference—their previous college experience—adding to either their comprehension or confusion when considering a new institution. They may be transferring following two successful years at a community college, looking for a fresh start after a poor experience at their first institution, or returning to college after stopping out for any variety of reasons. Transfer students also tend to be more focused, having previously selected a major or program of study, and have an idea of the career they want to enter. They often also have career, family, financial, and other obligations that can compete with their educational plans, which can create enrollment challenges for campuses.

As such, this significant enrollment market should receive the same planning time, attention, and energy as the first-time-in-college (FTIC) market. In fact, for some institutions, transfer enrollment may well be considered a primary market. Therefore, systems should be in place to ensure that transfer students are not only recruited, but also offered a seamless and easy enrollment process focused on helping them quickly move from entrance to degree completion.

While cost, financial aid, and academic reputation are among the primary student enrollment factors (Ruffalo Noel Levitz, 2016), there are three additional motivating factors for transfer students. Paying attention to them is important in building an effective transfer recruitment plan.

1. Maintaining credit for courses they have already taken.
2. Academic advising.
3. Career counseling and placement.

Note that maintaining credit is by far the most important consideration among transfer students. They want to know how much credit they will receive toward their general education requirements for degree completion as well as toward the requirements in their major field.

It is also important to recognize that transfer students usually make their decisions fairly quickly. It is common for the first point of contact (inquiry) to be the application, and as such, conversion and yield strategies are nearly the same. This compression of time means that campuses must be poised to respond quickly to transfer student needs.

Veterans

Many institutions are beginning to recognize the importance of having new student enrollment plans devised specifically for veterans. Enrollment offices must work in partnership with veterans' services and determine how their funding (often supported by the government), prior learning credit, and transfer credits are processed. As the institution considers marketing to recruit more students with military experience, the campus must review partnership opportunities with the Transition Assistance Program (TAP). The law creating TAP established a partnership among the Department of Defense, Department of Veterans Affairs, and Department of Transportation, as well as the Department of Labor Veterans' Employment and Training Services (VETS) to give employment and training information to armed forces members within 180 days of separation or retirement (U.S. Department of Labor, 2011).

International recruitment

Over the past decade, international student mobility has grown enormously. As a result, international student enrollment has become a key priority for many institutions around the world, particularly in countries that are the largest recipients of international student enrollment. According to the OECD Education Indicators Report, countries receiving the most inbound international students include the United States, the United Kingdom, Germany, France, and Australia. With a declining domestic pool of high school graduates (in the United States, Canada, Australia, New Zealand, and the United Kingdom) combined with growing reliance on tuition revenue, the focus on international students has never been greater. Institutions considering entering or expanding in the international market should adopt a five-step approach:

1. Conduct a thorough campus readiness assessment and institutional audit of corresponding personnel, structures, and programs.
2. Draft strategies and corresponding goals.
3. Execute effectively.
4. Measure outcomes.
5. Revise strategies and continue the cycle.

Assessing campus readiness to recruit and support international students

An audit of existing data and analysis reports (international enrollment data and graduation rates), financial and human resources, current recruitment strategies, communication plans, financial aid strategies, the college's website, and technological capabilities as they relate to the needs of prospective international students should be the first step in the development of an international recruitment and student support strategy. If the institution has a clearly defined international mission, philosophy, and agreed-upon goals, the fundamentals of a domestic recruitment plan can work well in international student markets. Institutions must have a thorough understanding of the various educational systems, world markets, demographics, migration patterns, and country-specific aid and funding streams.

Consideration of the institution's current state needs to include such features such as campus location, academic and support services, housing options, and existing international opportunities that help attract, retain, progress, and graduate international students. The first feature, location, is often confounded with the other features of regional demographics and ethnic mix. We are familiar with having to frame benefits of our campus locations for domestic students, regardless of whether they are urban, rural, or regional. For international students, locations outside of globally familiar cities (e.g., New York, Chicago, Toronto, Los Angeles) must often be analyzed for features that will assist in providing international students with comforts sufficient to aid in their transition to campus and their ongoing persistence. These features may include pockets of ethnic diversity, access to religion or places of worship, immigrant or expatriate communities with native language ability, and dietary options germane to the student's country of origin. Institutions may have exceptional domestic recruitment operations, but being truly global and enrolling a significant international student population requires knowledge of the local culture to be able to nuance the "excellence" messages to both the student and his/her parent.

The institutional self-assessment must also extend to academic and support services for international students. Are faculty and staff professionally trained to meet the needs of international students? Are they given professional development so they are equipped to properly handle academic, support, and disciplinary issues for students from a variety of cultural backgrounds? Organizations such as the Institute for International Education (www.iie.org), World Education Services (www.wes.org), and the American Association of Collegiate Registrars and Admissions Officers (www.aacrao.org) have excellent resources for these purposes.

Another opportunity for institutions to excel is in international student housing options. One size does not fit every culture, and institutions that take the time to understand the individual student needs as well as the cultural needs for the country of origin will increase the likelihood of having content students in campus housing.

International students, parents, and extended families use global measures like rankings to quickly and easily identify world-class programs for them to pursue. If globally ranked programs are already offered, an institution is most likely already attracting international enrollees. The caveat is that the institution must have a responsive admissions and enrollment process to ensure international applicants are not implicitly turned away due to factors such as admissions offer timing, lack of responsiveness, poor communication (either in English or applicant's native language), or lack of financial aid or scholarship.

Institutions must also evaluate the alignment of current academic offerings with programs in demand by international students. There are many quality sources of secondary data to answer the "student demand" question. The Institute of International Education's annual reports and myriad data-rich surveys, studies, and analyses are an excellent place to begin to determine whether an institution's academic offerings match up with the academic interests of international students and their families. Enrollment managers have often been asked to try and use international enrollment as a panacea for enrollment shortfalls in underperforming domestic programs. There are two main reasons why this presumption is misdirected. First, international students channel their academic interests in a relatively narrow band of academic programs and offerings. They will not be persuaded easily, if at all, to pursue studies in other areas. Second, their list of possible institutions to apply to is commonly tied to external quality measures like rankings, graduate success, career success, and/or famous alumni. Accordingly, programs that underperform domestically often cannot demonstrate success using these types of external quality measures.

For institutions that do not have highly-recognized quality academic programs, well-done academic pages on the institution's website can serve to support their recruitment efforts. The *2015 Ruffalo Noel Levitz International E-Expectations Report* noted that academics, cost, admissions, and financial aid are the four highest-ranked web content areas for international students.

Developing strategies and setting goals

Growth strategies may focus on one or more quadrants of the growth strategy matrix (see Chapter 6): market penetration, market development, program development, and/or diversification.

When considering which markets to focus on for international students, campus planners must consider both the offerings of competitors and the competitive conditions that exist based on what competitor institutions undertake in-country to support their enrollment goals. International recruitment plans need to be significantly more focused than a goal to "increase enrollment of international students." Instead, planners should identify specific target markets—countries, cities, provinces, or municipalities—for development based on an understanding of both institutional strengths and the educational needs arising in those target markets.

The majority (60 percent) of international students already have a particular school in mind, and this is their motivation for studying abroad (Ruffalo Noel Levitz, 2015). Therefore, schools with little or no brand recognition in various international markets must create opportunities for themselves. For instance, there are many excellent examples of leveraging competitor strengths to meet one's own international enrollment goals. International students are open to pathway options for their postsecondary needs, which may include articulation into graduate school from a local undergraduate school, or from an English as a Second Language (ESL) provider to an undergraduate program. Partnerships may be established that will benefit both institutions' enrollment and international profile, and could lower the total cost of enrolling students as a result.

Current activities like study abroad experiences, study tours, overseas summer programming, faculty exchanges or joint research projects, and international alumni programs have the benefit of established relationships and understanding in other countries. These activities can provide excellent opportunities for informal recruitment opportunities in addition to increased brand awareness.

> " A digital presence is essential, not only for admissions purposes, but to generate an appropriate volume of inquiries, allow for meaningful and in-depth browsing of an institution's offerings, and to build an institution's brand. "

International recruitment execution (do's and don'ts)

With strategies identified, the focus should turn to implementation and execution.

A digital presence is essential, not only for admissions purposes, but to generate an appropriate volume of inquiries, allow for meaningful and in-depth browsing of an institution's offerings, and to build an institution's brand by connecting with search engines, online measurement tools, and other indicators of quality.

Access to the Internet is ubiquitous in every major student market, but the tools available in those countries may differ. The most significant example is in China, where Facebook, Twitter, YouTube, and Google are not available. There are domestic alternatives, like Sina Weibo instead of Twitter and Baidu instead of Google search. The indexing services also function better with both native language content and native language indices. Institutions must, as a part of their planning, consider how they will either adapt or adopt the digital requirements of new international target markets and how they will service those markets with content in languages other than English. Communication in native languages can be used to aid comprehension, particularly for parents and other participants in the enrollment decision making process.

Many institutions use recruitment agents as a component of their in-country international enrollment strategy. The use of recruitment agents gives their partner institutions advantages of scale, a keen understanding of local market conditions, and native language communications (particularly with parents, who are key influencers in any international student's enrollment choice). Above and beyond those benefits, recruitment agents also can generate a significant pool of applicants at a relatively low cost to the institution. Recruitment agents are not a solution for all institutions, and should only be used with careful planning, contract negotiation, training, and quality assurance measures to make sure the institution's brand is protected and that the actions of the agent are centered on the best interest of the students they serve.

Another option for boots on the ground is for institutions to seek potential resources through their state government. Frequently, the economic development department within each state has officers stationed in various countries that provide support for U.S. corporations within their states through in-country help or by coordinating various trade mission programs, some of which are specific to education. Seeking their help for country information, contract negotiation, introductions to heads of schools, and language assistance is a cost-effective way to support in-country recruitment opportunities.

Institutions from advanced international destinations such as the United Kingdom and Australia have invested heavily in just-in-time admissions processing for international students. Students, parents, and their agents have come to expect immediate responses from the point of inquiring to the actual processing of the application. Timely responses, in addition to well-timed and effective communications delivered electronically to the student and parent, are the expectation, not the exception. Clearly articulated processes and requirements for the student, parent, and/or agent on the college's website will go a long way to keep a student engaged through enrollment. For most international students, the web is the only source of college/university information.

Measuring outcomes and adapting initiatives

As with any enrollment planning initiative, strategic or otherwise, ongoing assessment and evaluation of international recruitment and student success programs is essential. Well-written action plans will include the metrics that will determine plan success. Monitor those key metrics and adjust plans accordingly. Note the overarching recruitment fundamentals described earlier in this chapter and apply them to international recruitment efforts. Be sure to invest sufficient time for market development strategies; relationships must be developed and given time to mature. For student support initiatives, monitor persistence, progression, and retention metrics (see Chapter 12).

Plan assessment should then feed subsequent action plans and become part of the annual recruitment and retention planning cycle for international student initiatives.

Institutions are greatly enriched by the enrollment of international students. To do so effectively, efficiently, and strategically, institutions must realistically review their current abilities, designing an international plan that fits within the scope of the institution's mission, philosophy, and goals. A thorough consideration of all facets prior to the creation of such a plan will yield success and contribute to the institution's overall enrollment goals.

Conclusion

The purpose of this chapter is to share the essential elements of the recruitment plan and unite these elements with the strategic enrollment plan. The recruitment plan follows four very clear steps:

1. **Conduct a situation analysis.** This includes collecting, developing, and/or compiling all pertinent data and information.

2. **Set data-informed goals.** Use the data from the situation analysis to guide the establishment of recruitment goals. Goals should be quantifiable, measurable, and realistic. Most importantly, they should be mutually agreed upon by all whose efforts must achieve them. Finally, they should clearly be applicable to the overall goals of the SEP.

3. **Develop action plans.** Each key strategy requires a set of action or activity plans, complete with timetables and budgets. The activity plan describes the actions or tactics that will occur in order to implement the strategy and achieve the goal. The action plan should assign responsibility, as well as include clear beginning and end dates, measurable objectives when appropriate, and budget information.

4. **Track progress toward goals and the impact on net revenue.** If goals are quantifiable and measurable, tracking will obviously be much easier. Monitor key metrics rigorously and make adjustments as needed. As always, keep a close watch on recruitment-related net revenue. A loss of revenue could signal inefficiencies, goals that are too ambitious or unfocused, problems with financial aid awarding, or insufficient demand for some academic programs. No strategy should be done twice unless there is some proof that it worked.

Dialogue

Annual enrollment planning processes are focused on meeting annual institution-specific goals and objectives. In strategic enrollment planning, we seek to build a long-range enrollment plan that aligns fiscal health and enrollment. In building this foundation of success, institutions need to ensure they advance or integrate commonly held best practices into the plan as a part of their long-term efforts in the area of new student enrollment. One outcome of the planning process should be to ensure new student enrollment essentials remain strong while enhancing initiatives that are embedded into the new student enrollment plans.

Before proceeding, consider whether you have mapped out an institution-specific focus in these five areas:

1. How do you assess the effectiveness of your current new student enrollment strategies? If you are not assessing the effectiveness of these strategies on an annual basis, you are likely not using your operating and human resources in the most efficient manner. In addition, your new student enrollment essentials may be associated with traditional recruitment and admissions activities. Take a critical look at what you do to influence new student enrollment from an operating and human resource standpoint.

2. How do you involve others, outside the division of enrollment management, in new student enrollment planning? It's great to have a coordinated, interdepartmental approach to new student enrollment; however, as in the SEP process, it is even better to strengthen ownership of new student enrollment planning by including the academic- and student affairs-related service areas, as well as the business and finance and other administrative units at your institution. In this approach, new student enrollment becomes more holistic and is viewed as an institutional priority, rather than simply a divisional one.

3. What will your enrollment landscape look like in five years? In 10 years? How will your enrollment composition change during that time period? How will demographics impact your future enrollment? How will employment or career trends influence enrollment adaptations? What type of student will you be serving? If you are not constructing the what-if scenarios for new student enrollment planning, then you should not be surprised when your enrollment results don't meet expectations.

4. If you have graduate programs, where does graduate enrollment planning fit into your overall plan development? Often, new graduate student enrollment planning is not integrated into the institution's enrollment planning and management enterprise, as it should be in a carefully considered strategic plan (see Chapter 13 for an overview of graduate enrollment).

5. What are the costs to recruit a student? What are those costs by subpopulation? Where are gaps in resources being spent in comparison to market or demographic trends? (For example, are you continuing to invest more in traditional, new student recruitment when, in fact, you should be building an infrastructure to ease the process for transfer students?)

Writing the annual recruitment plan alone will not ensure that new student enrollment goals are met. Implementation is the key to your success.

CHAPTER 12

The Art and Science of Student Success Relationship Management

By Tim Culver

For decades, the major focus of those working in the areas of student success and retention has been to raise overall retention and graduation rates. While these continue to be the most critically important measures, this chapter argues that the traditional measures of fall-to-fall retention and graduation rates within a given number of years are insufficient on their own. What is needed is a more systematic, complementary approach to measurement that keeps educators in closer contact with students—an approach expressed by the student success relationship management model (Figure 12-1). This chapter describes the student success relationship management model as part of the student engagement stream and shows how to use it to monitor students' progress, set goals more precisely, and plan more effectively. This planning process should be integrated into your strategic enrollment plan and long-term enrollment management.

CHAPTER HIGHLIGHTS

- **Enrollments grow with focus on persistence to completion**

- **Benchmarks guide effectiveness of efforts**

- **Influence and targeted approaches matter**

Today, the pressure is on to improve student success outcomes in higher education. Demands for accountability and mounting concerns about access are prompting educators to rethink traditional approaches to retention management and look for new solutions. At the same time, higher education is witnessing unprecedented changes in its students, including a lack of preparedness, greater diversity, and "swirl"—the phenomenon described by experts such as Adelman (2006) in which many students enroll simultaneously at multiple institutions, attend classes intermittently rather than go straight through college, are decreasingly part of the traditional-age range (18 to 22), and hold down competing responsibilities, such as part-time jobs.

In response to this new environment, educators must make a paradigm shift toward a more precise model for measuring desired outcomes. Throughout this book, there have been references to the student engagement stream. Most of the discussion has focused on building search campaigns and comprehensive inquiry management leading to increased new student enrollment. The subsequent part of the student engagement stream includes the continuing student stages that follow the student from the period between admission/deposit through successful completion of the credential or, for many community college students, successful transfer to another institution.

Figure 12-1: Student Success Relationship Management

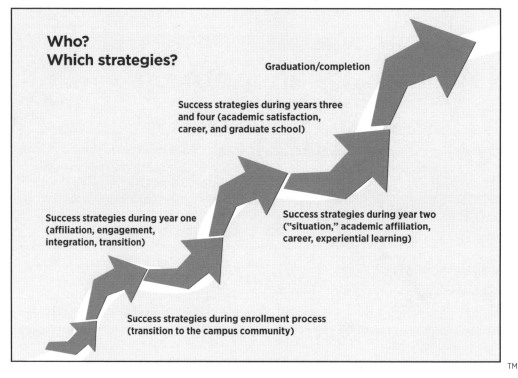

Essential to any discussion about the stages of student enrollment is the concept that retention begins with recruitment. Enrollment professionals, such as admissions staff, recruiters, financial aid staff, and student success teams, must co-manage the enrollment stages that impact overall completion. A prime example of this is the time between acceptance or deposit and the first day of class. At some institutions, students make the decision to attend many months before classes begin. During the time between this decision and the beginning of classes, students and their families experience many decision points that may impact whether or not they actually begin their chosen coursework.

The phenomenon wherein students commit to a particular college but do not matriculate at that college is known to many enrollment professionals as "melt." Student success teams should be working with enrollment management teams to reduce melt by implementing strategies geared toward reducing the number of students who commit/deposit and then don't attend on the first day of classes. This bridging concept is focused on moving students down the engagement stream by working collaboratively to ensure students and their families are prepared with the proper information to commit to their final enrollment and extend the relationship created during the recruitment process.

Once the student has enrolled, student success professionals from throughout the campus should form a student success planning team in order to assist students and their families with navigation of the first-year experience and transition into and through the second year. From our experience we have learned that if students in four-year schools persist and progress to the fifth term, they are far more likely to complete their degree. In other words, attrition is usually low single digits beyond that point. For our community college partners, we have learned that if students can persist and progress to the third or fourth term, they are more likely to earn a credential and/or transfer to a four-year school. Of course, this isn't the case for all schools but it is usually a good indicator.

The outcomes that should be measured as students continue along the engagement stream are persistence, progression, retention, and completion. For the arithmetically inclined, consider this theoretical formula:

Persistence + Progression + Retention = Completion/Graduation

TM

Student Success Relationship Management

Persistence

For the purpose of this discussion, persistence is defined as term-to-term return. Students who have consistent return patterns from fall to spring to fall, and beyond, are more likely to complete or graduate in a timely manner. In terms of measurement, persistence is more precisely defined as the enrollment headcount of any cohort compared to its headcount on the initial official census day, commonly measured on day one or the census date of terms two, three, four, and so on, but also measured at ongoing points in time to determine persistence rates on any given day of any given term. The examples below illustrate this concept:

> **Example 1:** On January 9, 2015, the first day of term two, 90 percent of an institution's fall 2014 first-time-in-college (FTIC) cohort persisted from the cohort's official term one census taken on October 3, 2014.

> **Example 2:** On August 27, 2015, the first day of term three, 70 percent of the institution's fall 2014 FTIC cohort persisted from the cohort's official term one census taken on October 3, 2014.

At most colleges and universities, students can persist from the first term to the second term without having truly progressed. Almost all institutions of higher education allow students a probationary term in order to show improvement. In effect, students could fail every course in term one and return for term two. While federal financial aid regulations regarding satisfactory progress have recently changed, most institutions continue to allow an appeal term in order for students to get back on track.

Progression

Progression is defined as the rate at which a cohort participates in any activity that an institution has determined to be correlated with persistence, such as course completion rates and academic probation. Students who have successfully persisted have at least satisfied the academic and financial aid policies of the institution. However, in many cases, this is not enough to ensure continuing progress. For example, students who meet the bare minimum requirements for progression may have a much harder time later in their persistence toward completion. This is especially true for students who have developmental education requirements in areas such as math, English, and reading. Students who progress in the math sequence with a grade of C in the first developmental math course may not be as successful in subsequent math courses as if they had achieved an A or a B.

> **Example 1:** Of the students in the fall 2015 FTIC cohort that took Sociology 101 during term one, 75 percent completed the course successfully (grade of C or higher) by day one of term two, January 10, 2016.

> **Example 2:** Of the students in the fall 2015 FTIC cohort that were placed on probation at the end of term one, 40 percent were removed from the probation list by the end of term two.

At the very heart of progression is the idea that, if students successfully persist and progress, they will retain to the next fall, barring unforeseen circumstances.

Retention

This metric within the student engagement stream is defined as the fall-to-fall return rate of any cohort or subpopulation within the cohort. Most campuses are accustomed to reporting this outcome via the Integrated Postsecondary Education Data System (IPEDS) and appropriate state agencies, but retention is really much more complex than that. Some of the seminal work on student retention was completed by Ruffalo Noel Levitz founders Lee Noel and Randi Levitz. According to Noel, Levitz, and

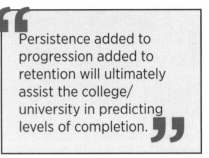

> Persistence added to progression added to retention will ultimately assist the college/ university in predicting levels of completion.

Saluri (1985), "Re-enrollment or retention is not then the goal; retention is the result or byproduct of improved programs and services in our classrooms and elsewhere on campus that contribute to student success." Other researchers have also presented reasons why students retain and achieve success. According to the Theory of Involvement outlined by Astin (1999), students who live in residence halls or hold part-time jobs on campus, for example, may show higher retention outcomes than students who do not.

Continuing this thought process leads us directly to completion. As suggested in the formula presented earlier, persistence added to progression added to retention will ultimately assist the college/university in predicting levels of completion. However, this topic should be considered within the context of institution type.

Completion/Graduation

For many years, colleges have focused on the concept of graduation. Since most reporting agencies require institutions to report graduation rates, most benchmarks use graduation as the standard, and the term "graduation" (150 percent of time) is normative in the higher education lexicon. In the current environment of accountability, it makes sense to change this conversation to emphasize on-time completion, rather than graduation, at more than 100 percent of time as the standard. On-time completion rate can be defined as:

> The rate at which a cohort persists and progresses with academic and co-curricular outcomes which are congruent with on-time completion.

> **Example 1:** Of the students in the fall 2013 FTIC cohort, 65 percent returned to term five and completed 60 hours of coursework (assume 120 for the degree) which counted toward graduation within the declared major (a progression measure supporting on-time completion).

> **Example 2:** Of the students starting AAS programs in fall 2013, 45 percent completed all degree requirements by May 2015.

The Voluntary Framework of Accountability (VFA), an initiative created by the American Association of Community Colleges in 2011, developed some outcomes that include percentage of students that earn an associate's degree without transfer; percentage of students that earn an associate's degree with transfer; percentage of students that earn an award of less than an associate's degree (certificate) without transfer; percentage of students that earn an award of less than an associate's degree (certificate) with transfer; percentage of students that transfer to a four-year institution with no degree or certificate; percentage of students that transfer laterally (attendance at another community college); percentage of students that are still enrolled during the sixth academic year; percentage of students that left institution, no award or transfer, but in good academic standing (30 credits or more, 2.0 GPA or higher); and percentage of students that left the institution who were not in good academic standing. Because graduation is not always the ultimate or best completion indicator, institutions may need to reconsider or redefine completion measures linked to institutional goals as they develop their key performance indicators (see Chapters 4 and 8).

Common data elements

Now that we have defined persistence, progression, retention, and completion, let us discuss the common data elements that colleges and universities should be collecting in order to inform student success planning efforts. The first part of this discussion will focus on data relating to persistence and progression, which in turn lead to retention and completion outcomes. The second part of the discussion will address benchmarking for effective planning.

Leading and lagging indicators

Note that persistence and progression data should be date-, year-, and cohort-specific. Persistence and progression measures are based on concrete behavioral outcomes, such as the acts of registering for, attending, and completing a class. Many institutions have developed a list of subpopulations within the cohort and track them regularly. Consider this example of subpopulations from Montana State University-Billings (2011):

- Main campus
- College of Technology
- College of Arts and Sciences
- College of Business
- College of Allied Health
- College of Education
- Undecided students
- Provisional admits
- AS294 students
- AS101 students
- SOS students
- Residential students
- Full-time students
- Part-time students

> "Persistence and progression measures are based on concrete behavioral outcomes, such as the acts of registering for, attending, and completing a class."

Table 12-1 outlines common data elements that should be tracked for each cohort or subpopulation deemed relevant by the institution. It should be noted that this list is not all-inclusive and should be adapted and customized for each institution.

Table 12-1: Common Data Elements

Persistence data (leading indicators)	Progression (leading indicators)	Retention data and retention outcome	Completion outcome
Weekly tracking of the number of students registered by cohort or subpopulation (once registration is open)	Course completion and course success	First-year student return rates by cohort or subpopulation	Less than a year, certificate, diplomas, transfer; two-, three-, four-, five-, six-, seven-, eight-year outcomes
Persistence at purge for non-payment	Academic probation and suspension	Second-year student return rates by cohort and subpopulation	
Fall-to-spring return rates by cohort or subpopulation	Satisfactory academic progress (SAP)	Third-year student return rates by cohort and subpopulation	
Persistence at drop/add and census	Student achieving less than 2.0 GPA in first term	Fourth-year student return rates by cohort and subpopulation	
Spring-to-fall return rates by cohort or subpopulation	Developmental course completion		
	Major declaration		
	Degree/Completion plan completed		
	Credit hours attempted/earned ratios		
	Student motivation data (first term, end of first term, beginning of second year, etc.)		
	Statistical identification of risk factors and/or student attributes that correlate with retention		
	Student satisfaction data that correlate with retention		
	Engagement data that inform the retention and completion outcomes		

TM

Benchmarking

Any discussion about the use of common data elements for planning should include reference to accurate industry benchmarks. Many agencies, such as the Consortium for Student Retention Data Exchange (CSRDE), ACT, and Ruffalo Noel Levitz, provide regularly updated benchmarks relating to aspects of college persistence and retention. Table 12-2 provides examples of persistence, progression, and retention benchmarks compiled by Ruffalo Noel Levitz (*Student Retention Indicators Report for Two-Year and Four-Year, Public and Private Institutions*, 2015).

Table 12-2: Examples of Persistence, Progression, and Retention Benchmarks

First-year student return rates

	Four-year private			Four-year public			Two-year public
	All	Lowest selectivity	Highest selectivity	All	Lowest selectivity	Highest selectivity	All
Persistence rates from term one to term two of 2013-2014 academic year							
25th percentile	87.0%	85.0%	91.0%	87.0%	84.0%	90.0%	75.0%
Median	91.0%	88.0%	92.0%	90.0%	87.0%	92.0%	80.0%
75th percentile	93.8%	91.0%	95.0%	92.8%	90.0%	95.0%	84.0%
Persistence rates from fall 2013 to fall 2014							
25th percentile	69.0%	61.0%	76.0%	67.3%	65.0%	74.0%	52.0%
Median	77.0%	69.0%	80.0%	74.0%	68.0%	77.0%	56.0%
75th percentile	81.3%	77.0%	84.0%	79.8%	74.0%	83.0%	62.0%

Second-year student return rates

	Four-year private			Four-year public			Two-year public
	All	Lowest selectivity	Highest selectivity	All	Lowest selectivity	Highest selectivity	All
Persistence rates from term one to term two of 2013-2014 academic year							
25th percentile	91.0%	88.3%	93.0%	90.0%	87.0%	92.8%	81.0%
Median	93.0%	92.0%	95.0%	92.0%	90.0%	94.0%	84.5%
75th percentile	96.0%	94.0%	96.0%	95.0%	92.0%	96.0%	89.0%
Persistence rates from fall 2013 to fall 2014							
25th percentile	81.0%	73.0%	85.0%	80.0%	68.0%	84.0%	NA
Median	86.0%	81.5%	88.0%	83.0%	80.0%	87.0%	NA
75th percentile	90.0%	85.0%	92.0%	87.8%	82.0%	91.0%	NA

TM

Source: Ruffalo Noel Levitz, 2015 Student Retention Indicators Report

Ultimately, each institution must develop its own set of performance measures in response to its distinctive student attrition patterns, while remembering that national benchmarks can provide helpful points of comparison. With this approach, retention teams can link enrollment and budget data to specific activities and programs. For the most effective year-to-year comparisons, it's advisable to store and analyze three to five years of comparative data, focusing on degree-seeking students.

By measuring and monitoring students' progress every step of the way, an institution is better equipped to accomplish its goals. The advantages of tracking persistence and progression rates in addition to overall retention and graduation outcomes include closer contact with students, more timely identification of student needs, the ability to measure the enrollment impact of specific strategies and tactics, the ability to justify expenditures for student success initiatives, and greater accountability for student success every step of the way.

Integrated strategic enrollment planning

Against this backdrop of retention principles, student success relationship management and associated metrics, completion concepts, common data elements, and benchmarks, it is time to move the conversation into the realm of strategic planning. This begins with a look at the use of data to inform strategies, followed by fundamental approaches for improving completion/graduation outcomes, including academic advising, early- and frequent-alert systems, and student engagement; managing expectations throughout the student lifecycle; and the role of data analysis in planning for new programs or services.

Use of data to inform decision making

Many colleges and universities begin to plan and prioritize before they have the right data and information to proceed. For example, we all believe that effective academic advising and support are strategies that have proven useful at most institutions and are verified by the literature. The use of Supplemental Instruction (SI), developed by Deanna C. Martin at the University of Missouri at Kansas City in 1973, has been shown to improve course success and eventual retention rates at many institutions, but where should this strategy be placed in our efforts? Should it be in math and natural sciences, because that's where many beginning students have trouble? Or should it be employed in social sciences? A careful analysis of the data will make an institution better informed as it prioritizes strategies.

The concept of milestone achievement and momentum point analysis may be helpful for prioritizing strategic efforts. Leinbach and Jenkins (2008) used a longitudinal approach to determine which milestones at a community college should be achieved in order to increase the likelihood of continued momentum toward completion. Examples included declaration of major, completion of developmental courses, and persistence through sequences. Careful analysis of data will help determine which milestones are not being achieved and thus impeding momentum toward completion. As another example, students who are undecided about a major at the time of admission are often less likely to complete than students who have declared a major. If that is the case, then intrusive and intentional advising and career strategies might be prioritized early in the student experience. Thus, the milestone of major declaration may be set as a priority and the institution will fund a corresponding strategy in order to encourage student momentum toward completion.

Academic advising

Ruffalo Noel Levitz conducts biannual best practices research among two-year and four-year public and private institutions across the United States. The 2015 report, *Student Retention and College Completion Practices at Four-Year and Two-Year Institutions*, revealed that, in addition to honors programs, mandatory advising was ranked as one of the top retention tools by respondents at all three institution types. ACT (Habley and McClanahan, 2004) found that advising almost always ranks among the top three most effective strategies for retention. In fact, when students are asked to rank the importance of academic advising, it is almost always in the top two, sometimes ranking even higher than instructional effectiveness (Ruffalo Noel Levitz, 2015). Given this, it is clear that colleges and universities must strategically plan for academic advising with respect to the model to be used, related staffing implications, course availability, and degree planning.

> " Advising almost always ranks among the top most effective strategies for retention. "

Advising models and their implications

Academic advising models can be categorized into one of three organizational structures, as described by Pardee (2004). The models are either centralized, with professional and faculty advisors housed in one academic or administrative unit; decentralized, with professional or faculty advisors located in their respective academic departments; or shared, with some advisors meeting with students in a central administrative unit (i.e., an advising center), while others advise students in the academic department of their major discipline.

According to Pardee, the chosen model should be carefully considered with the following elements in mind:

- What is the enrollment at the institution? For a large college or university, an advising center, either the self-contained (centralized) model or one of the shared structure models, would be an efficient choice with respect to benefits from economies of scale.

- What is the administrative structure of the institution, and what is the reporting line for advising? If the provost, vice president, or dean of academic affairs is responsible for advising, then faculty will very likely be involved with advising, either through a decentralized or shared structure. To what extent is the faculty interested in and willing to devote time to advising? If the faculty are recognized and rewarded for advising, a decentralized structure is feasible. It is also cost-effective, as no space or funding is needed to establish an advising center.

- What is the overall nature of the institution's academic policies, curriculum, and degree programs? A wide range of academic programs, high program selectivity, and complex graduation requirements increase the practicality of a centralized or shared model. In a central office, it is easier for a coordinator to train advisors, thus ensuring that complex policies and program options are understood and accurately conveyed to students.

- What is the institution's mission, and how does academic advising relate to the mission? If the institution and its programs are oriented toward career preparation, a decentralized structure, such as the faculty-only model, would be appropriate. Faculty, as experts in their field, may be better prepared to advise students on course selection, internships, and career options.

- What is the composition of the student body and what are students' special needs? An institution with a sizable proportion of unprepared, undecided, or re-entry students should devote financial and other resources to specialized advising that is effectively offered in a centralized or shared structure, such as the split model. On the other hand, if the majority of students are academically prepared and have declared majors, then a more decentralized structure would be appropriate.

Pardee concluded that, "There is growing recognition among advising professionals and researchers that a shared structure can incorporate the best features from the decentralized and centralized structures. An ideal shared structure would take advantage of the expertise of faculty advising in their departments (decentralized), while relying on professional advisors in a central administrative unit to meet the special needs of students, such as incoming freshmen, academically at-risk students, minority students, student athletes, or undecided students."

Campuses can use Pardee's three-tiered approach to guide a long-term strategic planning effort that includes consideration of budget implications and the time required to implement improvements to academic advising.

Course availability

In addition to selecting an appropriate advising model, colleges should ensure that courses are offered and available as promised. If they are not, academic programs should list what courses will be offered when and make sure they are offered in a way that will allow most students to follow the necessary sequence of prerequisites. In rotating course schedules, institutions must determine whether the courses are really offered in such a way that timely completion can occur. If not, are reasonable substitutions made? Only within this framework can proper degree planning occur.

Degree planning

Having an up-to-date degree plan on file for a particular student may be the ultimate indicator of an effective advising relationship. Some colleges call them academic plans, while others call them plans of study or individualized graduation or completion plans. Whatever an institution calls this plan, students and their families must be made aware that the plan is the implicit promise made to them at the time of enrollment. Strategically, the advising model must support the degree-planning process via electronic or other methods, making it possible for students to easily track progress toward the ultimate credential outcome.

Early- and ongoing-alert systems

Once strategies are in place to ensure a student has been given accurate guidance for degree planning and is set on the path to completion, the next strategic element to embrace is early and continuous intervention. Most commonly known as early-alert systems, these activities and approaches provide structure for faculty and staff as they attempt to help students persist and progress.

Early-alert programs enhance student success by identifying students' concerns or challenges as soon as possible and providing them with appropriate assistance so that they can stay on track and accomplish their academic goals. According to the *National Freshman Motivation to Complete College Report* (Ruffalo Noel Levitz, 2016), 95 percent of incoming freshmen express a strong desire to finish a college degree, and approximately half will not achieve this goal (ACT, 2015).

While students may leave at any time during the student lifecycle due to a variety of circumstances, the fact is that most students who do not persist leave during the first term or year, or perhaps during the second year. Early-alert systems help campuses:

- Identify at-risk students:
  - —In advance of enrollment: dropout-prone students who could benefit from institutional intervention;
  - —After enrollment: students experiencing academic, social, and/or personal problems that might be ameliorated by institutional intervention;
- Zero in on motivational factors, including each student's attitude and receptivity to assistance;
- Monitor each student's performance, attendance, and behavior; and
- Intervene when appropriate.

Identifying at-risk students during the first year

There are two approaches that best serve to identify students who might be more at risk for attrition. The first uses historical institutional data and logistic regression analysis to produce a predictive model based on how students have retained in the past. The second approach combines the results of the predictive model with the student motivation assessment to provide a powerful tool for prediction, early-alert, and advising.

Predictive modeling for early alert and advising during the first year

For many years, colleges and universities have been maintaining early-alert systems that employ a mid-term alert. At some point during the term, if a student shows evidence of not being successful, his or her instructor is expected to send a referral to a student service office. Examples of triggers might include poor test grades, lack of attendance, behavior issues in class, and lack of engagement. While these referrals are valuable and raise issues that should be addressed, they really aren't "early" in most cases. (Think of the "leading versus lagging" indicators discussed earlier in this chapter.) A true early alert can be accomplished by creating a predictive model based on what is known about the student at the time of admission or on past first- or second-term student behaviors related to factors such as enrolled courses or residency. The Ruffalo Noel Levitz predictive modeling for retention program is called the Student Retention Predictor™.

Using three to five years of historical financial aid and admissions data, appending additional socioeconomic or other data, and using retention as a dependent variable, colleges can establish which variables among the data set have the strongest relationship to retention. In other words, at the time of admission and based on historical attrition patterns, it is possible to predict which students will most likely retain. If an institution possesses this information, it is able to implement an early-alert system using this identification process. This predictive model allows the institution to prioritize its resources based on the entire risk distribution of the incoming class.

Figure 12-2: Risk Distribution of the Incoming Class

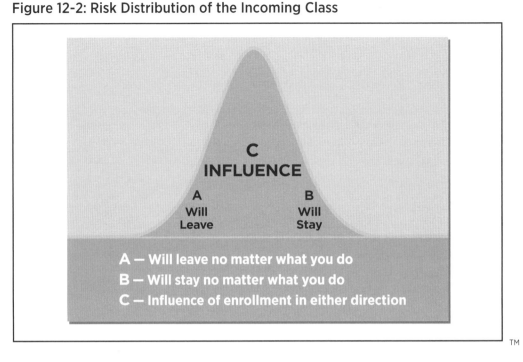

C
INFLUENCE

A
Will
Leave

B
Will
Stay

A — Will leave no matter what you do
B — Will stay no matter what you do
C — Influence of enrollment in either direction

For example, most institutions pay more attention to the upper or lower quartiles in the risk distribution, spending most of their time with the students who are more likely to leave or stay despite any actions they may take (Figure 12-2). The fallacy of this approach is that there are more students in the middle of the risk distribution than at either extreme. Predictive modeling will show the entire range of risk and empower the campus to prioritize resources for the greatest return on investment of time and budget (Figure 12-3).

Figure 12-3: Risk Distribution by Student Model Score

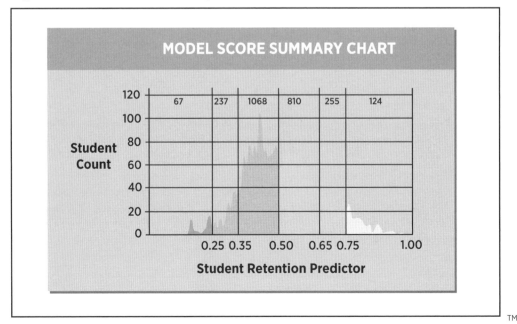

MODEL SCORE SUMMARY CHART

| 67 | 237 | 1068 | 810 | 255 | 124 |

Student Count

0.25 0.35 0.50 0.65 0.75 1.00

Student Retention Predictor

Continuous intervention via understanding of student transitions throughout the student lifecycle

The final question that colleges should consider in developing their early and ongoing intervention services is what students need as they persist and progress to their second, third, and fourth years. From the literature, it is clear that much attention has been paid to first-year and senior-year (for four-year institutions) transitions, but little attention has been paid to second- and third-year transitions. Momentum point or milestone achievement analysis focuses on student persistence and progress throughout the college experience.

As Leinbach and Jenkins (2008) explain, "Understanding how students actually progress through their college programs is essential in developing strategies and choosing appropriate interventions to improve student outcomes. The challenge is to build expertise and capacity in college and state agency research departments to transform raw student unit record (SUR) data into meaningful information of practical use for policymakers and practitioners." As described in an earlier example, if a student achieves the milestone of completing a developmental math course, then that momentum point in time will likely move him to the next math course in the sequence. If not, the momentum has been stopped or delayed.

This same concept can be applied to second-, third-, and fourth-year students. In *Helping Sophomores Succeed* (Hunter et al., 2010), the authors contend that there is little attention paid to the second year. "It is much easier to define the beginning and the ending periods of college, because they are more distinct, pronounced, and therefore amenable to redress." According to the authors, when the second year begins may depend on time in college or credits earned. Noting that the primary objectives of the second year are selecting a major and developing purpose, they recommend institutions focus their intervention and advising efforts with second-year students on these two purposes.

As second-year students develop their purpose and move on to their third year, career closure and connecting career and academics assume greater importance. Second-year and third-year student success initiatives typically feature opportunities that focus on academic concerns, degree planning, leadership, majors, careers, community service, finances, and social relationships.

Institutions should never assume that once a student enters his or her last year, decisions have already been made about career or transition to graduate school. Many fourth-year students find themselves in the predicament of not taking all the required courses or needing to repeat courses to complete their degree. Advising and degree checks near the end of the second and third years by faculty advisors and degree audit systems are desirable components of the ongoing and frequent outreach effort.

Student satisfaction and engagement and their relationships to completion

Implicit in this discussion of persistence strategies is the need to conduct student satisfaction assessments and use what our students are telling us. As someone once said, "All you have to do to find out what students need is ask them." One of the basic principles of planning for success is to rely on your assessment results and use them continuously as your students transition through the student lifecycle to completion.

Aligning student and institutional priorities

Each year, Ruffalo Noel Levitz publishes national student satisfaction and priorities reports. The information serves as a benchmark for colleges and universities and informs the strategic student success planning process. For example, almost every year, students from all institution types rank instructional effectiveness or academic advising as their most important priority. At the same time, faculty and staff within those same institutional types may not rank instructional effectiveness or academic advising as their top priority. This type of incongruence may lead to planning that is misguided, underfunded, understaffed, and ultimately doesn't contribute to the desired completion outcomes.

Engagement influences completion

Similarly, Kuh, Kinzie, Schuh, and Whitt (2005) concluded, "Student engagement has two key components that contribute to student success. The first is the amount of time and effort students put into their studies and other activities that lead to experiences and outcomes that constitute student success. The second is the ways the institution allocates resources and organizes learning opportunities and services to induce students to participate in and benefit from such activities." Based on consistent findings among student development theorists (Astin, 1999; Chickering and Gamson, 1987; Chickering and Reisser, 1993), colleges and universities should attempt to create environments where students experience frequent faculty-to-student contact, cooperation among students, active and collaborative learning approaches, prompt feedback, time on task, high expectations, and a respect for diverse ways of learning.

Dialogue

This chapter has discussed the continuing student stages of enrollment, common data elements, and benchmarks needed for the annual and strategic planning process; fundamental strategies for encouraging student persistence and completion; and how satisfaction and engagement levels impact the planning process. Leaders at colleges and universities must now confront a few common issues that may be inhibiting the success of the planning process on their campuses.

First, many campuses adhere to the notion that student success is everyone's responsibility; this is often embraced as a paradigm by most faculty and staff. Even in the unlikely event that this is true, it doesn't mean that improvements in outcomes will automatically happen as a result. These things rarely happen by chance. Campuses must organize their efforts to create better outcomes and appoint a strategic success leader to collaboratively lead the process. It is true that student success does belong to the entire village, but the village cannot make it happen without a chief.

Second, the data needed to inform planning for the continuing student stages must be collected over a four-, five- or six-year period. Having focused on the first year for decades, it is time to focus on the overall completion outcome using data collected throughout the student lifecycle.

Third, those data must be used to plan for the desired ultimate completion outcome. Institutions cannot be fixated on first-year retention rates, even though it is still true that most students who leave the institution will drop out during the first year. Knowing persistence and progression data over the entire student lifecycle will greatly improve and inform planning.

Lastly, these six basic indicators of successful retention approaches should be considered by institutions as they plan for the achievement of completion outcomes:

1. Are retention programs highly structured and integrated with other programs/services?

2. Has the institution assessed student satisfaction, developed a better understanding of student motivation, and integrated data analysis into the process of improving the student experience?

3. What level of quality classroom engagement and outcomes-based learning occurs on campus?

4. What data ensure a student-centered dynamic is embedded into institutional practices?

5. How are faculty, staff, and students empowered to develop relationships with one another?

6. What intrusive and intentional strategies are implemented on campus? Are they effective? This is known as "front-loading" or, as Lee Noel once said, "giving them what they need before they know they need it."

CHAPTER 13

Attracting and Retaining Adult, Online, and Graduate Students

By Sue Dietrich, Sheila Mahan, and William Husson

Enrollment of adult learners

In an age of declining growth rates of traditional-aged enrollments, many colleges and universities are taking an important look at developing or expanding their offerings to adults in the classroom, online, or both. Forty-four percent of all undergraduate students are now older adults, as defined by NCES (25 years of age and over). For this older age group, enrollment through 2022 is projected to increase by 20 percent, compared to only 9 percent for students 24 and under. By 2022, adult learners are expected to total 10.1 million, compared to 13.6 million traditional-aged learners, 24 years of age and under (NCES, 2014). How does the adult learner differ, and how do our approaches need to vary to attract and retain this large segment of potential students? Understanding adult learner characteristics can help institutions form an effective strategy for this population.

> **CHAPTER HIGHLIGHTS**
>
> ■ Adult learner enrollment represents opportunity for revenue growth
>
> ■ Today's student views distance learning as valuable option
>
> ■ Graduate enrollment strategies extend from recruitment through retention

Figure 13-1: Projected Enrollment Growth, From 2010 to 2021, by Age Range

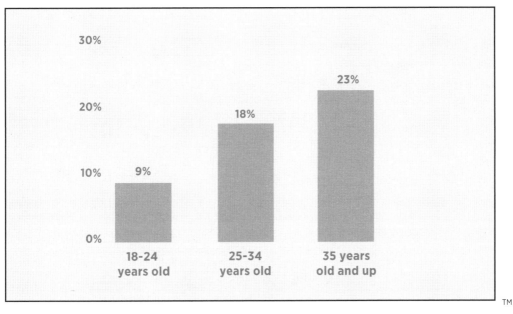

Source: NCES: Projections of Education Statistics to 2022

Thanks to the pioneering efforts of academics and researchers of adult learning such as Malcolm Knowles, Patricia Cross, Stephen Brookfield, and Sharan Merriam, we now know much more about the learning needs and characteristics of the adult learner. Adult learners have significantly different characteristics from traditional-aged learners in many respects. A study of over 47,000 undergraduate adult learners who completed the Ruffalo Noel Levitz Adult Student Priorities Survey™ at 150 institutions between fall 2011 and spring 2014 indicated the following top nine reasons adult students enrolled at undergraduate colleges. Academic reputation and availability of evening/weekend courses are of primary importance.

Table 13-1: Factors That Contributed to Adult Learner Enrollment

Factor	Importance percent
Academic reputation	82%
Availability of evening/weekend courses	80%
Future employment opportunities	79%
Campus location (close to home/work)	79%
Financial aid/scholarship opportunities	79%
Cost	76%
Personalized attention prior to enrollment	73%
Recommendations from family/friends/employer	63%
Size of institution	60%

™

Source: Ruffalo Noel Levitz, 2014-15 National Adult Student Priorities Report

How a program is designed becomes a key consideration. Here are some program design strategies that appeal to the adult learner:

- Offer accelerated terms. Offer classes in five-, eight-, or 10-week formats, with classes meeting once a week for a longer class session. Adults have valuable life experiences that often enable them to grasp and retain, learning more readily than a student direct from high school. While they have multiple priorities (spouse, children, parents, job, community, health, etc.), they are typically highly motivated to complete their educational goals. With proper curriculum and program design, adults absorb content efficiently.

- Provide adult and career-relevant courses. When possible, consider adjusting your general education requirements to have relevance to the adult learner. For example, a communications requirement may be met through coursework in report writing, non-verbal communication, business communication, or business presentations. A foreign language requirement (difficult to master in even a full semester), could be fulfilled through a cultural diversity class or a computer language course.

- Recognize prior learning, both through other colleges and life experience. How prior credit is transferred can impact the total time and expense required for goal achievement. Restrictive transfer credit policies and slow or limited evaluation and recognition of military and professional training decreases the likelihood of enrollment.

- Actively engage the learner. Adults want their learning to help them solve problems. Problem-based learning enables application of theory to problem-solving, creating relevancy and meaning. Classes that provide opportunity for adults to share their experience through small group discussion, teamwork, and projects appeal to their learning style. Faculty who incorporate real-life experience can merge theory with application, replicating the business world where individuals continuously learn from colleagues and experts in the field.

Recruitment strategies

An adult-friendly program design is essential for success in managing the classroom enterprise. However, the management of recruiting and initial enrollment for older adults differs dramatically from the traditional-age recruitment process. While many of the mechanisms look familiar, the approach differs regarding the messaging, the timelines, the contact technology, and the sales strategy.

Figure 13-2: Lead Generation for Adult Learners

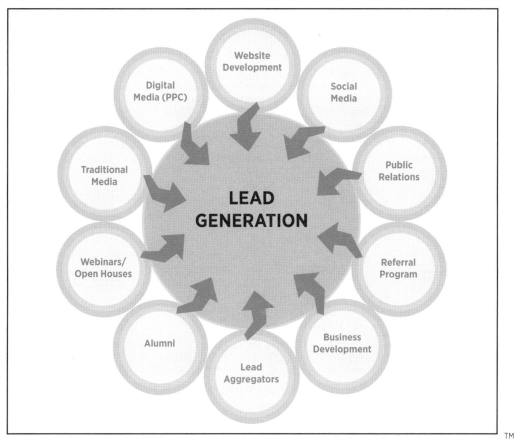

Website development: How does the adult student learn about your college? While the campus website is key in the recruitment of any student population, it is especially important for the recruitment of adult learners where name acquisition for solicitation is expensive and often met with poor results. Not surprisingly, many adults over the age of 24 are technology-savvy and use Internet search engines and college search sites to discover and study multiple colleges. Busy adults lack the time to search traditional program information to see if it will fit their needs. Institutions need to provide access to adult program information on the home webpage and ensure that key webpages are written for search engine optimization (SEO). It is a good idea to enlist web and interactive marketing professionals to assist in these fundamental strategies. Organic search results can yield quality leads on a small budget. In addition, be sure your website contains content-rich, interactive, self-service information, as the adult typically conducts stealth research before initiating an application. Video testimonials, degree credit calculators, video interviews with faculty, and career information provide methods for the adult to become familiar with your college on their own terms (Maslowsky, 2012).

Though Internet searches and college websites are the two methods prospective adult students most often use to learn of adult program opportunities, other marketing strategies are also important. Traditional "snail mail" flyers and postcards to the home and emails are effective communication strategies, followed closely by television and website advertising. Radio ads, newspaper ads, billboards, and bus/train ads round out the methods by which adults search for enrollment options. A contemporary form of adult marketing, paid interactive Internet advertising, should seriously be considered to drive the prospective adult student to visit your website.

Referrals: While web and paid advertising support inquiry pool development, the single most important source of information for the adult learner is referrals, including current or former students, friends, family, and coworkers (Aslanian, 2013).

How can you generate more referrals? It is no surprise that satisfied students are more likely to generate referrals than dissatisfied students. In fact, research conducted by Ruffalo Noel Levitz shows a strong relationship between satisfaction and willingness to recommend an institution, as shown in Figure 13-3.

Figure 13-3: Adult Learner Satisfaction and Willingness to Recommend an Institution

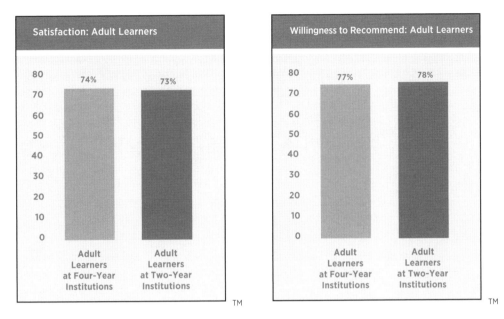

Source: Ruffalo Noel Levitz, 2015-16 National Adult Learners Satisfaction and Priorities Report

Other effective recruitment strategies center on developing relationships and are grassroots in nature. Efforts can be focused within a 40-minute drive of the adult's work or home. Key strategies include:

- **Business development:** Cultivate business and organizational relationships. Conduct needs assessments with human resource managers and offer to deliver a one-hour seminar, lunch and learn, or online course free of charge on-site. Conduct job fairs and invite area businesses to participate. Find ways to assist businesses, and they will likely assist you.

- **Public relations:** Get involved in the community. Ensure that you are a member of and represented at as many events and organizations as possible, including the chamber of commerce, clubs, military events, social services, government, and charitable organizations. Small events like food drives or volunteer activities can provide positive publicity as well.

- **Linkage with local universities, community colleges, and vocational/technical schools:** Consider forming partnerships and creating articulation agreements both upward and downward. With an effective prior learning experience program, you can also form articulation agreements with businesses, the military, and organizations that serve adult learners. A simple example: The American Council on Education (ACE) has recommended state licensure for realtors to require three credits in Introduction to Real Estate, which you offer. Ask a specific agency if you can email or contact all their realtors to advise them of this offering.

Enrollment strategies

The enrollment strategy for the adult learner needs to take into account the current dynamic and changing marketplace. Since the advent of online programs, predominately for adult learners, there are a host of competitors in all markets, many with substantial recruiting budgets. However, within a radius of 50 to 100 miles of your campus, you still stand a good chance of being a top choice in the consumer's opinion. This will only prove true if you adopt focused and timely recruiting strategies similar to your competition. This will require your enrollment counselors to quickly follow up on all leads. In fact, it has been said that a lead is only active for 24 hours, and the first university to personally talk to a prospective student is the one most likely to covert the lead into an application. Attempt to reach the prospect by phone first and follow up with email. Design a communication strategy that is persistent but not pesky. Provide information about your program, the value of an education, and testimonials in a well-planned communication strategy. Attempt to meet the prospect either in-person or in real time with visual chat or telephone call. The adult is busy and may not have time to meet you on campus. A tour is not high on their priority list. Answer their financial questions. Process their transcript evaluations quickly.

Once adult learners have committed to the learning experience, it is important to enable them to begin studies almost immediately. Have a class or program they can start within a few weeks to reduce the chance that they will wander elsewhere. Adults can be impatient. The phrase, "We want what we want when we want it," was written with the adult in mind. Keep them engaged by getting them started.

As with traditional enrollment, track your inquiries by lead source and degree program. Monitor rates through the inquiry to information session to application to acceptance to enrollment rates. Understand which of your enrollment counselors have the highest conversion rate and establish benchmarks. A solid customer relationship management (CRM) system will enable you to track your interactions and generate the data you need to customize your marketing efforts.

Attracting and enrolling adult students are only the first steps in the process. It is also essential that you are prepared to help them succeed once they enroll.

Retention strategies

Adults often re-enter higher education with a unique set of concerns. Fear of failure is strong, particularly if they were not college-bound out of high school or had a negative college experience. While commitment to completion may be high, so are insecurities. Quite often, sincere reassurance can help build self-efficacy and persistence. Toward that goal, the following five strategies may help you build an adult student retention plan.

- As part of the program of study, build in a required orientation course. Not unlike traditional-age learners, adults often know little about college processes, degree requirements, time management, learning outcomes, and the use of technology. A well-designed orientation course, as part of the degree and completed within the first term, provides a solid foundation.

- Requisite knowledge for advanced coursework is critical. How this knowledge is provided is equally critical. Consider building assessment into required coursework for adult learners that is sequenced prior to an advanced course, but not required in the first block of credit attempted. This provides an opportunity for the adult to become familiar with the learning process. It also provides content knowledge closer to the time at which it can be applied.

- Provide timely academic advising to establish a relationship with the adult learner. Adults need to see how they can complete what they have started. They need to have contact with a person who can help them, academically and logistically. This is typically the role of academic advisors or success coaches. Continued encouragement can assure the fearful adult that they are capable; frequent contact can identify areas where the student may need additional help.

- Build in weekly touchpoints during the adult student's first term. Calling the student once a week (initially) and asking how things are going provides opportunity to identify student concerns and take immediate action on behalf of the student. Surveys while the student is enrolled as well as upon the completion of the semester and year provide longer-range data for planning purposes, while a calling program provides a chance for immediate intervention.

- Create early-alert systems. Faculty who monitor and report non-attendance during the first two weeks can provide valuable information to support ongoing student touchpoints. Academic indicators such as poor grades on first assignments provide additional opportunities for early intervention and referral of resources. There are now early-alert detection systems built into student information systems, reducing the need for a manual process. Exploration of software packages may be useful in your strategy formulation.

Summary

The adult learner represents a significant portion of higher education enrollment today and a real opportunity for significant revenue growth. Colleges and universities should carefully integrate such programs into their mission. Meeting the needs of this market segment requires a different approach in recruitment, enrollment, program design, and teaching methods. Colleges that address these differences will gain students who are satisfied learners, proud alumni, and supportive members in the community.

Enrollment of online learners

With the growth of the Internet and computers in the home, online learning programs slowly began to emerge in the mid-1990s. Dial-up connections made it cumbersome, employers were skeptical, most faculty were equally skeptical, and federal financial aid could not be used. As technology improved, online learning grew incrementally in popularity and acceptance. By 2005, electronic learning management systems were adopted across many campuses. Faculty and students alike began to see the value in the convenience. Faculty began to explore creative ways to teach concepts and engage learners beyond classroom-based lecture and discussion. Today's learner expects wireless connectivity in their dorm room or home, like ice from a refrigerator door. They also expect to communicate and learn via online modalities, just as they do in traditional settings.

As colleges and universities consider strategic enrollment planning, most acknowledge that the ability to deliver quality online learning experiences will position them for the evolving needs of the 21st century learner. With the advent of massive open online courses (MOOCs), adaptive learning, and competency-based learning, the ways in which our students learn will continue to change. Students will log in to class at a place and time of their choice. The availability of online courses and entire degrees will factor into enrollment decisions. Institutions that use technology to its fullest will help students learn more efficiently and deeply, focusing on areas in which their learning is most shallow (adaptive learning) and demonstrating mastery and depth of knowledge (competency).

Distance learning today

According to data published by the U.S. Department of Education, we have seen a dramatic increase in student participation in distance learning. Enrollments at Title IV institutions grew from 4.3 million (20 percent of total enrollment) in 2008 to 5.5 million (nearly 26 percent) in 2012. That is an increase of 1.2 million enrollments in a four-year period (NCES, 2014). Clearly, today's student views distance learning as a viable alternative or supplement to ground-based learning.

Table 13-2: Fall 2012 Distance Learning Enrollments by Type of Title IV Institution

Type, All Degree Levels	Total Enrollment, All Degree Levels	Exclusively Distance Program Enrollment	Percentage of Total Enrollment	One or More Distance Course	Percentage of Total Enrollment	Total All Distance Learners	Percentage of Total Enrollment
Public	14,996,480	1,249,000	8.3	2,407,000	16.0	3,656,000	24.4
For-Profits	2,175,000	925,500	42.6	143,200	6.6	1,068,700	49.2
Private Non-Profits	3,975,540	467,500	11.8	259,800	6.5	727,300	18.3
All Types	21,147,000	2,642,000	12.5	2,810,000	13.3	5,452,000	25.8

TM

Source: NCES, 2014 Digest of Education Statistics

Undergraduate students enrolled in distance learning: Trends as of fall 2012

- In 2012, the total number of distance learning undergraduates was almost 4.6 million, up from 4.3 million in 2008.

- Over 2.5 million undergraduates enrolled in course distance learning (CDL).

- More students pursued entire degrees via distance learning (DDL). In 2012, 11 percent of undergraduates were enrolled in DDL programs compared to only 4 percent in 2002.

Graduate students enrolled in distance learning: Trends as of fall 2012

In earlier studies, distance learning data collection focused on undergraduate enrollment only. The 2014 NCES data breaks out the student level to include graduate enrollment.

- Of the 2,910,715 graduate students enrolled nationwide in fall 2012, a full 22 percent pursued their entire graduate degree exclusively via distance learning delivery.

- Another 7.8 percent of graduate students pursued at least one course via distance delivery.

- In total, nearly 30 percent of graduate students enrolled in at least one course offered via distance delivery.

Graduate programs lend themselves to distance delivery modalities. The students are experienced learners, generally adults who have been out in the work world, and have family commitments. They are highly motivated, realizing that an advanced degree will give them the edge needed to get ahead professionally. If a strategic enrollment plan includes graduate programs (see the next section of this chapter), it would be prudent to include delivery options that include distance learning.

Student and faculty perceptions of online learning

Learners today seek the convenience of distance delivery, particularly via online modalities, much as we now seek the convenience of our TV DVR. According to the 2015-16 Ruffalo Noel Levitz *National Online Learners Satisfaction and Priorities Report*, online learners are generally satisfied with their online learning experience. This is true for students enrolled online at both four-year and two-year institutions. These data represent the perceptions of more than 118,000 students completing the Priorities Survey for Online Learners™ while enrolled online at 132 institutions between fall 2012 and spring 2015. See Figure 13-4.

Figure 13-4: Student Satisfaction and Likelihood to Re-Enroll

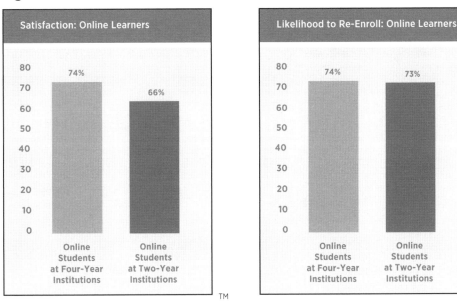

Source: Ruffalo Noel Levitz, 2015-16 National Online Learners Satisfaction and Priorities Report

While the majority of students are satisfied and feel that the online program is a good fit for them, approximately one-quarter of the four-year students and one-third of the two-year students were not satisfied and would not re-enroll in their current program if they had to do it all over again. This is important for institutions to consider as they work to recruit and retain online learners at their own institutions.

Skepticism related to online learning effectiveness has waned due in large part to wider adoption by faculty. With wider adoption, we have seen more studies in which online learning outcomes compare favorably to ground-based learning.

The U.S. Department of Education (2010) published a meta-analysis of 50 study effects, 43 of which were drawn from older learners, and found that, "Students in online conditions performed modestly better, on average, than those learning the same material through traditional face-to-face instruction" (Means, 2010). In the 2013 *Survey of Faculty Attitudes on Technology* published by Inside Higher Ed and Gallup, 71 percent of faculty who taught in the online course format agreed that students can achieve equivalent learning outcomes when compared to in-person courses. Despite this positive news, only 40 percent of the faculty who had never taught an online course felt online learning could achieve comparable outcomes.

Strategies for implementing online learning

Online courses offer tremendous convenience and flexibility. They also provide great efficiency and flexibility for administrators and faculty. Online courses require no management of physical classroom space, and faculty scheduling is less restrictive. In addition, adjunct faculty can reside in a different state, providing a broader pool of faculty candidates.

While distance learning programs will surely grow in the coming years, there are many challenges in moving from on-ground instruction to online learning. These challenges can be intimidating to campuses and prevent them from taking advantage of this learning modality. The following seven strategies can help your campus ensure a smooth launch of its online programs.

1. **Establish a clear vision for online distance learning.** One of the greatest obstacles to online learning is fear that the culture, mission, and purpose of the institution will change. This fear can be felt by faculty, alumni, staff, students, and board members. By establishing a clear vision for online learning, you reassure constituents that convenience in learning does not automatically lessen the quality of the educational experience or outcomes. Sufficient research on the efficacy of online learning now exists and can be used to assuage fears. Researching other colleges with successful online distance learning programs can also be helpful in demonstrating the many positive benefits of online learning.

2. **Establish a comprehensive financial plan.** As with all major endeavors of a university, a clear financial plan outlining all the assumptions, revenue expectations, anticipated expenses for staffing, faculty, marketing, and support services should be carefully prepared. The most helpful tool for this plan is an integrated spreadsheet pro-forma. Your university financial officer can help create the spreadsheet. The pro-forma will confirm that important issues have been addressed and will lead to the development of a comprehensive budget.

3. **Create a recruiting strategy.** Marketing online programs requires different strategies. A call-center-like approach should be considered with enrollment counselors who interact with potential students on the phone and online. While lead sources will be similar to traditional recruitment categories, your strategy should include a much stronger emphasis on the website, pay-per-click advertising, social media, and online lead providers. In addition, the marketing plan should clearly outline the SWOT (strengths, weaknesses, opportunities, and threats) analysis, an overview of the competition, and budgetary and personnel expenses.

4. **Secure internal and external regulatory approvals.** Internal approval processes should be carefully followed including both administrative and faculty protocols. When an institution offers more than 50 percent of a degree program online, approval from the regional accrediting association may be required before student recruitment can begin. Allow approximately six months from time of submission of your change document for approval. If your degree program is also professionally accredited (business, nursing, medical), additional time may be required. If you plan to offer the online program in other states, or expect learners from other states to enroll, state approvals may also be necessary.

5. **Establish the delivery of services for distance learners.** Services previously delivered face-to-face must be translated into electronic delivery. Web meeting tools can be used for academic and financial aid advising. The ability to register online, pay tuition and fees, and view academic progress should be available through the student information system. Access to library resources is also an important consideration for the online learner. Prior to implementation, a planning session with all affected departments will identify electronic alternatives to face-to-face services.

6. **Employ an experienced instructional designer.** Converting a course from on-ground to online can seem daunting. An instructional designer familiar with the Learning Management System (LMS) and experienced in teaching online (possibly even an existing faculty member) can be instrumental in the successful adoption of an online program. Hire a full-time or part-time instructional designer to provide assistance in course design.

7. **Clarify the organizational and governance structure for online programs.** Some of the most divisive issues involved in establishing and continuing online programs emanate from governance considerations. The key considerations are relative autonomy, strong support from university leadership, and clear lines of authority and responsibility. The structural framework needs to address the organizational relationship between the faculty's prerogative to manage and assure the curriculum content and quality, the supervision of a strong marketing outreach, the assurance of just-in-time student support services, and the creation of a multi-month schedule with an outline of clear expectations for the performance of all stakeholders. This task will require the online leadership to have the budgetary and discretionary authority to effectively manage the programs.

Strategies for growing online learning enrollment

Competition for the online learner is fierce. An early 2015 search using the Institute of Education Sciences College Navigator online tool (http://nces.ed.gov/ collegenavigator) revealed more than 500 institutions offering online options. At two-year public institutions, 27 percent of degree-seeking students are distance learners; at four-year publics, 22 percent; at four-year private, nonprofit, 16 percent; and at four-year private, for-profits, 67 percent. For graduate students, 24 percent of degree-seeking students at public institutions were distance learners; the rate was 23 percent at private nonprofits, and 82 percent at for-profit privates (NCES, 2014). As you identify strategies for growing online enrollment, first-time students who may wish to earn an associate degree or complete their first two years of college should not be ignored, as they represent a substantial potential online population. If you are a private nonprofit, getting into the game as quickly as possible is a large opportunity for you.

To grow online enrollment, you should offer degrees that are in demand and most widely known at your institution. Initially, your ground-based enrollment may dip in those program areas as more students gravitate to online (seat-shifters), but over time, total enrollment in the degree field should increase at a greater rate than if you had not offered the online option.

Recent research by Clinefelter and Aslanian (2015) suggests that for prospective undergraduate students, business administration is by far the most popular online major, with nursing, computer science and engineering, information technology, engineering, and sociology rounding out the top six. For prospective graduate students, the top four areas of study are identical, with early childhood education and counseling psychology/psychotherapy rounding out the top six.

Health jobs are expected to grow at the greatest rate between 2014 and 2024. According to the Bureau of Labor Statistics, the employment of registered nurses will increase by 16 percent; nursing assistants will increase by 17 percent; and licensed practical and vocational nurses will increase by 16 percent.

Adult learners are particularly attracted to flexible online study. As noted in the first section of this chapter, recruiting the adult learner requires different strategies and messages, as well as attractive transfer credit policies, credit for prior learning, and the potential to accelerate degree programs and course offerings.

Online learners will find your program through several channels:

- A referral from a friend, colleague, or employer.
- A web search for online programs.
- Web advertisements, often supported with television, radio, and direct mail.

Check your website to determine if there is a link for online and adult learners on the homepage. Be sure your search engine optimization includes online or distance delivery keywords. Expect to invest in advertising dollars, as the online learner typically needs to hear your message more than once before taking action. In fact, most online learners will range outward from your campus by as much as 100 miles, making it harder to ensure your message is heard via traditional media. Direct mail to selected zip codes can spread your message inexpensively. Radio spots on satellite radio or Pandora can also reach a wide geographic market.

As you build your recruitment strategy, consider the factors that students weigh in their decision to enroll. According to the 2015-16 Ruffalo Noel Levitz *National Online Learners Satisfaction and Priorities Report*, students at both four-year and two-year institutions indicated that convenience and flexible pacing were the most important factors in their decision to enroll in their online program. Online learners clearly require their courses to fit into their lives and allow them to participate when it is convenient for them.

Table 13-3: Factors in the Decision to Enroll at Four-Year Institutions

Factor	Importance percent
Convenience	96%
Flexible pacing for completing a program	93%
Work schedule	92%
Program requirements	89%
Reputation of institution	86%
Financial assistance available	85%
Cost	83%
Ability to transfer credits	82%
Future employment opportunities	81%
Distance from campus	60%
Recommendations from employer	58%

TM

Table 13-4: Factors in the Decision to Enroll at Two-Year Institutions

Factor	Importance percent
Convenience	93%
Flexible pacing for completing a program	88%
Cost	88%
Work schedule	87%
Ability to transfer credits	85%
Program requirements	84%
Financial assistance available	82%
Future employment opportunities	79%
Distance from campus	76%
Reputation of institution	75%
Recommendations from employer	57%

TM

Source: Ruffalo Noel Levitz, 2015-16 National Online Learners Satisfaction and Priorities Report

As noted in Tables 13-3 and 13-4, many factors influence the decision of a student to enroll in an online course, as at least 80 percent of students listed nearly all of these items as factors in their decision to enroll. Institutions need to make sure they address these issues for online learners. Work schedule, program requirements, and reputation of the institution are more important to four-year students, while cost, ability to transfer credits, and distance from campus are more important to students at two-year institutions.

Retaining the online learner

How can we mitigate online course and program attrition? Consider these causes and cures:

1. **The online learner may feel less engaged with faculty and fellow students.** Creating a social element to the learning environment, such as posting pictures and sharing background information, can help create a classroom environment of support. Having students work collaboratively in teams can also foster engagement.

2. **The amount of time it takes to complete coursework online may be more than the student anticipated.** In the recruitment process, it is important to be honest about the workload and expectations. Time management skills should be reviewed with the learner.

3. **Online learners can be anxious for immediate feedback.** Faculty must be responsive but also establish realistic expectations for the learner. A 24- to 48-hour turnaround time on student inquiries may be appropriate, while graded assignments may require a 72-hour turnaround time.

4. **Technology can be frustrating and confusing for students and faculty alike.** Build in an orientation session for learners and faculty to become familiar with proper use of the learning management system. Provide screenshots and how-to guides.

5. In a Ruffalo Noel Levitz study (2015) of retention practices, the single most important factor in retaining online learners was a "Mandatory training program for online faculty." **The greatest influence on student satisfaction with the learning experience is typically the instructor.** The best classroom-based instructor may not be the best online instructor. Training, development, student feedback, and peer mentoring can provide the instructor with the greatest tools for success in the online environment.

6. **In the same study, both two-year and four-year (public and private) institutions indicated that technical support for online connection issues is a best practice.** When the learner has forgotten his or her password or has difficulty loading an assignment that is due, a help center should be available with a clearly visible phone number or email address.

7. **Not all learners are ideal candidates for online learning.** Before choosing the online route, students should be exposed to the learning management system and the pros and cons of learning in this method; assess their comfort with reading, writing, and technology; and enter into an online classroom knowing his/her strengths and potential weaknesses.

8. **When a student struggles academically, academic support services should be as available for online learners as they are for on-campus students.** Other support services such as financial aid, career counseling, and learning resources must be accessible online.

9. **Assessment of learning outcomes for students, courses, and programs is imperative.** Comparing outcomes from students in the same courses offered on-ground and online should occur and be used to improve the teaching/learning process.

Summary

Learners today are adept with electronic technology in many facets of their lives. Online learning has established a firm foothold in all sectors of American higher education. To date, online learning has been focused on the working adult learner, but in the future this modality will extend to all aspects of the collegiate experience. Now is the time to embrace online and distance learning and incorporate this element into the strategic plan.

Enrollment of graduate students

Any discussion of graduate student enrollment issues—recruitment, persistence, and financial aid—must begin with a caveat about the perils of generalization given the diversity and complexity of graduate enrollment management. Academic doctoral enrollment is dramatically different from master's enrollment, which is also very different from graduate professional students (e.g., law). Graduate students are a mix of full-time students and those who study part-time while they continue working, returning adults, and recent baccalaureate recipients. Financial aid at the graduate level includes both traditional assistantships and merit scholarships that offer discounts. Suffice it to say, discipline-based differences affect trends, issues, and conventional wisdom about enrollment.

One thing is certain, however: everything related to graduate enrollment management requires the same level of intentionality and strategic thinking as the undergraduate enterprise. Graduate enrollment can contribute to a healthy overall enrollment picture. The National Center for Educational Statistics data reveals growth of 54 percent in master's degrees awarded and 42 percent in doctoral degrees awarded between 2001-02 and 2011-12 (NCES, 2014). But challenges have emerged in the last few years that remind us that, if improperly managed or taken for granted, graduate enrollment can drain energy and divert resources.

Trends in graduate enrollment and fields of study

The story of new and overall graduate student enrollment in recent years has been one of sudden change. Following a very robust period of growth through most of the first decade of the 21st century, the last few years have seen some steep declines in new graduate student enrollment in some disciplines—including mainstay graduate programs such as education, humanities and arts, and, to a lesser degree, business and social sciences.

The slow economic recovery, a growing student reluctance to assume additional debt, and competition from new sectors and delivery sources have all been mentioned in connection with these enrollment declines. In many parts of the country, cutbacks in public school funding and recent changes where teachers' educational attainment no longer factors into salary increases have contributed to a dramatic loss of student interest in education programs, both for new teacher prospects and career teachers seeking advanced degrees. These changes in new student enrollment are translating into graduate enrollment declines in these and other fields.

Table 13-5: Change in New Enrollment by Program Areas

Field of Study	One-year change, 2012 to 2013	One-year change, 2012 to 2013, in new enrollment	One-year change, in overall graduate enrollment
Arts/Humanities	-2.5%	-1.1%	-2.6%
Education	-2.2%	-3.1%	-4.5%
Business	-1.1%	1.6%	-0.6%
Health Sciences	3.1%	7.3%	4.5%
Math and Computer Science	17.4%	9.2%	8.5%
Biological and Agriculture Sciences	-1.8%	2.5%	1.0%
Social and Behavioral Sciences	-2.1%	0.1%	-0.3%
Engineering	6.9%	4.5%	3.8%

TM

Source: Council of Graduate Schools

In contrast to these losses is the growth of new and overall graduate student enrollment in math and computer science, health sciences, engineering, and (more modestly) in biological and agricultural sciences (Table 13-5).

NCES data on graduate degrees awarded confirms these trends. Though the number of graduate degrees awarded in virtually all fields has increased (led by business and education), there has been a dramatic increase in degrees awarded in the health professions, especially in recent years. Other fields that saw growth in master's degrees awarded included business, education, engineering, public administration and social services, and psychology. Though the number of degrees is smaller, the growth rate for homeland security and law enforcement master's degrees has also been substantial in recent years (NCES, 2014).

Table 13-6, also from the Council of Graduate Schools, provides a snapshot of degrees awarded by broad field in 2012-13. It is essential to localize these numbers in order to estimate potential markets in each institution's primary, secondary, and tertiary markets.

Table 13-6: Graduate Degrees and Certificates Awarded by Degree Level and Broad Field, 2012-13

Broad field	Doctoral Degrees		Master's Degrees		Certificates	
Total	70,920	100.0%	522,350	100.0%	34,416	100.0%
Arts and Humanities	5,632	9.0%	25,476	5.8%	1,144	4.2%
Biological and Agricultural Sciences	8,005	12.8%	14,672	3.3%	780	2.8%
Business	2,141	3.4%	98,112	22.3%	4,541	16.5%
Education	8,585	13.7%	95,592	21.7%	8,536	31.0%
Engineering	8,793	14.0%	37,036	8.4%	1,443	5.2%
Health Sciences	9,988	15.9%	49,654	11.3%	3,848	14.0%
Mathematics and Computer Sciences	3,307	5.3%	21,612	4.9%	1,080	3.9%
Physical and Earth Sciences	5,144	8.2%	7,101	1.6%	196	0.7%
Public Administration and Services	569	0.9%	27,333	6.2%	781	2.8%
Social and Behavioral Sciences	8,353	13.3%	32,821	7.5%	1,918	7.0%
Other fields	2,252	3.6%	30,316	6.9%	3,230	11.7%

TM

Source: CGS/GRE Survey of Graduate Enrollment and Degrees

The growth of online programs—as well as other distance learning models, such as low residency programs—has been an important part of the overall growth in graduate enrollment.

Critical elements of graduate recruitment

As they navigate this changing and challenging environment, many institutions are learning that they cannot simply create a new graduate program or rely on word of mouth and expect to fill classes. Instead, they need to be intentional and proactive in building their graduate student enrollments, use marketing strategies to both generate and sustain student interest in their programs, and provide prospective students with a smooth pathway to enrollment as well as solid student services tailored to their needs.

Institutions also need to have clear graduate enrollment goals, including program capacity, master's vs. doctoral enrollment targets, and funding allocations to ensure alignment of expectations across the institution.

Organization, leadership, and planning

Unlike the focused recruitment efforts of undergraduate admissions—which are typically the responsibility of a single unit—graduate recruitment involves participation by staff and offices across an institution. Both central administrative offices and graduate program staff must be actively engaged in recruitment efforts. It is essential, therefore, that an institutional organization is in place that supports coordinated graduate recruitment (not just graduate admissions) with clear roles and expectations for the recruitment of new graduate students.

The most successful institutions typically reflect a "shared responsibility" model, where some recruitment functions are performed centrally on behalf of all graduate programs and other responsibilities reside clearly with the head of the graduate program, most often a faculty member. Table 13-7 shows a sample of the division of labor for graduate recruitment.

Table 13-7: Graduate Recruitment Functions

Graduate Recruitment Functions Typically Performed Centrally	Graduate Recruitment Functions Typically Performed at Program Level
■ Leadership and planning, including goal setting ■ Recruitment and admissions support including application processing, information system, and data reports ■ Web support, including SEO for graduate program pages and recruitment-oriented content ■ Other institutional marketing and communication support, including program materials, and email communication support ■ University outreach via participation in graduate fairs and campus visit programs ■ Graduate funding support ■ Coordination of recruitment efforts	■ Commitment to recruitment, including tracking of interest ■ Discipline-specific outreach ■ Timely response to inquiries ■ Regular communications with inquiries, applicants, and admits ■ Participation in campus visit programs ■ Expeditious application review ■ Faculty involvement with recruitment including inquiry and admitted student interaction ■ Strategic use of financial aid (scholarships, assistantships) to support new student recruitment goals

TM

According to the 2014-15 Ruffalo Noel Levitz *National Adult Students Satisfaction and Priorities Report*, based on responses from 34,823 graduate students at 150 institutions completing the Adult Student Priorities Survey™, students indicated the following factors were important in their decision to enroll (Table 13-8).

Table 13-8: Factors in Decision to Enroll for Graduate Students

Factor	Importance percent
Academic reputation	81%
Availability of evening/weekend courses	77%
Future employment opportunities	76%
Campus location (close to home/work)	72%
Cost	71%
Financial aid/scholarship opportunities	70%
Personalized attention prior to enrollment	65%
Recommendations from family/friends/employer	56%
Size of institution	50%

TM

Source: Ruffalo Noel Levitz, 2014-15 National Adult Student Priorities Report

As Table 13-8 illustrates, graduate students are influenced by the quality of the academic experience and the reputation of the graduate program when they search for a program. Cost and financial aid are considerations, of course, but program quality is paramount. These characteristics are best communicated by the faculty in the program, and they should be active components of graduate student recruitment.

Given the distribution of effort required, annual recruitment plans by both administrative offices and the graduate programs are needed to ensure that each is pursuing strategies to achieve the program goals. Also critical is a single point of coordination.

Marketing strategies

Graduate programs need marketing strategies aimed at building student interest throughout the recruitment funnel—especially at the top—as well as proactively managing applications and yield efforts. But many graduate programs do not begin interaction with prospective students until they apply. There are a range of both traditional and relatively new techniques to build the inquiry pool, including test score name purchases, travel to graduate fairs and feeder colleges, pay-per-click Internet advertising, and online listings. Institutions should be prepared to experiment with a range of outreach strategies over several graduate recruitment cycles, and to monitor prospective student traffic based on these investments.

Also critical is reaching the "influencers" of graduate students—people who help shape their pool of potential institutions. These influencers typically include faculty members in the disciplines and professionals in the field. Faculty must be involved in discipline-specific recruitment through participation in conferences, publication in journals, and other avenues that publicize the program.

The corporate community may influence graduate student enrollment decisions. Outreach to employees can include company visits, corporate discounts, and preferred program status on corporate intranets.

Once a student expresses interest in a graduate program, multiple communication flows and campus visit opportunities have been found to be effective. There are clear best practices that work as noted in the *2012 Marketing and Student Recruitment Practices Report for Master's-Level Graduate Programs Report* by Ruffalo Noel Levitz, in partnership with the National Association of Graduate Admissions Professionals (NAGAP).

Web resources

A strong graduate program website is another key marketing resource. Webpages should be designed to attract prospective graduate students and address their key motivations and priorities. Content should feature faculty achievements, student success, and program outcomes. Moreover, each program page should be search engine optimized and mobile-friendly.

Yield strategies

Like their undergraduate counterparts, graduate students do much comparison shopping, and often make their final enrollment choice by comparing several programs to which they have been admitted. The application review process should be streamlined and expedited and the decision communicated quickly to the student. Follow-up contact by faculty and students should be part of the yield process. Admitted students should have an immediate opportunity for advisement and enrollment as a holding strategy.

Financial aid for graduate students

Graduate programs are increasingly competing for students via financial aid and merit scholarships strategies (including discounting), along with traditional assistantship awards. As competition increases for graduate students, institutions must ensure that price is carefully considered. A review of National Student Clearinghouse data for non-enrolling graduate students should be part of each year's planning process to ensure that the institution's graduate tuition and financial aid are in line with competitors (and that perceived competitors are the actual competitors for students).

As with undergraduate recruitment, possible merit awards should be made as early as possible, ideally along with the admit letter. In addition, financial aid offices should be prepared to assist graduate students by providing a high level of individual service to help them fully manage their financing.

Graduate student persistence and degree completion

Until recently, it has been rare to hear discussions about graduate student retention. The assumption seems to have been that if an institution successfully recruits a student, that student will persist through the degree program. But in this competitive and challenging environment for graduate enrollment, attention to student success and persistence must be part of the strategy to ensure solid graduate enrollment.

The Council of Graduate Schools (CGS) has sponsored two recent initiatives to help institutions support degree completion by graduate students—the Ph.D. Completion Project and the Master's Completion Project. Descriptions of these projects can be found at the CGS website (cgsnet.org), as well as tools to measure persistence.

These initiatives have revealed wide variation in degree completion by program and by level. For example, at the master's level, 66 percent of students in STEM fields completed their degree, while 86 percent of students in MBA programs completed after four years. Rates for men and women differ by program as well (Allum, 2014). Other studies have revealed difference in persistence among full-time vs. part-time students.

As with every other element of enrollment management, institutions should begin with an understanding of the current state, a review of the current persistence and enrollment patterns of graduate students, and—as the CGS data makes clear—should be developed at the program and degree level.

Once the program's current state is clear, appropriate interventions and enhancements should be undertaken. For example, if the program loses a large number of students at the end of the first semester or first year, special efforts to reach out to students at these critical stages may help the institution successfully retain those students. Academic and career advisement should be readily available, perhaps even intrusive in the early stages of the graduate career. An institutional orientation coupled with program-based sessions for new graduate students can also head off problems and create a community among the students that may support retention. Other institutional services, financial aid, veterans' services, etc., should be prepared to serve graduate students as well.

Some level of attrition is beyond the control of an institution, of course. According to the CGS study, students who persisted attributed their success to motivation and family support (non-financial). Those who did not persist most often described interference from work as the reason. But if these variables are on the radar, program advisors may be able to help students work around them.

Enrollment planning at the graduate level

Graduate enrollment in an institution's overall enrollment management strategy requires a range of decision factors:

- Current programmatic strengths and likely program demand.
- Demographics in the markets from which the institution expects to draw students.
- Delivery modes—online, blended, or in-person—and other convenience factors important to graduate students.
- Career pathways and the ability to provide preparation through internships and research programs.
- Institutional capacity to provide the necessary space, staffing, services, and investments to support successful graduate enrollment.

Dialogue

Enrollment planning can hardly be called strategic if it does not at least consider adult, online, and graduate students. The growth strategy matrix (see Chapter 6, Strategy Identification) helps an institution consider adult students as either a new market or an existing market warranting deeper penetration. Expanding online course offerings is often a market penetration strategy, while a strategy that offers fully online programs often fits within both the program development and the market development quadrants. New graduate programs fit within the program development quadrant. As your institution studies its approach to adult, online, and graduate students and programs, consider the following:

- What is your current proportion of adult student enrollment? Does expanding your service to adult students fit within the mission of your institution? Do your adult enrollment trends reflect national trends, and are you on track to have 40 percent of your students in the adult category? If not, is that by design?

- Are your current programs and services designed to meet the needs of adult students and their competing priorities? It is not enough to simply recruit adult students. Service hours and delivery options need to allow students to balance their lives, and campus personnel need training and support to best serve the nontraditional student population.

- What is the current balance of online enrollment at your institution? Do you fit the national profile, with at least a fourth of your students taking at least one online course? Do you have the infrastructure in place to grow your online enrollment? Do you understand how your current online strategy (or lack thereof) is affecting the market share of your programs within at least your primary market?

- If graduate programs are within your missional scope, has your institution found the right balance of centralizing enrollment services and functions while allowing sufficient departmental and program level autonomy? Are you as intentional about managing your graduate recruitment processes and metrics as you are for your undergraduate processes?

- Do you understand how your current graduate programs are distinctive from your competitors? Are you monitoring your market share trends? Do you have a specific plan for recruiting your own undergraduates and alumni to your graduate programs?

CHAPTER 14

Lessons Learned

By Lewis Sanborne

For nearly a decade, Ruffalo Noel Levitz has had the privilege of guiding a number of colleges and universities through the strategic enrollment planning process. The work takes effort, patience, and perseverance, but it can be transformative for institutions. The majority of colleges and universities in North America do not have the luxury of more students desiring to enroll than their capacities will allow. The majority do not have burgeoning endowments and substantial operating surpluses. And so the majority do need to plan thoughtfully and strategically to ensure long-term institutional health. We close this book with a series of lessons learned, with the aim of providing campus leaders a set of considerations and guidelines for making informed decisions about launching the process and doing it well.

CHAPTER HIGHLIGHTS

- **Consider readiness factors prior to SEP launch**

- **Success requires leadership, data, and communication**

- **Change requires resources**

Readiness

In the concluding chapter in the first edition of this book, Craig Engel asked, "Are you ready to eat the oyster?" What could be more appropriate than beginning the end of this book with a question about readiness? Before launching a strategic enrollment planning project, institutional leaders must consider a number of factors. As Kevin Crockett makes clear in Chapter 1, the landscape of higher education in the United States is changing, and pressures are increasing—from competition, from governments and government agencies, from families and students, from financial institutions. Jumping into the process without first determining institutional readiness, though, is more likely to lead to frustration than to a robust, productive SEP document. What should campus leaders consider before launching SEP?

Leadership readiness

Leadership is essential both from an institutional and project perspective. At the institutional level, the president or chancellor must commit fully to the process. That means identifying the right lead(s) for the project and then giving them the time, voice, and authority to bring the project to life. The support and engagement of three key players is absolutely essential: the chief academic officer, the chief financial officer, and the chief enrollment officer. If those three are not all committed to the project, failure is likely. The voices of these institutional leaders must also consistently reinforce the value of the SEP project to the institution. Ultimately, these leaders must commit resources to implementing action plans and strategies that emerge from the process. Don't even start if you know that there will be no resources at the end of the planning process.

Identification of the SEP project lead is vital as well. If a single individual, the person must have the confidence of senior leadership and the respect of the faculty. He or she should have a track record of prior project accomplishment and the ability to bring diverse campus constituents together to work on behalf of the institution as a whole, not in the interests of empire building or turf maintenance. Many institutions will opt for co-chairs of the SEP project to bring both enrollment and academic leadership together. Institutions that adopt that approach need to ensure that the co-chairs will truly share the workload and leadership tasks. A symbolic faculty co-chair will seldom satisfy the need for faculty involvement, engagement, and support.

Data readiness

Few institutions will have all the data they need to complete the SEP process before they start it, but there must be a willingness to work hard to collect, organize, and make sense of data in ways that many colleges and universities simply haven't taken the time or invested the effort in before. Ruffalo Noel Levitz suggests various versions of data collection tables to support SEP, and I would hazard a guess that none of our SEP campus partners have ever had everything on the lists. Campuses that are already data-centric and have a history of data-informed decision making will typically move through the SEP process at a faster rate than those that are not. SEP can, however, help a campus make the transition to being data-centric in decision making. Quite simply: do not launch SEP if you are not willing to commit to disciplined data collection and analysis and the use of that analysis for decision making.

Workload capacity

One of the greatest challenges of doing SEP well is the time that the project takes, from the project leads, from the data folks, from the working group chairs and action plan authors, from the communication plans and plan authors, from the finance leads, and basically everyone who touches the project. Seldom have I seen someone given formal release time from their regular responsibilities to do the hard work of strategic enrollment planning; SEP work fits into the classic 'other duties as assigned' category. Something has to give, though. Institutional leaders are well advised to give SEP leaders a break from other committee work or course overloads. SEP project leads must also acknowledge the demands on project participants and be sensitive to the demands of the academic calendar, especially when setting deadlines and considering the time necessary to complete tasks.

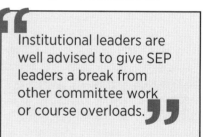

> Institutional leaders are well advised to give SEP leaders a break from other committee work or course overloads.

Change readiness

Strategic enrollment is all about change. We all know the cliché: *If you continue to do what you have always done, you will continue to get the same results.* SEP is about environmental and internal scanning followed by the development of strategies and action plans based on those scans that lead to new initiatives and different approaches. It is exciting because the process is creative and imagines a future state shaped by the project participants. Yet implementation requires change from the top to the bottom of the institution. Change is often hard on college campuses for two reasons.

First, change in itself is unsettling to people who are comfortable in what they do. Often these people are not sufficiently aware that the world around them is changing, and that if they do not change, their comfortable routines are likely to be severely disrupted, even to the extent that layoffs may be in the offing. For these change-resistant folks, the broad sharing of SEP situation analyses can be illuminating.

Second, if prior planning efforts have not led to visible and meaningful change, there is likely to be cynicism that this new process will lead to more of the same. Schools that have had bad experiences with prior planning projects (the creation of glossy documents with no changes in programs, processes, behaviors, or outcomes; or competitive proposal development approaches that led to the same old winners and losers) are more likely to struggle to get buy-in to the SEP process.

For these reasons SEP requires commitment from the top, a well-crafted communication plan, and then action that is justified by the data.

Pitfalls to avoid and practices to adopt

One of the most frequent questions Ruffalo Noel Levitz hears from institutions either thinking about launching SEP or in the midst of the launch phase is frequently phrased like this: "What are the most common errors schools make that limit the effectiveness of the SEP process?" The flip side of the pitfalls question is the success question: "What characteristics and practices lead to effective SEP projects?" The answers to both questions are surprisingly similar; the difference is all in perspective and degree. Successful projects do the following things well, while less successful SEP projects typically manage at least one of the following dimensions poorly:

- Leadership
- Data orientation
- Communication and buy-in

Leadership

SEP leadership pitfalls come in two primary forms: lack of support from the president and cabinet/senior team and ineffective project lead or co-leads. If the president, provost, and chief financial officer are not firmly behind and vocally in front of the project, then its likelihood of success is significantly diminished. SEP cannot be led if only the chief enrollment officer believes in the process. Ultimately, resource allocation (or reallocation) will have to occur, and that does not happen—certainly not at the level required for strategic enrollment initiatives—without support from the top. The voices of the president and senior leadership throughout the project are not just symbolic gestures. Virtually every time they have the ear of the campus community, they should promote SEP and express appreciation for the hard work many are doing. These messages reinforce to the entire campus community that SEP is vital to the future of the institution.

Effective leadership for SEP must come from the project lead or co-leads as well. Those leading the project must have the respect of the entire campus community, but especially of the faculty. SEP's power comes from its placement of the academic enterprise at the center, so academic leadership and the rank and file faculty must have confidence that the person(s) leading the project will honor shared governance and engage the faculty throughout the process. Finding the right lead(s) can be challenging, for the person must have a thorough understanding of strategic enrollment planning, must be respected on campus, understand how to work with data and the data team, be highly organized, and be an effective communicator. He or she must be able to see the big pictures—the college or university or system AND the broader context within which the institution exists.

Leadership vignette one

A large (25,000 students plus), comprehensive public institution had set aggressive enrollment goals as part of its institutional strategic planning process. The chancellor made broad pronouncements about where the school was headed. To help reach those lofty goals, SEP was launched and housed in the enrollment division of the university. The person identified to lead the project was an exceptionally strong enrollment manager, and the resulting strategic enrollment plan was heavy on undergraduate marketing, recruitment, and financial aid strategies. New student enrollment results were impressive and far exceeded goals and timelines. Retention and graduation rate improvements were modest, however, and graduate enrollment was largely stable. Overall SEP results were mixed and could be traced back, not to weak leadership, but to leadership that did not have a sufficiently broad sphere of influence. This project would likely have had better results if it had been facilitated by co-leaders from the student success and graduate divisions. The larger issue, though, was that senior leadership did not sufficiently push engagement with the project from all university divisions.

Leadership vignette two

At a small private college, the designated SEP lead held the reins of the project tightly. He formed the SEP council well, but kept the working groups small (fewer than six) and did not include faculty beyond those already present on the council. He also struggled with multi-tasking. Leadership of SEP was an add-on to an already full plate, and the day-to-day tasks of bringing in the new class consistently meant that SEP tasks were delegated late, and so completed at the last minute, more often by a single individual rather than by working groups or small teams of dedicated internal experts. The president gave the SEP project good attention and worked hard to keep the SEP process and the institutional strategic planning process in sync, but a broad institutional commitment—from either the rank and file faculty or staff—was never achieved. Ultimately the faculty felt out of the loop, and when program proposals came before the academic policy body, approvals were withheld and planners were forced to start the program development process over, with the higher levels of faculty participation that should have been part of the project from the start. Results at this institution were delayed for at least a year.

Data orientation

A strategic enrollment planning project is often the first time many campuses truly become data-centric. Many campuses manage by anecdote. Effective SEP requires a commitment to a data-informed approach that challenges assumptions and anecdotes, and regularly scans the environment and the institution. Schools that have not been data-centric before can become so through the SEP process, but they must be willing to make that change. I have seen a small school with no full-time institutional research person and no history of data-informed decision making become completely committed to a data-informed approach through SEP. It can be done. But I have seen schools with much larger IR and assessment shops refuse to move away from anecdote or they continue to defer to the loudest, or the most senior, or the apparently politically connected. Doing SEP without embracing a data-centric approach usually means you are not doing SEP at all. It's just business as usual.

Data win vignette

A small (fewer than 1,000 students), private, faith-based institution had no person dedicated to institutional research. Data reporting was managed through the registrar's office. Campus leadership knew, however, that their approach to enrollment and institutional planning would need to become data-informed. Prior to launching SEP, they conducted comprehensive recruitment and retention planning projects. For both projects, they mined what historical data they could from their administrative computing system and built the baselines they would need for both planning and assessment moving forward. Recruitment funnels helped them identify weak spots in processes and communication flow. Retention data led to a substantive redesign of advising and re-registration processes. When it was time to launch SEP, they were still not strong in data, but their recruitment and retention metrics were already improving, and they knew it. The campus community began to rally around their newfound, data-informed processes. Both new and continuing enrollment began to improve, in large part because they were focusing their efforts in the areas where their data suggested they could improve.

Communication and buy-in

The SEP process must not unfold behind closed doors with a small group of campus leaders who determine the enrollment future of the college. The organizational structure must engage a substantial proportion of the community (see Chapter 3), but more importantly, outreach and communication must be intentional and frequent well before the project is launched.

Communication vignette

A community college in a major population center in its state had seen a trend of declining enrollments despite a growing population base and excellent outcomes for its graduates both in terms of transfer and job placement. The college struggled, however, to manage multiple campuses and to integrate its large, non-credit programming division into the college culture. Knowing this decentralized structure had historically been a challenge for the college, the SEP leadership team was intentional about ensuring representation from each campus on the SEP council and on every working group. They built a structure like the one described in Figure 3-3 (Chapter 3). Equally as important, however, the SEP leads frequently traveled to each campus to present updates and to seek input on the project. Faculty and staff at all locations felt as if they had ownership of the project, and when the time came to implement initiatives, folks were on board and projects quickly began to produce positive results.

Additional lessons from the trenches

Begin with the end in mind

In truth, the plan document itself is less important than the planning process. What ultimately gets done is the result of the work ethic and dedication of those charged with implementation, not necessarily related to the quality of the plan writing or the quality of paper upon which the plan is printed or the digital storage medium on which it is shelved. That said, a written plan as one concrete outcome of the process is essential. Boards and presidents don't like to see institutional resources spent on such a comprehensive project and then not have any documentation that the work was done. The idea of a written strategic enrollment plan can be daunting, especially if the plan drafting begins at the end of the process. Memories become hazy, and the tasks of the moment—bringing in that next fall cohort for example—will pull even the most disciplined writer away from the SEP draft and into the problems of the present. To ensure a written document, start writing it as soon as you begin the process. Identify the primary plan author and construct the plan outline during one of the first SEP council or steering committee meetings, noting the primary audiences for the document and their likely expectations for the finished product. Then write the plan as you go. As the strategy set and action plans come together, the plan document will be ready for their inclusion.

> To ensure a written SEP document, start writing it as soon you begin the process.

Check for broad inclusion, but not full representation

One of the greatest challenges of effective SEP is often encountered at the beginning of the process, when the organizational structure for the project is formed. There is a temptation to ensure that each key division of the school is represented on the SEP steering team. Unfortunately, a representative body will make for too large of a group. Strive for no more than a dozen members. Remember, managing a college or university is not leading a democracy: everyone will not get a vote. Creation of a strategic enrollment plan is not about making everyone happy. Some key players must be present on the team: chief enrollment officer, chief academic officer or designee, chief finance officer or designee, representatives from financial aid and student success, some strong faculty. But do not, at the steering team level, try to include every area. Remember, the working groups will require subject matter experts (and additional faculty). Check for representation across all the working groups, not for the steering team. Group dynamics are such that the larger a group, the slower the process.

Project enrollment conservatively; budget aggressively

Time and again, at every kind of institution—public, private, two-year, four-year—I see a reluctance among SEP action plan authors to actually assign numbers to their plans. They will identify action steps, but plan authors and teams seem reluctant to claim actual enrollment impact from their prospective efforts. They are just as shy about identifying the real dollars that persons, technology, and spaces will require to make new initiatives happen. At its core, SEP is about change, and change takes resources.

On the enrollment projection side, it is essential that plan authors dig back into the data in the situation analyses to identify the performance indicators their plans will influence. Plan authors should then integrate those metrics into the assessment plans for their initiative. Estimated enrollment impacts should naturally and logically follow from the expected change in metrics based on the steps built into the initiative. How many students are represented by a 2 percent increase in yield, a 5 percent reduction in melt, or a 1 percent increase in cohort retention? Do not worry during the plan draft stage that plan A and plan B may have overlapping impact. During the prioritization stage any deduplication can be applied to plans and excessive enrollment projections trimmed down to reasonable levels.

On the budgetary side, especially in the plan drafting stage, do not worry that costs seem to be mounting quickly. These are not real dollars yet. Too often plan authors try to minimize budget projections because they think their plan will more likely be funded if a large enrollment impact can be realized with little or no investment. This is quite simply bad business. In truth, sharp-eyed finance professionals will spot underfunded plans and any hope for a persuasive advantage will be lost. Ultimately, plans will be prioritized—some moved forward, and some not—based on the potential interactions among numerous plans. Budget honestly, and others working on the SEP project and those who will be charged with the hard decisions will have reasonable information upon which to base their decisions.

One more note about budgeting: when SEP works well, chief financial officers are engaged in the process, and either they or their designee will work with plan authors to build accurate budget pro formas. When it is time to approve plans, these engaged CFOs are much more likely to facilitate these initiatives because they have seen the data-informed process from which they have been developed. The SEP council will not need to provide contextual remediation to gain approval from the finance division because the finance division has been engaged from the outset.

Build in evaluation and assessment

Another challenge at the action plan drafting stage is the creation of evaluation and assessment plans. Two points of advice: first, link enrollment justifications to evaluation; second, know that some steps are not necessarily complicated; they were completed or not—simplify!

One reason plan authors are reluctant to claim enrollment impact is because they have not sufficiently linked their enrollment projections to existing metrics and rates. For example, if enhanced communications and outreach strategies will be developed to increase yield rates, then the enrollment impact should come from a reasonable increase in those yield rates. Plan evaluation will, in part, be accomplished by analysis of the actual change in yield rates.

Another piece of plan evaluation will be the accomplishment of key steps in the timeframe stipulated in the plan: on time, on budget, and of the desired quality. Simple yes/no answers will provide substantive portions of any evaluation plan. Don't make it harder than it needs to be.

Mini case studies

Four-year, faith-based institution

A largely traditional, residential school decided to launch strategic enrollment planning, not because it wanted to grow its traditional undergraduate population, but because it needed to diversify its enrollment and revenue streams. The traditional student population was at capacity and entering student cohorts were managed with a waiting list. Residence hall occupancy rates were consistently above 95 percent; science labs were in use from 8 a.m. to 10 p.m., Monday through Thursday and all day Friday. Night classes had been added to meet student demand for courses, but as evening enrollment rates increased, participation in co-curricular and service programs had begun to decline, a serious concern for this highly missional campus. The study abroad program was relieving some of the on-campus pressure, but it too was at capacity. While undergraduate enrollment was strong, the data deep dive raised concerns about market share. Many in the tightly defined set of peer institutions had capacity and were growing, so while enrollment was stable, market share was in decline. A price sensitivity study and econometric modeling suggested that there was no real opportunity to increase price or net revenue per student, and that any attempt to do so would likely result in an enrollment decline. Yet costs were on the rise.

One focus area in this school's strategic enrollment plan was an investment in personnel and technology to expand its online offerings. The institution hired an expert from outside the university, and faculty received the support necessary to convert select courses for online delivery. Traditional undergraduate students were permitted to enroll in one online course each semester, and these same courses were made available for prospective high school and transfer students. Evening course enrollment immediately declined and participation rates in the co-curriculum rebounded. A niche master's degree program with modest on-campus enrollment was identified for conversion to online to reach the institution's market pockets across the country. In the first fall it was offered, the program enrolled many times over the number of students needed to break even. By the end of the first year, that one master's program was so successful, faculty from other departments asked to adapt their programs for online delivery.

Not every SEP initiative at this campus was as successful, but they were able to address issues central to mission, student engagement, course scheduling, outreach, and enrollment by focusing the broad online strategy to accomplish multiple specific ends.

Four-year, regional, comprehensive, public university

A medium-sized institution in a tristate region had experienced several years of slow enrollment decline. Furthermore, it was challenged with retention and graduation rates that had been running slightly lower than its peer institutions. Its two largest competitors were the local community college and another four-year public, about 30 miles away but across the border in a neighboring state. A border-state scholarship program had been somewhat effective, but because it required high academic performance for renewal, retention rates for out-of-state students were poor, functioning as a drag on overall retention. Competition for students was fierce and exacerbated by state-level policies that had made the community college a nearly free option for in-state students.

During the strategic enrollment planning process, campus leaders decided to restructure the border-state scholarship as a border-region tuition rate. This allowed a targeted expansion of the counties covered by the new pricing structure and led to a substantial increase in new out-of-state students in the first year of the program. With satisfactory academic progress requirements now consistent for in-state and out-of-state students, retention rates rebounded. One reason this strategy was so effective was that the recent enrollment declines had created capacity. The institution was able to accommodate net new students from out of state in existing classes served by existing programs. Expenses were related primarily to marketing and recruitment efforts, leading to a substantial return on the initial investment for this program.

Two-year public college

A community college near a major metropolitan area, with very sophisticated institutional research and effectiveness efforts, was monitoring a steady decline in the enrollment of adult students. Market share for the direct-from-high-school population was strong and trending positively, but the decline in the adult market was troublesome. A significant population of workers migrated into the college's district each day for work, which should have bolstered enrollment, but did not actually seem to be doing so. Analysis of recent completions showed that adult students were choosing shorter programs, those of less than 30 credits, rather than associate degrees.

Because adult student enrollment showed the steepest decline, a number of strategies to remedy that trend were developed. Among the initiatives were improved services and enhanced onboarding programs for adults, improved scheduling and registration processes to ensure that students could get the courses they needed when they needed them, a centralized program and processes for prior learning assessment, and an institutionwide commitment to building a service culture. These strategies were selected because of their potential to provide direct benefits to adult students, but the college anticipated a much broader impact from these initiatives. Themes of the strategic enrollment plan are feeding into the next version of the institutional strategic plan. It is too early to report results, but preliminary data is encouraging.

A few final words

When I assumed leadership for Ruffalo Noel Levitz strategic enrollment planning services, I wasn't sure I was going to like the job. As the years have slipped by, and the number of campuses I have worked with has grown, I have come to love what I do. Strategic enrollment planning can be transformative for the colleges and universities that do it well. Is it for every campus? Of course not; all of the pitfalls described here come from actual campus partners. But all of the successes are real as well.

During an SEP assessment exercise a while back, I was conducting interviews with campus leaders from SEP projects that had been completed for at least two years. The majority of the campus partners I talked to could point to enrollment results that, in hindsight, made it clear the investment had been worth it. But what struck me was the consistent testimony that by far the greater benefit of the process was a change in organizational culture. Faculty were now paying attention to enrollment metrics, not just in their own programs, but institutionwide. Almost everyone on campus now understood that every interaction with both prospective and current students was influential and made a difference to the health of the college. Folks saw that what they did made a difference, not just to the institution, but to its students.

That's why I love leading campuses through strategic enrollment planning: the process allows us to bring the benefits of higher education to more people. Sure, the colleges and universities I work with are stronger after the process than they were before, but that strength expands the number of individuals who have access to higher education, can find ways to afford it, and can be successful at it. That's what it's all about. Whether your school serves fewer than 1,000, more than 30,000, or any number in between, our work touches individual student lives and brings the benefits of education to the people and communities that we serve.

Strategic enrollment planning is a lot of work, but so are most things that make a difference in the world.

Happy Planning,

REFERENCES

ACT. (2015). *2015 National collegiate retention and persistence-to-degree rates.* Iowa City, IA: Author. Retrieved from http://www.act.org/content/act/en/research.html

ACT. (2015). *The condition of college and career readiness 2015.* Iowa City, IA: Author. Retrieved from http://www.act.org/content/act/en/research.html

Adelman, C. (2006). *The toolbox revisited: Paths to degree completion from high school through college.* Washington, DC: U.S. Department of Education. Retrieved from http://www2.ed.gov/rschstat/research/pubs/toolboxrevisit/toolbox.pdf

Allen, E., and Seaman, J. (2016). *Online report card: Tracking online education in the United States.* Boston, MA: Babson Survey Research Group and Quahog Research Group, LLC. Retrieved from http://onlinelearningsurvey.com/reports/onlinereportcard.pdf

Allum, J. (2014). *Graduate enrollment and degrees: 2003 to 2013.* Washington, DC: Council of Graduate Schools. Retrieved from http://www.cgsnet.org/ckfinder/userfiles/files/GED_report_2013.pdf

American Association of Community Colleges (2011). *Voluntary framework of accountability.* Washington, DC: Author.

Anctil, E. (2008). Selling higher education: Marketing and advertising America's colleges and universities. *ASHE Higher Education Report*, Volume 34, No. 2. San Francisco, CA: Jossey-Bass.

Andreasen, A. (1985). Backward market research. *Harvard Business Review*, May-June 1985.

Aslanian, C. B., and Clinefelter, D. L. (2013). *Online college students 2013: Comprehensive data on demands and preferences.* Louisville, KY: The Learning House, Inc.

Astin, A. W. (1999). Student involvement: A developmental theory for higher education. *Journal of College Student Development*, 40(5).

Astin, A. W. (2003). From number crunching to spirituality. In *Higher education handbook of theory and research, Volume 18.* London, England: Kluwer Academic Publishers.

Atkins, K. (2010). Strategically planning to change. *New Directions for Student Services*, 2010: 17–25. doi: 10.1002/ss.372

Baer, M., and Stace, P. (1997). Enrollment management. In J. Martin and J. Samuels (Eds.), *First among equals: The role of the chief academic officer.* Baltimore, MD: Johns Hopkins University Press.

Barr, M. (2002). *Academic administrator's guide to budgets and financial management.* San Francisco, CA: Jossey-Bass.

Bean, J. P. (1990). Strategic planning and enrollment management. In D. Hossler, J. P. Bean, and Associates, *The strategic management of college enrollments.* San Francisco, CA: Jossey-Bass.

Black, J. (Ed.). (2001). *Strategic enrollment management revolution.* Annapolis Junction, MD: AACRAO.

Bok, D. (2006). *Our underachieving colleges: A candid look at how much students learn and why they should be learning more.* Princeton, NJ: University of Princeton Press.

Bolman, L., and Deal, T. (1997). *Reframing organizations: Artistry, choice, and leadership* (Second Ed.). San Francisco, CA: Jossey-Bass.

Brookfield, S. (1984). Self-directed adult learning: A critical paradigm. *Adult Education Quarterly*, 35, 59-71. Thousand Oaks, CA: Sage Publications.

Brookfield, S. (1991). *Understanding and facilitating adult learning: A comprehensive analysis of principles and effective practices.* San Francisco, CA: Jossey-Bass.

Brookfield, S. (1984). *Adult learners, adult education and the community.* Milton Keynes, England: Open University Press.

Brookfield, S. ed. (1985). Self-directed learning: From theory to practice. *New Directions for Continuing Education*, No. 25. San Francisco, CA: Jossey-Bass.

Barkley, E.F., Cross, K.P., Major, C.H. (2005). *Collaborative learning techniques. A handbook for college faculty.* San Francisco, CA: Jossey-Bass.

Bryk, A. S., and Schneider, B. (2003). Trust in schools: A core resource for school reform. *Educational Leadership,* 60(6).

Bryson, J. (1995). *Strategic planning for public and nonprofit organizations: A guide to strengthening and sustaining organizational achievement* (Revised Ed.). San Francisco, CA: Jossey-Bass.

Bryson, J. (2004). S*trategic planning for public and nonprofit organizations: A guide to strengthening and sustaining organizational achievement* (Third Ed.). San Francisco, CA: Jossey-Bass.

Bureau of Labor Statistics (2014). *Occupational outlook handbook.* Washington, DC: Author. Retrieved from http://www.bls.gov/ooh/

Chickering, A. W., and Gamson, Z. F. (1987). Seven principles for good practice in undergraduate education. *AAHE Bulletin,* 39(7).

Chickering, A. W., and Reisser, L. (1993). *Education and identity* (Second Ed.). San Francisco, CA: Jossey-Bass.

Christensen, C., and Eyring, H. (2011). *The innovative university: Changing the DNA of higher education from the inside out.* San Francisco, CA: Jossey-Bass.

Clinefelter, D. L. and Aslanian, C. B. (2014). *Online college students 2014: Comprehensive data on demands and preferences.* Louisville, KY: The Learning House, Inc.

College and University Professional Association for Human Resources. (2015). *Professionals in higher education salary survey.* Knoxville, TN: Author.

College Board. (2013). *Education pays 2013.* Trends in Higher Education Series. New York, NY: Author. Retrieved from www.collegeboard.org

College Board. (2014). *College-bound juniors and sophomores.* Trends in Higher Education Series. New York, NY: Author. Retrieved from www.collegeboard.org

College Board. (2015). *Trends in college pricing.* Trends in Higher Education Series. New York, NY: Author. Retrieved from www.collegeboard.org

College Board. (2015). *Trends in student aid.* Trends in Higher Education Series. New York, NY: Author. Retrieved from www.collegeboard.org

Collins, J. (2001). *Good to great: Why some companies make the leap ... and others don't* (First Ed.). New York, NY: Harper Business.

Complete College America (2011). *Time is the enemy.* Washington, DC: Author. Retrieved from http://www.completecollege.org/docs/Time_Is_the_Enemy.pdf

Consortium for the Advancement of Adult Higher Education. (March, 2014.) *Chronicle, program enrollments.* Phoenix, AZ: Author. Retrieved electronically 10/27/14 at https://sites.google.com/a/caahe.org/caahe-chronicle-march-2014/home/program-enrollments.

Cope, R. (1981). *Strategic planning, management, and decision making.* AAHE-ERIC/Higher Education Research Report, No. 9, Washington, DC: American Association for Higher Education.

Cross, K.P. and Zusman, A. (1977). *The needs of non-traditional learners and the responses of non-traditional programs.* Berkley: University of California.

Cross, K.P. (1981). *Adults as learners. Increasing participation and facilitating learning.* San Francisco, CA: Jossey-Bass.

Dickeson, R. (1999). *Prioritizing academic programs and services: Reallocating resources to achieve strategic balance.* San Francisco, CA: Jossey-Bass.

Dickeson, R., (2010). *Prioritizing academic programs and services: Reallocating resources to achieve strategic balance* (Revised). San Francisco, CA: Jossey-Bass.

Doerfel, M., and Ruben, B. (2002). Developing more adaptive, innovative, and interactive organizations. In B. Bender and J. Shuh (Eds.), *New Directions for Higher Education*, 118. San Francisco, CA: Jossey-Bass.

Dolence, M., and Norris, D. (1994). Using key performance indicators to drive strategic decision making. In V. Borden and T. Banta (Eds.), Performance indicators to drive strategic decision making. *New Directions for Institutional Research*, 82. San Francisco, CA: Jossey-Bass.

Doran, G. T. (1981). There's a S.M.A.R.T. way to write management's goals and objectives. *Management Review.* November 1981, 70(11).

Durkin, D. (2010). Growing with the flows. *Continuing Higher Education Review*, 74, 2010.

Eagan, K., Stolzenberg, E. B., Ramirez, J. J., Aragon, M. C., Suchard, M. R., & Hurtado, S. (2014). *The American freshman: National norms fall 2014.* Los Angeles: Higher Education Research Institute, UCLA.

Eagan, K., Stolzenberg, E.B., Bates, A.K., Aragon, M.C., Suchard, M.R., Rios-Aguilar, C.R. (2015). *The American freshman: National norms for fall 2015.* Los Angeles, CA: Higher Education Research Institute, UCLA.

Education Trust, The. (2015). *College results online.* Retrieved from http://www.collegeresults.org

Ehrenberg, R. G., and Webber, D. A. (2010). Student services expenditures matter. *Change*, 2010, 42.

Eleuterio, T. (2015). *Delaware cost study.* Newark, DE: University of Delaware.

Ellis, S. E. (2010). Introduction to strategic planning in student affairs: A model for process and elements of a plan. In S. E. Ellis (Ed.), Strategic planning in student affairs. *New Directions for Student Services*, (132). San Francisco, CA: Jossey-Bass.

Ginsberg, B. (2011). The strategic plan: Neither strategy nor plan, but a waste of time. Washington DC: *The Chronicle of Higher Education*, July 17, 2011.

Habley, W. R., and McClanahan, R. (2004). *What works in student retention?* Iowa City, IA: ACT. Retrieved from http://www.act.org/research/policymakers/reports/retain.html

Hadley, J., Lanzerotti, L., and Nathan, A. (2014.) *Revisit your strategy and repeat the process.* Boston, MA: The Bridgespan Group. Retrieved from http://www.bridgespan.org/Publications-and-Tools/Strategy-Development/Living-Into-Your-Strategic-Plan/Steps-Overview/Step-6-Revisit-Your-Strategy-and-Repeat-the-Pr-(1).aspx

Haines, S. (2000). *The systems thinking approach to strategic planning and management.* Boca Raton, FL: CRC Press, LLC.

Heifetz, R., Grashow, A., and Linsky, M. (2009). Leadership in a permanent crisis. *Harvard Business Review*, 87(7/8). Retrieved from http://www.ocvets4pets.com/archive17/Leadership_in_a__Permanent__Crisis_-_HBR.org.pdf

Henderson, S. E. (2005). Refocusing enrollment management: Losing structure and finding the academic context. AACRAO, *College and University*, 80(3).

Hunter, M. S., Tobolowsky, B. F., Gardner, J. N., Evenbeck, S. E., Pattengale, J. A., Schaller, M. A., and Schreiner, L. A. (2010). *Helping sophomores succeed: Understanding and improving the second-year experience* (First Ed.). San Francisco, CA: Jossey-Bass.

Institute of International Education. (2015). *Open doors 2015: Report on international educational exchange.* New York, NY: Author. Retrieved from http://www.iie.org/Research-and-Publications/Open-Doors

Jaschik, S. and Lederman, D. (ed) (2013). *The 2013 Inside Higher Ed survey of faculty attitudes on technology.* Washington, DC: Inside Higher Ed and Gallup. Retrieved from https://www.insidehighered.com/booklet/survey-faculty-attitudes-technology

Karabel, J. (2005). *The chosen.* New York: First Mariner Books.

Keller, G. (2004). *Transforming a college: The story of a little-known college's strategic climb to national distinction.* Baltimore, MD: Johns Hopkins University Press.

Kena, G., Aud, S., Johnson, F., Wang, X., Zhang, J., Rathbun, A., Wilkinson-Flicker, S., and Kristapovich, P. (2015). *The condition of education 2015.* Washington, DC: NCES, US Department of Education. Retrieved from https://nces.ed.gov/pubsearch/pubsinfo.asp?pubid=2015144

Kinkead, J. (Ed.). (2011). *Advancing undergraduate research: Marketing, communications, and fundraising.* Washington, DC: Council on Undergraduate Research.

Knowles, M. (1950). *Informal adult education.* New York, NY: Association Press.

Knowles, M. (1962). *A history of the adult education movement in the USA.* New York, NY: Krieger.

Knowles, M. (1975). Self-directed learning. Chicago: Follet.

Knowles, M. (1984). *The adult learner: A neglected species* (3rd Ed.). Houston, TX: Gulf Publishing.

Knowles, M. (1984). *Andragogy in action.* San Francisco, CA: Jossey-Bass.

Kotler, P. (1999). *Kotler on marketing: How to create, win, and dominate markets.* New York, NY: Simon and Schuster.

Kotler, P., and Fox, K.F.A. (1985). *Strategic marketing for educational institutions.* Englewood Cliffs, NJ: Prentice-Hall, Inc.

Kuh, G. D. (2008). *High-impact educational practices: What they are, who has access to them, and why they matter.* Washington, DC: AAC&U.

Kuh, G. D., Kinzie, J., Schuh, J. H., and Whitt, E. J. (2005). *Student success in college: Creating conditions that matter* (First Ed.). San Francisco, CA: Jossey-Bass.

Lake, N. (2006). *The strategic planning workbook* (Second Ed.). Philadelphia, PA: Kogan Page.

Leinbach, D. T., and Jenkins, D. (2008). Using longitudinal data to increase community college student success: A guide to measuring milestone and momentum point attainment. *CCRC Research Tools No. 2.* New York, NY: Community College Research Center, Teachers College, Columbia University. Retrieved from http://ccrc.tc.columbia.edu/Publication.asp?uid=570

Lesick, L. (2009). *A Gazette Minute with Larry Lesick.* West Palm Beach, FL: The Greentree Gazette.

Leslie, D. W., and Fretwell, E. K. (1996). *Wise moves in hard times: Creating and managing resilient colleges and universities.* San Francisco, CA: Jossey-Bass.

Lumina Foundation. (2016). *A stronger nation 2016.* Indianapolis, IN: Author. Retrieved from https://www.luminafoundation.org/resources

Martin, D.C. and Arendale, D.A. (Eds.) (1994, Winter). Supplemental Instruction: Improving student achievement and persistence. *New Directions for Teaching and Learning.* San Francisco: Jossey-Bass.

Maslen, G. (2014). Mass movement of the world's students. *University World News.* January 31, 2014. Retrieved from http://www.universityworldnews.com/article.php?story=20140129200018337

Maslowsky, C. (2012). Top five ways to market higher education to adult students. *The evolllution* (blog). Retrieved from http://www.evolllution.com/opinions/top-five-ways-to-market-higher-education-to-adult-students/

Massey, R. (2001). Developing a SEM plan. Chapter from J. Black, *The strategic enrollment management revolution.* Washington, DC: American Association of Collegiate Registrars and Admissions Officers (AACRAO).

Means, B., Toyama,Y., Murphy. R., Bakia, M., and Jones, K. (2010). *Evaluation of evidence-based practices in online learning: A meta-analysis and review of online-learning studies.* Washington, D.C.: U.S. Department of Education.

Moody's Investors Service. (2015). *2015 outlook for U.S. higher education.* New York, NY: Author.

National Association for College Admission Counseling (NACAC). (2014). *State of college admission report.* Arlington, VA: Author.

National Association of College and University Business Officers (NACUBO). (2015). *2015 Tuition discounting study.* Retrieved from http://www.nacubo.org/Research/NACUBO_Tuition_Discounting_Study.html

National Center for Education Statistics (NCES). (2010). *Digest of education statistics.* U.S. Department of Education. Retrieved from http://nces.ed.gov/programs/digest/d10/

National Center for Education Statistics (NCES). (2012). *Digest of education statistics.* U.S. Department of Education. Retrieved from http://nces.ed.gov/programs/digest/d12/

National Center for Education Statistics (NCES). (2014). *Projections of education statistics to 2022.* U.S. Department of Education. Retrieved from https://nces.ed.gov/pubsearch/pubsinfo.asp?pubid=2014051

National Center for Education Statistics (NCES). (2015). *Projections of education statistics to 2022.* U.S. Department of Education. Retrieved from https://nces.ed.gov/programs/digest/current_tables.asp

National Center for Education Statistics (NCES). (2014). *Enrollment in distance education courses, by state: Fall 2012.* U.S. Department of Education. Retrieved from http://nces.ed.gov/pubs2014/2014023.pdf

National Center for Education Statistics (NCES). (2015). *Enrollment in distance education courses, by state: Fall 2012.* U.S. Department of Education. Retrieved from http://nces.ed.gov/programs/digest/d15/tables/dt15_311.15.asp

National Conference of State Legislatures (NCSL). (2016). *Performance-based funding for higher education (webpage).* Retrieved from http://www.ncsl.org/research/education/performance-funding.aspx

National Student Clearinghouse. (2015). *Current term enrollment estimates, fall 2015.* Herndon, VA: Author. Retrieved from https://nscresearchcenter.org/currenttermenrollmentestimate-fall2015/

Newman, F., Couturier, L., and Scurry, J. (2004). *The future of higher education: Rhetoric, reality, and the risks of the market.* San Francisco, CA: Jossey-Bass.

Newton, B., and Smith, J. (2008). Steering in the same direction: The importance of academic and student affairs relationships to student success. *College and University*, 84(1). Washington, DC: AACRAO.

Noel, L., Levitz, R., and Saluri, D. (1985). *Increasing student retention: Effective programs and practices for reducing the dropout rate* (First Ed.). San Francisco, CA: Jossey-Bass.

OECD. (2013). *Education indicators report.* Paris, France: OECD Publishing. Retrieved from http://www.oecd.org/education/skills-beyond-school/EDIF%202013--N%C2%B014%20%28eng%29-Final.pdf

Norris D., and Poulton N. (2008). *A guide to planning and change.* Ann Arbor, MI: Society for College and University Planning.

Pardee, C. F. (2004). *Organizational structures for advising.* NACADA Clearinghouse of Academic Advising Resources. Retrieved from NACADA Clearinghouse of Academic Advising Resources: http://www.nacada.ksu.edu/Resources/Clearinghouse/View-Articles/Organizational-Models-for-Advising.aspx

Paulsen, M. B., and Smart, J.C. (2001). *The Finance of higher education: Theory, research, Policy and practice.* New York, NY: Agathon Press.

Peters, T. J., and Waterman Jr., R. H. (1982). *In search of excellence.* New York, NY: Harper & Row.

Poock, M.C., and LeFond, D. (2001). How college-bound prospects perceive university web sites: Findings, implications, and turning browsers into applicants. *C&U Journal*, 77(1).

Radford, A. W. (2011). *Learning at a Distance: Undergraduate Enrollment in Distance Education Courses and Degree Programs. Stats in Brief.* NCES 2012-154. National Center for Education Statistics.

Rowley, D., Lujan, H., and Dolence, M. (1997). *Strategic change in colleges and universities: Planning to survive and prosper.* San Francisco, CA: Jossey-Bass.

Ruffalo Noel Levitz. (2012). *Marketing and student recruitment practices for master's-level graduate programs.* Cedar Rapids, IA: Author. Retrieved from https://www.RuffaloNL.com/papersandresearch

Ruffalo Noel Levitz (2014). *Recruitment funnel benchmark report for four-year institutions.* Cedar Rapids, IA: Author. Retrieved from https://www.RuffaloNL.com/papersandresearch

Ruffalo Noel Levitz. (2015). *Discounting report.* Cedar Rapids, IA: Author. Retrieved from https://www.RuffaloNL.com/papersandresearch

Ruffalo Noel Levitz. (2015). *High school students' and parents' perceptions of and preferences for communication with colleges.* Cedar Rapids, IA: Author. Retrieved from https://www.RuffaloNL.com/papersandresearch

Ruffalo Noel Levitz (2015). *International E-Expectations.* Cedar Rapids, IA: Author. Retrieved from https://www.RuffaloNL.com/papersandresearch

Ruffalo Noel Levitz. (2015). *Marketing and student recruitment practices at four-year and two-year institutions.* Cedar Rapids, IA: Author. Retrieved from https://www.RuffaloNL.com/papersandresearch

Ruffalo Noel Levitz. (2015). *National Online Learners Priorities Report.* Cedar Rapids, IA: Author. Retrieved from https://www.RuffaloNL.com/papersandresearch

Ruffalo Noel Levitz. (2015). *Retention indicators report.* Cedar Rapids, IA: Author. Retrieved from https://www.RuffaloNL.com/papersandresearch

Ruffalo Noel Levitz. (2015). *Student retention and college completion practices report for four-year and two-year institutions.* Cedar Rapids, IA: Author. Retrieved from https://www.RuffaloNL.com/papersandresearch

Ruffalo Noel Levitz. (2016). *National student satisfaction and priorities report.* Cedar Rapids, IA: Author. Retrieved from https://www.RuffaloNL.com/papersandresearch

Ruffalo Noel Levitz, OmniUpdate, CollegeWeekLive, & NRCCUA. (2014). *E-expectations report: The online expectations of prospective college students and their parents.* Cedar Rapids, IA: Author. Retrieved from https://www.RuffaloNL.com/papersandresearch

Ruffalo Noel Levitz, OmniUpdate, CollegeWeekLive, & NRCCUA. (2015). *2015 E-expectations report: What 10 years of research has told us about college e-recruitment.* Cedar Rapids, IA: Author. Retrieved from https://www.RuffaloNL.com/papersandresearch

Schroeder, C. C. (1999). Partnerships: An imperative for enhancing student learning and institutional effectiveness. In J. H. Schuh and E. J. Whitt (Eds.), Creating successful partnerships between academic and student affairs. *New Directions for Student Services*, No. 87. San Francisco, CA: Jossey-Bass.

Selingo, J. (2013). *College unbound: The future of higher education and what it means for students.* Boston: Houghton Mifflin Harcourt.

Sevier, R. (2000). *Strategic planning in higher education: Theory and practice.* Washington, DC: CASE Books.

State Higher Education Executive Officers (SHEEO). (2015). *State higher education finance FY 2015.* Boulder, CO: Author. Retrieved from www.sheeo.org

Steiner, G, Miner, J, and Gray, E. (1992). *Management policy and strategy* (Second Ed.). Old Tappan, NJ: MacMillan Publishing.

Stewart, A., and Carpenter-Hubin, J. (2000). The balanced scorecard: Beyond reports and rankings. *Planning for Higher Education*, 29(2).

Terenzini, P. T., Pascarella, E. T., and Blimling, G. S. (1996). Students' out-of-class experiences and their influence on learning and cognitive development: A literature review. *Journal of College Student Development*, 37(2).

Tingley Advantage. (2013). *The importance of dashboards (blog).* June 20, 2013. Toronto, ON: Author. Retrieved from http://www.thetingleyadvantage.com/2013/06/the-importance-of-dashboards.html

Troop, D. (2014). Moody's Issues Negative Outlook for Higher Education. Washington, DC: *The Chronicle of Higher Education*, July 14, 2014. Retrieved from: http://chronicle.com/blogs/bottomline/moodys-issues-negative-outlook-for-higher-education/

Tunis, H., and Harrington, M. (June 9, 2013). *The Learning Organization: Strategic Planning and Evaluation.* Los Angeles, CA: Center for Nonprofit Management.

U.S. Department of Education. (2011). *Meeting President Obama's 2020 college completion goal.* Retrieved from http://www.ed.gov/news/speeches/meeting-president-obamas-2020-college-completion-goal

U.S. Department of Education (2010, Revised). *Evaluation of evidence-based practices in online learning: A meta-analysis and review of online learning studies.* Retrieved from https://www2.ed.gov/rschstat/eval/tech/evidence-based-practices/finalreport.pdf

U.S. Department of Education. (2014). *Enrollment in Distance Education Courses, by State: Fall 2012.* Publication NCES 2014-023. Retrieved from http://nces.ed.gov/pubs2014/2014023.pdf

U.S. Department of Labor. (2014). Bureau of Labor Statistics, Economic News Release, Table 4, *Fastest growing occupations, 2012 and projected 2022.* Retrieved from http://www.bls.gov/news.release/ecopro.t04.htm

U.S. Department of Labor. Bureau of Labor Statistics. (2014). Economic News Release, *Employment Projections: 2012-2022 Summary.* Retrieved from http://www.bls.gov/news.release/ecopro.toc.htm

U.S. Department of Labor. Bureau of Labor Statistics. (2014). Economic News Release, Table 8, *Occupations with the largest projected number of job openings due to growth and replacement needs, 2012 and projected 2022.* Retrieved from http://www.bls.gov/news.release/ecopro.t08.htm

U.S. Department of Labor, Veterans' Employment and Training Service. (2011). *Transition assistance program manual.* Retrieved from https://www.dol.gov/vets/programs/tap.htm

Van Der Werf, M., and Sabatier, G. (2009). *The college of 2020: Students.* Washington, DC: Chronicle Research Services: The Chronicle of Higher Education.

Vanover Porter, M. (2010). When the price is right. *NACUBO Business Officer*, March 2010.

Whitney, R. (2010). Involving academic faculty in developing and implementing a strategic plan. In S.E. Ellis (Ed.), Strategic planning in student affairs. *New Directions for Student Services.* San Francisco, CA: Jossey-Bass.

Western Interstate Commission for Higher Education. (2012). *Knocking at the college door: Projections of high school graduates.* Boulder, CO: Author. Retrieved from http://www.wiche.edu/knocking-8th

Western Interstate Commission for Higher Education. (2016). *Knocking at the college door: State profiles.* Boulder, CO: Author. Retrieved from http://www.wiche.edu/knocking-8th

Zlotkowski, E. (Ed.). (1998). *Successful service-learning programs: New models of excellence in higher education.* Bolton, MA: Anker Publishing.

ABOUT THE AUTHORS

Scott Bodfish — CHAPTER 10

Scott Bodfish is vice president of the market research division of Ruffalo Noel Levitz and has more than 14 years of experience on campus in strategic planning and institutional research. During his career at Ruffalo Noel Levitz, Mr. Bodfish led the development of new research services designed to help campuses make data-informed decisions regarding pricing strategy and new program development.

With particular interest in researching the student college choice process, Mr. Bodfish has designed and implemented research studies focusing on all aspects of enrollment management and student retention. These include policy formation; predictive modeling of inquiries, applicants, and matriculants; financial aid modeling and analysis; non-enrolling students; and student success and retention.

Prior to joining Ruffalo Noel Levitz, Mr. Bodfish served as director of institutional research and planning support at Wilkes University (PA) and Sweet Briar College (VA), where enrollment management teams achieved 20 percent average increases in freshman class size. He has also taught philosophy courses at institutions such as St. Louis Community College (MO), the University of Missouri-Columbia, and Randolph-Macon Women's College (VA).

Mr. Bodfish holds an MA from Washington University (MO).

Wes Butterfield — CHAPTER 10

Wes Butterfield has served more than 40 small and large four-year public and private campuses across the United States throughout his 12-year consulting career at Ruffalo Noel Levitz.

Mr. Butterfield has assisted campuses achieve enrollment and net revenue goals through the strategic use of financial assistance, increasing the effectiveness of student recruitment through Forecast*Plus*™ predictive modeling, and optimizing their enrollment management efforts.

Before coming to Ruffalo Noel Levitz, Mr. Butterfield served as director of admission for Cornell College (IA). His primary responsibilities included supervising the admissions staff and assisting with the development, creation, and execution of the overall recruitment plan. During his tenure at Cornell, the admissions staff stopped a three-year decline in entering student enrollment. Further accomplishments included creating the college's first comprehensive recruitment plan and revamping the scholarship program to provide greater access to the college for students and their families. His 15 years of on-campus higher education experience were spent in enrollment management at Cornell College and in college advancement at both Cornell College and the University of Iowa Foundation.

Mr. Butterfield is currently enrolled in a PhD program at the University of Iowa.

Sarah Coen — CHAPTER 11

Sarah Coen offers 25 years of experience in new student marketing, recruitment, financial aid, orientation, and staff development. As Ruffalo Noel Levitz senior vice president for consulting services, Ms. Coen has served more than 50 institutions in the United States and Canada, including small and large four-year private, two-year public, and four-year public institutions. In addition, she has worked with system-level projects in both Louisiana and Maine.

Before her position at Ruffalo Noel Levitz, Ms. Coen was dean of admissions at Transylvania University (KY). During her tenure at Transylvania, she helped engineer record gains in applications, freshman enrollment, and net revenue. In addition, academic quality and freshman-to-sophomore retention rates increased, resulting in the largest enrollment in the university's 225-year history.

Ms. Coen speaks nationally on the topics of recruitment plan development, effective strategies for marketing and recruitment, and on using data to make informed decisions to grow enrollment. She previously served as director of admissions at Commonwealth College (VA) and director of admissions at the University of Michigan-Dearborn. She holds a master's degree in public administration from Central Michigan University.

Kevin Crockett — CHAPTER 1

Kevin Crockett is enrollment management division president at Ruffalo Noel Levitz. He consults directly with campuses on effective leadership and strategy development for admissions, marketing, recruitment, retention, and student financial aid. An experienced enrollment manager, Mr. Crockett has served more than 300 institutions and systems throughout North America.

Prior to joining the firm, Mr. Crockett served as dean of admissions and enrollment management at Cornell College (IA), where he enrolled the three largest consecutive entering classes in school history—culminating in record opening enrollment.

Mr. Crockett is an inspirational speaker on enrollment management topics and frequently appears at higher education conferences to share significant enrollment trends and innovative strategies. He holds an MA in higher education administration from the University of Iowa with concentrations in policy analysis and leadership studies.

Marilyn Crone — CHAPTER 7

Marilyn Crone offers 18 years of experience in higher education, serving private institutions in the United States and Canada, following 15 years in the financial services industry. She is vice president for enrollment management at Seattle University where she has led collaborative efforts to create and implement undergraduate and graduate strategic enrollment plans in addition to overseeing the undergraduate admissions, graduate admissions, student financial services, office of the registrar and operations, university retention initiatives and summer programs.

Prior experience includes multiple roles as a management consultant at Trinity Western University (BC), enrollment management consultant for Quest University Canada (BC), then a start-up private university, and vice president for enrollment and retention management at Baylor University (TX).

Ms. Crone holds an MBA from Baylor University and completed the Harvard Institute for Educational Management. She has served on numerous non-profit boards.

Tim Culver, PhD — CHAPTER 12

Tim Culver leads the retention consulting services of Ruffalo Noel Levitz, offering counsel to help institutions develop, implement, and evaluate plans for improving enrollment, student success, persistence, retention, and degree completion rates. He has consulted with more than 50 four-year and two-year institutions and brings expertise in a wide range of areas of enrollment management, including but not limited to retention planning, Title III and Title V grants, enrollment planning, developmental education, and institutional assessments.

Prior to joining Ruffalo Noel Levitz, Dr. Culver served as director of the student success center at Shawnee State University (OH). He wrote and received federal Title III grants resulting in the implementation of a new instructional support services model. At Shawnee State, he used his passion for teaching as well, designing a curriculum for and teaching developmental mathematics courses.

Dr. Culver has been a member of several national and state organizations including the National Association of Student Personnel Administrators, the National Association for Developmental Education, and the National Academic Advising Association. He holds a PhD from Colorado State University, an MEd from the University of Dayton (OH), and an MBA from Marshall University (WV).

Sue Dietrich, EdD — CHAPTER 13

Sue Dietrich is Ruffalo Noel Levitz associate vice president, with over 35 years of both hands-on and consulting expertise in the areas of adult, online, and graduate services. She brings her passion for the nontraditional learner to her consulting work in strategic enrollment, operations, student retention, accreditation, and new program development.

Prior to joining Ruffalo Noel Levitz, Dr. Dietrich was senior vice president of a higher education consulting firm dedicated to developing and implementing innovative programs for nontraditional learners. She assisted 40 colleges and universities in the design and development of undergraduate and graduate degrees, online and face-to-face, helping over a quarter million nontraditional learners complete degree programs over a 30-year career. Dr. Dietrich founded and served as executive director for the Consortium for the Advancement of Adult Higher Education for 25 years. Dr. Dietrich was dean of students at Danville Area Community College, veterans affairs director at Pepperdine University, enrollment advisor at the University of Redlands, and director of admissions and records at the University of Phoenix.

A lifelong learner herself, Dietrich holds a doctorate in educational leadership from Nova Southeastern University and a master's in adult higher education from Arizona State University.

Gary Fretwell — CHAPTER 4

As a senior vice president for Ruffalo Noel Levitz, Gary Fretwell has been a strong catalyst for enrollment success on over 700 campuses throughout North America. His recommendations and guidance have helped institutions establish strategic and tactical enrollment plans for both graduate and undergraduate programs.

In addition to providing consulting support, Mr. Fretwell frequently has delivered hundreds of presentations on strategic enrollment management, development of campuswide retention programs, graduate and professional school recruitment, and mobilizing campus divisions to achieve enrollment success.

Over the course of his 40-year career in higher education, Mr. Fretwell served as vice president for enrollment and student affairs at Millsaps College (MS) and held a variety of posts at Tulane University (LA) and the University of South Florida. Mr. Fretwell holds an MA from Stetson University (FL).

Jim Hundrieser, PhD — CHAPTERS 2 and 8

Jim Hundrieser is Associate Managing Partner, Association of Governing Boards (AGB) Institutional Strategies. Dr. Hundrieser's enrollment management expertise covers strategic enrollment planning, student recruitment, student retention, strategic planning, institutional planning and assessment, and student life.

Prior to joining AGB, Dr. Hundrieser led at team at Plymouth State University to transform and re-engineer their marketing, recruitment, and admissions efforts. The results led to enrolling the largest first-year class in the university's history as well as significantly increasing the number of inquiries, applications, and the profile of the incoming class.

As a former vice president at Noel-Levitz, he consulted with more than 50 colleges and universities to create comprehensive strategic enrollment plans, long-range enrollment plans, and recruitment and retention strategies. His recommendations and guidance helped institutions establish comprehensive enrollment management initiatives for both graduate and undergraduate programs.

In his spare time, he delivers national and regional presentations and conducts campus workshops on topics ranging from building a strong recruitment program to improving the quality of student life and learning. He holds a PhD in leadership and education from Barry University (FL) and serves as a faculty member in the College of Education.

William Husson, PhD — CHAPTER 13

William Husson is academic dean emeritus at Regis University, where he served for more than 30 years. Bill served as the vice president for professional studies and strategic alliances, during which time he oversaw the operations of undergraduate and graduate programs enrolling more than 12,000 students annually at 11 campuses in Colorado, Nevada, and Virginia, and throughout the U.S. and internationally via distance learning. He is currently an associate consultant with Ruffalo Noel Levitz.

Dr. Husson is a trustee at Alliant University in San Diego, (CA), and is the president of the SCOPE International board of directors. He also serves on the board of The Regis Company (formerly Regis Learning Solutions corporation), a leadership training company.

He received his bachelor's and master's degrees from St. Thomas College and Theological Seminary before earning his PhD in human and organizational systems with a specialization in adult education from Fielding Graduate University.

Joyce Kinkead, PhD — CHAPTER 8

Joyce Kinkead is an academic and administrator with 35 years of experience in higher education. She offers extensive expertise in the areas of student recruitment, retention, financial aid, academic advising, institutional research, academic planning and assessment, and classroom instruction.

Dr. Kinkead served as the associate vice president for research at Utah State University as well as the vice provost overseeing undergraduate education and enrollment management. She enhanced the undergraduate research program, increased the number of students accepted to the National Conference on Undergraduate Research, administered the university's New Faculty Research Grant Program, and created the Utah Conference on Undergraduate Research, among other accomplishments. For her high-profile work in undergraduate research, she was named a Council on Undergraduate Research Fellow (2012). In addition to her administrative duties, she is a professor of English. She was named the Utah Professor of the Year by the Carnegie Foundation and CASE in 2013.

A prolific scholar and writer, Dr. Kinkead has authored 12 books and dozens of journal articles and book chapters. She has presented at numerous regional, state, national, and international conferences. Dr. Kinkead holds a PhD from Texas A&M University–Commerce and is a native of Missouri.

Evelyn (Bonnie) Lynch, EdD — CHAPTER 5

Evelyn Lynch spent more than 35 years in higher education as a faculty member and as an academic administrator. Her last position before retirement was executive director of the Lehigh Valley Association of Independent Colleges. This academic consortium, governed by the presidents of the six private colleges in the Lehigh Valley, facilitates collaborative academic opportunities and shared purchasing contracts for approximately 18,000 students and 5,000 faculty and staff.

Prior to her work at Lehigh Valley, Dr. Lynch served as president of Saint Joseph College (CT) where she created a strategic vision for the college and facilitated a comprehensive plan for student recruitment and retention. Dr. Lynch held previous leadership positions at East Stroudsburg University of Pennsylvania, Arkansas State University, Ball State University (IN), and Minnesota State University-Moorhead.

Dr. Lynch has published and presented on developmental disabilities, teacher preparation, and education. She received her EdD from Indiana University.

James Mager, PhD — CHAPTERS 3 and 5

With more than 40 years of experience in higher education as an administrator and consultant, James Mager specializes in strategic enrollment planning, student recruitment, student retention, enrollment management research, and operations analysis.

Dr. Mager was associate vice president for Noel-Levitz until his retirement in 2010. In addition to campus consulting, Dr. Mager was instrumental in the research and development of the firm's strategic enrollment planning process and many of its national reports and strategic white papers.

Previously, he held a variety of enrollment management positions at The Ohio State University from 1971 to 2002. As associate vice president for enrollment management at OSU, he led the offices of admissions, first-year experience, financial aid, and the university registrar. Previously he served as director of admissions and financial aid and as a systems analyst. Enrollment results credited to Dr. Mager's leadership include significantly better academically prepared freshman classes, increases in student retention and graduation rates, larger transfer student classes, and greater race-ethnic and geographic diversity. In 2006 Dr. Mager received The Ohio State University Distinguished Service Award.

Dr. Mager received his doctorate in industrial systems engineering from Ohio State.

Sheila Mahan — CHAPTER 13

Sheila Mahan has served as an associate consultant for Ruffalo Noel Levitz for 12 years, working with more than 20 campus partners, focusing on both graduate and undergraduate, adult, and online enrollment at public and private institutions.

Previously, Ms. Mahan served as assistant vice president for academic affairs at the University at Albany, State University of New York, supervising recruitment and retention as well as planning across all areas of enrollment management. Her work with graduate admissions led to enhanced recruitment as well as improvements in customer service and technology, while also producing greater organizational and services coordination. Additional areas of responsibility included course planning and management and the application of information technology to student services. Prior to joining the University at Albany, she was on the faculty at Hudson Valley Community College (NY).

Ms. Mahan holds a master's degree from the State University of New York at Binghamton.

Brian Ralph, PhD — CHAPTER 6

Brian C. Ralph is president of William Peace University in Raleigh, (NC). Previously, he served Queens University of Charlotte (NC) as vice president for enrollment management, where he oversaw traditional undergraduate admissions, student financial services, residence life, student activities, athletics, multi-cultural affairs, the center for active citizenship and health and wellness services. He also co-chaired the university retention committee. Dr. Ralph also served as vice president for enrollment management and marketing at Bethany College (WV). As a Ruffalo Noel Levitz senior associate consultant, he specializes in strategic enrollment planning, recruitment and admissions processes, marketing and promotions strategies, and marketing communications.

An excellent speaker, Dr. Ralph has presented on numerous occasions at national higher education conferences. He completed the Institute for Educational Management at Harvard University and received his PhD in organizational communication and culture from Ohio University.

Lewis Sanborne, PhD — CHAPTER 14

Lew Sanborne is Ruffalo Noel Levitz's leader in strategic enrollment planning. He offers nearly three decades of experience in higher education and enrollment management, with a range of expertise including annual and strategic enrollment planning, student success and retention, quality service, and leadership and organizational development. He has consulted with more than 60 two-year and four-year institutions to support both their intermediate and long-range enrollment and fiscal goals.

Prior to joining Ruffalo Noel Levitz, Dr. Sanborne served at St. Ambrose University (IA) in a number of positions, including dean of the College for Professional Studies and associate vice president for enrollment management, as well as holding status in the English department. Earlier in his career, he led efforts at St. Ambrose that resulted in an increase of first- to second-year retention from 71.5 to 79.5 percent.

Dr. Sanborne is a member of the Society for College and University Planning and holds a PhD in higher education administration from Illinois State University as well as an MA in English, BA in English, and BA in English education from Idaho State University.

Ruth Sims — CHAPTER 9

Ruth Sims spent over 25 years of her career serving higher education. Most recently senior vice president for marketing and research at Noel-Levitz, she consulted with campuses on market research, marketing strategy, and communications development. She was a driving force behind the firm's national prominence as a center for market research, specializing in image analyses, communication strategies, and market positioning.

Ms. Sims consulted with more than 175 colleges and universities, overseeing projects that ranged from market research studies and direct marketing to publications and website development services for clients.

Prior to joining the firm, Ms. Sims managed creative services for a Citicorp subsidiary and served as a marketing executive for US Bank. She holds a master's degree in communications from the University of Denver (CO).

Robert Van Cleef — CHAPTER 4

Robert Van Cleef is the strategic advisor and executive director of institutional research at Gordon College (MA). In his current position, Mr. Van Cleef advises the college's cabinet in spheres of institutional strategic planning, competitive strategy, strategic enrollment management, and execution of priority change initiatives. Collaborating through influential committees—including recruitment, retention and persistence, institutional advancement, provost's council, and others—the College has enjoyed multiple years of record recruitment and gains in retention under his counsel. He played a formative role in the development of the college's brand and web strategy.

As an associate consultant with Ruffalo Noel Levitz, Mr. Van Cleef's expertise bridges the strategic enrollment planning and market research service areas.

Mr. Van Cleef holds an MBA from Amberton University (TX) with a concentration on strategic leadership. He also holds a Master's Certificate of Project Management (MCPM) from Boston University (MA), and the internationally recognized PMP certification from the Project Management Institute. He has co-presented at the National Conference on Student Recruitment, Marketing, and Retention and AACRAO National Conference.